Manchester
November '90

Time and the Other

Time and the Other
HOW ANTHROPOLOGY MAKES ITS OBJECT

Johannes Fabian

COLUMBIA UNIVERSITY PRESS   NEW YORK

Library of Congress Cataloging in Publication Data

Fabian, Johannes.
  Time and the other.

  Bibliography: p.
  Includes index.
  1. Anthropology—Philosophy.   2. Time.   I. Title.
GN345.F32   1983   306'.01   82-19751
ISBN 0-231-05590-0
ISBN 0-231-05591-9 (pbk.)

p 10 9 8 7 6 5 4

Columbia University Press
New York   Guildford, Surrey

For my parents
And for Ilona

Contents

Preface and Acknowledgments

*"You see, my friend," Mr. Bounderby put in, "we are the
kind of people who know the value of time, and you are the
kind of people who don't know the value of time." "I have
not," retorted Mr. Childers, after surveying him from head
to foot, "the honour of knowing you—but if you mean that
you can make more money of your time than I can of mine,
I should judge from your appearance that you are about
right."*

Charles Dickens *Hard Times*

WHEN THEY APPROACH the problem of Time, certain
philosophers feel the need to fortify themselves with a ritual
incantation. They quote Augustine: "What is time? If no
one asks me about it, I know; if I want to explain it to the
one who asks, I don't know" (*Confessions,* book XI). In fact,
I have just joined that chorus.

It is difficult to speak about Time and we may leave it
to philosophers to ponder the reasons. It is not difficult to
show that we speak, fluently and profusely, *through* Time.
Time, much like language or money, is a carrier of significance, a form through which we define the content of relations between the Self and the Other. Moreover—as the
conversation between Mr. Bounderby, the factory owner,
and Mr. Childers, the acrobat, reminds us—Time may give
form to relations of power and inequality under the conditions of capitalist industrial production.

It occurred to me that this could be the perspective for
a critique of cultural anthropology. These essays, then, are
offered as studies of "anthropology through Time." The

reader who expects a book on the anthropology *of* Time—perhaps an ethnography of "time-reckoning among the primitives"—will be disappointed. Aside from occasional references to anthropological studies of cultural conceptions of Time, he will find nothing to satisfy his curiosity about the Time of the Other. I want to examine past and present uses of Time as ways of construing the object of our discipline. If it is true that Time belongs to the political economy of relations between individuals, classes, and nations, then the construction of anthropology's object through temporal concepts and devices is a political act; there is a "Politics of Time."

I took an historical approach in order to demonstrate the emergence, transformation, and differentiation of uses of Time. This runs counter to a kind of critical philosophy which condemns recourse to history as a misuse of Time. According to a famous remark by Karl Popper, "The historicist does not recognize that it is we who select and order the facts of history" (1966 2:269). Popper and other theorists of science inspired by him do not seem to realize that the problematic element in this assertion is not the constitution of history (who doubts that it is made, not given?) but the nature of the *we*. From the point of view of anthropology, that *we*, the subject of history, cannot be presupposed or left implicit. Nor should we let anthropology simply be used as the provider of a convenient Other to the *we* (as exemplified by Popper on the first page of the *Open Society* where "our civilization" is opposed to the "tribal" or "closed society," 1966 1:1).

Critical philosophy must inquire into the dialectical constitution of the Other. To consider that relation dialectically means to recognize its concrete temporal, historical, and political conditions. Existentially and politically, critique of anthropology starts with the scandal of domination and exploitation of one part of mankind by another. Trying to make sense of what happens—in order to overcome a state of affairs we have long recognized as scandalous—we can in the end not be satisfied with explanations which ascribe Western imperialism in abstract terms to the mechanics of power or aggression, or in moral terms to greed and wickedness. Aggression, one suspects, is the alienated bourgeois' perception of his own sense of alienation as an inevitable, quasi-natural force; wickedness projects the same inevitability inside the person. In both cases, schemes of explanation are easily bent into ideologies of self-justification. I will be searching—and here I feel close to the Enlightenment *philosophes* whom I shall criticize later on—for an "error," an intellectual misconception, a defect of reason which, even if it does not offer *the* explanation, may free our self-questioning from the double bind of fate and evil. That error causes our societies to maintain their anthropological knowledge of other societies in bad faith. We constantly need to cover up for a fundamental contradiction: On the one hand we dogmatically insist that anthropology rests on ethnographic research involving personal, prolonged interaction with the Other. But then we pronounce upon the knowledge gained from such research a discourse which construes the Other in terms of distance, spatial and temporal. The Other's empirical presence turns into his theoretical absence, a conjuring trick which is worked with the help of an array of devices that have the common intent and function to keep the Other outside the Time of anthropology. An account of the many ways in which this has been done needs to be given even if it is impossible to propose, in the end, more than hints and fragments of an alternative. The radical contemporaneity of mankind is a project. Theoretical reflection can identify obstacles; only changes in the praxis and politics of anthropological research and writing can contribute solutions to the problems that will be raised.

Such are the outlines of the argument I want to pursue. It lies in the nature of this undertaking that a great mass of material had to be covered, making it impossible always to do justice to an author or an issue. Readers who are less familiar with anthropology and its history might first want to look at the summary provided in chapter 5.

I don't want to give the impression that this project was conceived principally by way of theoretical reasoning. On the contrary, it grew out of my ordinary occupations as a teacher working mainly in institutions involved in the reproduction of Western society, and as an ethnographer trying to understand cultural processes in urban-industrial Africa (see Fabian 1971, 1979). In the act of producing ethnographic knowledge, the problem of Time arises concretely and practically, and many anthropologists have been aware of the temporal aspects of ethnography. But we have rarely considered the ideological nature of temporal concepts which inform our theories and our rhetoric. Nor have we paid much attention to intersubjective Time, which does not measure but constitutes those practices of communication we customarily call fieldwork. Perhaps we need to protect ourselves by such lack of reflection in order to keep our knowledge of the Other at bay, as it were. After all, we only seem to be doing what other sciences exercise: keeping object and subject apart.

Throughout, I have tried to relate my arguments to existing work and to provide bibliographic references to further sources. W. Lepenies' essay the "End of Natural History" (1976) is closely related to my views on the uses of Time in earlier phases of anthropology (although we seem to differ on what brought about the phenomenon of "temporalization"); P. Bourdieu has formulated a theory of Time and cultural practice (1977) in which I found much agreement with my own thought. H. G. Reid has been, to my knowledge, one of the few social scientists to employ the notion of "politics of time" (see 1972). My indebtedness to the work of Gusdorf, Moravia, Benveniste, Weinrich, Yates, Ong, and others is obvious and, I hope, properly acknowledged. I made an attempt, within the limitations of libraries at my disposal, to read up on the topic of Time in general. The literature I consulted ranged from early monographs on primitive time reckoning (Nilsson 1920) to recent studies of time-conceptions in other cultures (Ricoeur 1975); from philosophical (Whitrow 1963) to psychological (Doob 1971) standard works. I looked at interdisciplinary projects from the "Time and its Mysteries" series (1936–1949) to the work inspired by J. T. Fraser and the International Society for the Study of Time he founded (see Fraser 1966, Fraser et al., eds., 1972 ff). Special issues of journals devoted to Time have come to my attention from *History and Theory* (Beiheft 6:1966) to *Cahiers Internationaux de Sociologie* (1979). I should mention several highly original treatments of the topic, exemplified by G. Kubler's *The Shape of Time* (1962) and the work of M. Foucault (e.g., 1973). The one bibliography I found (Zelkind and Sprug 1974) lists more than 1,100 titles of time research but is badly in need of completing and updating.

As could be expected, many of the questions I raise occupied other writers at about the same time. This work came to my attention after these essays were completed (in 1978), too late to be commented on at length. Most important among these writings is undoubtedly Edward Said's *Orientalism* (1979 [1978]). Similarities in intent, method, and occasionally in formulations between his study and mine confirmed me in my ideas. I hope that my arguments will complement and, in some cases, elaborate his theses. Quite possibly, M. Foucault's influence explains why there is so much convergence between our views. There may also be deeper analogies in our intellectual biographies, as we found out in later conversations. I believe we both struggle to restore past experiences, which were buried under layers of "enculturation" in other societies and languages, to a kind of presence that makes them critically fruitful.

A remarkable study by Ton Lemaire (1976) provides background and much detail to chapters 1 and 2. Lemaire's is one of the best recent critical evaluations of cultural anthropology; unfortunately it is as yet not available in English.

Justin Stagl achieved in my view a breakthrough in the historiography of anthropology with his studies on early manuals for travelers and on the origins of certain social-scientific techniques, such as the questionnaire-survey (1979, 1980). His findings demonstrate a connection which I only suspected, namely a direct influence of Ramist thought in giving "method" to our knowledge of the Other. Much of what I discuss in chapters 3 and 4 takes on added significance in the light of Stagl's writings.

Stagl drew on the seminal work of W. Ong, as did J. Goody in his book *The Domestication of the Savage Mind* (1977) which provides valuable illustrations to issues treated in chapter 4, especially regarding the role of the visual in the presentation of knowledge. The section on Hegel's theory of symbols in that chapter is complemented by F. Kramer's essay "Mythology and Ethocentrism" (1977:15–64).

Some of the points I make in chapters 3 and 4 receive support from a recent study by Arens (1979) on cannibalism, one of the most persistent topics in anthropology, which is shown to have been primarily an "oppressive mental construct" derived from cosmological ideas about other times and places.

Finally, I found much confirmation, albeit of a negative sort (from the position taken in this book) in the work of G. Durand (1979; see also Maffesoli, ed., 1980). He seems to emerge as the major proponent of a neohermetic movement in French anthropology whose strategy it is to play the "imaginary" against prosaic positivism and pseudoscientific evolutionism. The effect is to revitalize "orientalism" and to reinstate the visualist rhetoric whose history has been critically studied by Yates and Ong (see chapter 4).

With few exceptions I shall not refer to these and other recent publications in the text or in the notes. I mention some of them now because they confirm my conviction that we are on the threshold of some major change in our conceptions of the history and present role of anthropology. Elements of a new understanding are being formulated here and there; mine is one attempt to show how they might be put together.

Much as I am indebted to readings, I owe most to my conversations with African workers and intellectuals. I hope that V. Y. Mudimbe, P. Lalèyê, Wamba-dia-Wamba, M. Owusu, and many others will recognize in these essays some of the exchanges we had through the years. A version of chapter 1 (including the plan for the book) was first read at the Department of Anthropology at Harvard University and I want to thank Michael Fisher for giving me the opportunity to formulate my thoughts. Perhaps even more important was to me another occasion when I presented these ideas in a panel discussion with the African philosopher M. Towa at the National University of Zaire in Kinshasa. I discussed chapter 3 with J. Habermas and his collaborators at the Max-Planck-Institute in Starnberg.

To Wesleyan University I am grateful for a sabbatical leave giving me time to write, and to students at Wesleyan University and the University of Bonn for letting me try out my thoughts in courses on the History of Anthropological Thought.

Ilona Szombati-Fabian helped generously with suggestions and critical response. Fredric Jameson, Martin Silverman, Bob Scholte, and Walter Ong read the manuscript and encouraged me. Although this may come as a surprise to him, I think that the time of close collaboration with Hayden White at the Center for the Humanities at Wesleyan University was important in giving shape to this project.

I want to thank Valborg Proudman and Hanneke Kossen for help and competent assistance of which typing versions of the manuscript was but a small part.

Amsterdam
November 1982

Time and the Other

Chapter One / Time and the Emerging Other

Apart from time there is one other means to bring about important change—force. If one works too slowly, the other will do it faster.

Georg Christoph Lichtenberg [1]

Of course the history and prae-history of man take their proper places in the general scheme of knowledge. Of course the doctrine of the world-long evolution of civilisation is one which philosophic minds will take up with eager interest, as a theme of abstract science. But beyond this, such research has its practical side, as a source of power destined to influence the course of modern ideas and actions.

Edward Burnett Tylor [2]

KNOWLEDGE IS POWER. That commonplace applies to anthropology as much as to any other field of knowledge. But commonplaces usually cover up for not-so-common truths. In this first chapter I want to set down some of the terms for an argument to be pursued throughout these essays: Anthropology's claim to power originated at its roots. It belongs to its essence and is not a matter of accidental misuse. Nowhere is this more clearly visible, at least once we look for it, than in the uses of Time anthropology makes when it strives to constitute its own object—the savage, the primitive, the Other. It is by diagnosing anthropology's temporal discourse that one rediscovers the obvious, namely that there is no knowledge of the Other which is not also a temporal, historical, a political act.

Perhaps this covers too much ground; *political* can mean anything from systematic oppression to anarchic mutual recognition. The epigrams chosen for this chapter are to indicate that our attention will mostly be directed to the oppressive uses of Time. Anthropology's alliance with the forces of oppression is neither a simple or recent one, as some moralizing critics would have it, nor is it unequivocal. The brief sketches of some of the historical contexts in which anthropological uses of Time developed have the main purpose of recounting a story whose conclusion is open-ended and contradictory. Anthropology may, during the period covered here, have succeeded in establishing itself as an academic discipline; it failed to come to a rest vis-à-vis a clearly defined Other.

From Sacred to Secular Time: The Philosophical Traveler

In the Judeo-Christian tradition Time has been conceived as the medium of a sacred history. Time was thought, but more often celebrated, as a sequence of specific events that befall a chosen people. Much has been said about the linear character of that conception as opposed to pagan, cyclical views of Time as an *éternel retour.*[3] Yet such spatial metaphors of temporal thought tend to obscure something that is of more immediate significance in an attempt to sketch the ancestry of Time's anthropological uses: Faith in a covenant between Divinity and one people, trust in divine providence as it unfolds in a history of salvation centered on one Savior, make for sacred conceptions of Time. They stress the specificity of Time, its realization in a given cultural ecology—the Eastern Mediterranean, first, and the circum-Mediterranean with Rome as its hub, later.

Decisive steps towards modernity, those that permitted the emergence of anthropological discourse, must be sought, not in the invention of a linear conception, but in a succession of attempts to secularize Judeo-Christian Time by generalizing and universalizing it.

Different degrees of universalizing Time had of course been achieved in an abstract form by earlier philosophical thought. In fact, "universal Time" was probably established concretely and politically in the Renaissance in response to both classical philosophy and to the cognitive challenges presented by the age of discoveries opening up in the wake of the earth's circumnavigation. Nevertheless, there are good reasons to look for decisive developments, not in the moments of intellectual rupture achieved by Copernicus and Galileo nor, for that matter, by Newton and Locke, but in the century that elaborated the devices of discourse we now recognize as the foundations of modern anthropology—the Age of Enlightenment.[4]

If we follow G. Gusdorf we may locate the starting point of these developments, a sort of barrier that had to be broken through, in one of the last attempts during the seventeenth century to write a universal history from the Christian viewpoint, Bossuet's *Discours sur l'histoire universelle* (first published in 1681).[5] Perhaps it is too simplistic to put Bossuet at the other side of a premodern/modern watershed, for in many ways he anticipated the Enlightenment genre of "philosophical history." His opposition to modernity is not so much in the detail of his methodological prescriptions as it is in the position that integrates his views: faith in the evangelical specificity of all of history as history of salvation. A brief reading of the introduction to the *Discours,* entitled "The General Plan of this Work," will illuminate the importance of Bossuet's treatise.

Bossuet's professed aim is to alleviate confusion caused by the multitude of historical fact. This is to be accomplished by teaching the reader to "distinguish different times (*temps*)" with the help of "universal history," a device which "is to the histories of every country and of every people what a general map is to particular maps" (1845:1, 2). In this analogy the universal is aligned with the general, which signals a certain ambiguity (one which, incidentally, is still with us in anthropology's quest for universals). *Universals* appears to have two connotations. One is that of totality; in this sense, universal designates the whole world at all times. The other is one of generality: that which is applicable to a large number of instances.[6] The important point, borne out by the body of the *Discours,* is that Bossuet does not thematize the first connotation. His account does not cover the world, it never leaves the circum-Mediterranean. Writing within the horizon of the history of, Christian religion, he does not see his perspective, nor does he look beyond his horizon. The former is self-evident as an article of faith, the latter is bounded by his political position at the French court of Louis XIV, whose succession to the Christian Roman Empire he takes for granted. Perspective and horizon of the *Discours* are tied together by the all-pervading intention to validate (albeit not uncritically) the political realities of his day by a history that is universal because it expresses the omnipresent signs of divine providence.

In contrast, Bossuet is quite conscious of problems implicit in the second connotation of *universal*. How can one present history in terms of generally valid principles? He argues that such a project rests on the ability to discern in the "sequence of things" (*suite des choses*) the "order of times." Methodologically this calls for an "abbreviation" of sequences in such a way that order can be perceived "at a glance" (*comme d'un coup d'oeil,* 1845:2). A long history of the "art of memory" is behind this remark, and a history of the visual reduction of temporal sequence—its "synchronic" understanding—lies ahead of it.[7]

A methodological device that opens the view over Time is the *epoch,* conceived, not in its currently most common understanding of a period or interval of time, but in a transitive sense derived from its Greek root. An epoch is a point ploring the past; every step he makes is the passage of an age" as from a place of rest, all that happened before or after, so that one may avoid anachronisms, that is, a kind of error which results in confusing the times." In exposing universal history one proceeds by treating a "small number of epochs" in secular and religious history, the outcome of which will be—and here Bossuet's methodology rejoins his faith—to make visible the "PERPETUAL DURATION OF RELIGION, AND . . . THE CAUSES OF THE GREAT CHANGES IN THE EMPIRES" (1845:3, 4). Thus both, the external, spatial boundaries of history and its inner continuity are of religion. Where mere sequence might cause confusion, the distinction of times in

the light of divine providence creates order. It demon-
strates the omnipresent work of salvation.

O. Ranum, the editor of a recent English version, reminds us that Bossuet used the term *discourse* in the title of
his work deliberately. He wanted to break with conventions
according to which highly stylized secular and religious histories were produced during the seventeenth century (see
Ranum 1976:xviii). Bossuet asserted his freedom to abbre-
viate, condense, and emphasize without being bound by the
then firmly established canon of historical facts each historian was expected to report. In this he anticipated the "philosophical history" which Voltaire opposed to mindless
chronicling and out of which the first projects of modern
anthropology were to grow. Less obvious, but equally important, is the model set by Bossuet for what one might call
sermonizing history, which is another possible connotation
of *discourse*. Bossuet wrote his work for the enlightenment
and education of the Dauphin (and his father, the Sun King).
It was meant as a refutation of attacks on the literal understanding of the Bible and as a defense of a Gallican, French-
centered, reformed Catholicism. In short, his "distinction of
times" is embedded in concrete political-moral concerns. He
expressed himself through discursive devices that were rhetorical in the classical sense: aimed to move and convince
the reader. His political intent and its rhetorical form were
to influence the writing of the *philosophes* and to become part
of anthropology's heritage as, in Tylor's words, a "reform-
er's science."

We set out to show in Boussuet's *Discours* an example
for a premodern treatise on universal history; now we seem
to end up with more similarities than dissimilarities if we
compare his method and devices to those of the Englighten-
ment philosophical histories. We are confronting here a well-
known problem in the interpretation of eighteenth-century
thought. On the whole, the *philosophes,* whom we recognize
in many respects as our immediate ancestors, achieved only
a sort of negative modernity. In the words of Carl Becker:
"Their negations rather than their affirmations enable us to
treat them as kindred spirits" (1963:30). Or, as Gusdorf puts

it, these thinkers replaced Bossuet's Christian myth with the "myth-history of reason" which, by and large, continued to use the conventions and devices of earlier periods. If one wants to show how Time became secularized in the eighteenth century and onward he must concentrate on the transformation of the *message* of "universal history" rather than on the elements of its code. The latter display a remarkable continuity with preceding periods down to the Greco-Roman canons of the arts of memory and rhetoric. The transformation of the message had to be operated on what we identified as the specificity of Christian "universality." Change also had to occur on the level of political intent or "judgment." It was on that level that the *philosophes* had to overcome Bossuet who "was never reluctant to judge all of the past in the light of the single most important event of all time: the brief passage of the man-god Jesus through a life on earth" (Ranum 1976:xxvi).

In fact, among the many expressions of change one could cite is the very transformation of one man's all-significant passage on earth into the *topos of travel*. In the Christian tradition, the Savior's and the saints' passages on earth had been perceived as constituent events of a sacred history. To be sure, this had occasioned much travel to foreign parts in the form of pilgrimages, crusades, and missions. But for the established bourgeoisie of the eighteenth century, travel was to become (at least potentially) every man's source of "philosophical," secular knowledge. Religious travel had been *to* the centers of religion, or *to* the souls to be saved; now, secular travel was *from* the centers of learning and power to places where man was to find nothing but himself. As S. Moravia had shown in his brilliant studies, the idea and practice of *travel as science,* prepared in Diderot's encyclopedia (1973:125–132), was definitively established toward the end of the eighteenth century, especially among the thinkers known as "ideologues" (see Moravia 1976). Two names, those of J. M. Degérando and C. F. Volney, are of special interest in this connection of travel and the secularization of Time.

It was Degérando who expressed the temporalizing ethos of an emerging anthropology in this concise and programmatic formula: "The philosophical traveller, sailing to the ends of the earth, is in fact travelling in time; he is exploring the past; every step he makes is the passage of an age" (Degérando 1969 [1800]:63). In this statement, the attribute *philosophical* echoes the militant enthusiasm of the preceding century for a science of man to be conceived by man and for man, one in which religious and metaphysical searches for mankind's origin and destiny were to give place to a radically immanent vision of humanity at home in the entire world and at all times. Now man is, in Moravia's words, "placed, without residue, inside of a world-horizon which is his own . . . to travel means, in this framework, not only to quench the thirst for knowledge; it also signifies man's most intimate vocation" (1967:942). It is in this sense of a vehicle for the self-realization of man that the topos of travel signals achieved secularization of Time. A new discourse is built on an enormous literature of travelogues, collections and syntheses of travel accounts.[8]

The manifest preoccupation in this literature, in its popular forms as well as in its scientific uses, was with the description of movements and relations in *space* ("geography") based primarily on visual observation of foreign *places*. However, this does not contradict the contention that elaborating a secular conception of Time was its underlying concern. Precisely because secular Time was its presupposition, logically speaking, or its signified, in semiotic parlance, the new discourse had (with exceptions to be mentioned later) no need to thematize Time. (Philosophical History, as is well known, was strangely ahistorical). Such distinction between intent and expression is an important principle of interpretation which will be more fully elaborated in chapter 3. It also invites consideration of the reverse case: A discourse in which Time is thematized may be about an atemporal referent.[9] As we shall see, nineteenth-century evolutionism is a case in point. At any rate, "philosophical travel," that is, the conception of travel as science, could leave the problem of Time theoretically implicit because travel itself, as witnessed by Degérando's statement, is instituted as a temporalizing practice.

Why this should be so is explained by the subsumption

of travel under the reigning paradigm of natural history. Moravia has shown that the project of scientific travel was consciously conceived to replace an earlier, enormously popular, genre of mostly sentimental and aesthetisizing tales of travel. The new traveler "criticized the *philosophes:* the reality of lived experience and of things seen was now opposed to a reality distorted by preconceived ideas" (1967:963). One also begins to reject the linkup, unquestioned by earlier voyagers, between travel in foreign parts and military conquest. According to La Pérouse, one of the most famous figures in this story, "the modern navigators only have one objective when they describe the customs of new peoples: to complete the history of man" (cited in Moravia 1967:964 f).

There is a significant double entendre in the verb *to complete.* As used by La Pérouse, it signifies belief in the fulfillment of human destiny: travel is the self-realization of man. It also has a more literal, methodological meaning and might then be translated as *filling out* (as in "to complete a questionnaire"). In the episteme of natural history[10] the exercise of knowledge was projected as the filling of spaces or slots in a table, or the marking of points in a system of coordinates in which all possible knowledge could be placed. It is therefore not surprising that with the rise of an ethos of scientific travel we also see the emergence of a genre of scientific preparation for travel quite different from the *instructiones* European potentates used to give to the early navigators and conquistadors. We know its modern offspring, the *Notes and Queries on Anthropology* which accompanied generations of anthropologists to the field.[11] Only recently have we rediscovered and come to appreciate such predecessors as Degérando's *The Observation of Savage Peoples,* issued from the short-lived activities of the Société des Observateurs de l'Homme. It is most revealing to find that a model of the genre was conceived by that natural historian par excellence, Linnaeus (*Institutio Perigrinatoris,* Uppsala, 1759).[12] This confirms, if confirmation is needed, beyond any doubt the roots of the new science of travel in natural-historical projects of observation, collection and classification, and description.

The new travelers did not mindlessly subscribe to empiricism and pure, positive description. Volney, one of the most eminent representatives of the genre, is also the one who advocated a critical stance based (and in this he is closer to the Romantic revolt against the Enlightenment) on explicitly historical, i.e., temporal considerations. During his voyages in Egypt and Syria he constantly had to face the dilapidated monuments of a once glorious past. Contrasting past and present became an intellectual concern as well as a literary device pervading his writings (see Moravia 1967:1008 f). It was elevated to a poetic-philosophical vision in his *Les Ruines ou Méditation sur les Révolutions des Empires*. Better than any commentary, the opening page from *Ruines* will illustrate the poignancy of contradictory experiences of past and present *and* the political nature of Volney's concern with Time:

In the eleventh year of the reign of *Abd-ul-Hamid,*
son of *Ahmed,* emperor of the *Turks,* at a time when
the victorious Russians took the Crimea and planted
their banners on the coast that leads to Constanti-
nople, I was travelling in the empire of the *Otto-
mans,* and I traversed the provinces which once had
been the kingdoms of *Egypt* and *Syria.*
    Carrying with me my attentiveness to every-
thing that concerns the well-being of man in society,
I entered the cities and studied the customs of their
inhabitants; I ventured into the palaces and observed the conduct of those who govern; I lost myself in the countryside and examined the conditions
of those who work the land. Seeing everywhere
nothing but pillage and devastation, nothing but
tyranny and misery, my heart was heavy with sad-
ness and indignation. Everyday I found on my road
abandoned fields, deserted villages, and cities in
ruins; often I encountered ancient monuments and
temples reduced to debris; palaces and fortresses,
columns, aqueducts, tombs. This spectacle turned
my spirit to medidating about times past, and it
caused in my heart thoughts that were grave and
profound. (Volney 1830:21 f)

When he later draws the "lessons from times past for times present" (thus the title of chapter 12) he finds consolation in a thought that rings with the optimism of the *phil-osophes:*

It is a man's folly that makes him lose himself; it is
up to man's wisdom to save him. The peoples are
ignorant, may they instruct themselves; their rulers
are perverted, let them correct and better themselves. Because that is the dictate of *nature: Since the
evils of societies come from cupidity and ignorance, mankind will not cease to be tormented until it becomes enlight-
ended and wise,* until they practice the art *of justice,*
based on the *knowledge* of their relations and of the
laws of their organisation. *(Ibid.* 90)

The difference between this new faith in reason and
Bossuet's old faith in salvation could not be expressed more
clearly. Bossuet preached understanding of a past that contained a history of salvation and divine providence. Volney
preaches, too, but has no recourse from the history of man.
To him, knowledge of the past is a sort of Archimedian
point from which to change an otherwise hopeless present.
There certainly is an element of romantic pessimism and
nostalgia in his reveries on the Orient's glorious past. At the
same time, if we consider the context and message of *Ruines*
in its entirety, we find, beneath the image of a dream which
the writer conveys to his readers, the pragmatic assertion
that it is *his,* the educated French traveler's, knowledge of
the past that counts. It is a superior knowledge, for it is not
shared by the Orientals caught in the present of their cities,
either deserted and dilapidating, or overpopulated and pu-
trid. Bossuet had evoked the same topos at the end of his
Discours, albeit with a different conclusion: "Egypt, once so
wise, stumbles along drunken, dizzy, because the Lord has
spread giddiness in its designs; she no longer knows what
she is doing, she is lost. But peoples should not fool themselves: When it pleases Him, God will straighten out those
who err" (1845:427).

Prefigured in the Christian tradition, but crucially
transformed in the Age of Enlightenment, the idea of a
knowledge of Time which is a superior knowledge has become an integral part of anthropology's intellectual equip-
ment. We recognize it in an outlook that has been charac-

teristic of our discipline through most of its active periods: The posited authenticity of a past (savage, tribal, peasant) serves to denounce an inauthentic present (the uprooted, *évolués*, acculturated). "Urban anthropology," inasmuch as it exposes counterimages to the pristine wholeness of primitive life, was in an obvious sense the byproduct of an advanced stage of colonization abroad and an advanced stage of urban decay at home. On a deeper level, as Volney's example reminds us, it was the point of departure for our discipline in that it expressed the consciousness and concerns of its urban, bourgeois founders.

From History to Evolution: The Naturalization of Time

Thanks to studies such as those by Burrow, Stocking, and Peel, our understanding of evolutionism, the paradigm under which, at least in England, anthropology gained its status as an academic discipline, is much improved. Nevertheless, there remains much confusion, some of it revived and perpetuated in various forms of neoevolutionary anthropology whose historical awareness does not seem to go beyond Leslie White.[13] A failure to distinguish between Darwin's and Spencer's views of evolution is responsible for a great deal of equivocal back-and-forth tracking between biological and sociocultural applications. On the other hand, an admixture of the two cannot simply be dismissed as an error. It stems from a tradition of equivocation fostered by Spencer himself (see Peel 1971:ch. 6) and perhaps by Darwin in his later stages. One way to get a grip on this slippery issue is to examine it in the light of a critique of anthropology's uses of Time.

If our conclusions in the preceding section are correct, the starting point for any attempt to understand evolutionary temporalizing will be the achieved secularization of Time. It resulted in a conception which contains two elements of particular importance to further developments in the nineteenth century: 1) Time is immanent to, hence coextensive with, the world (or nature, or the universe, depending on the argument); 2) relationships between parts of the world

(in the widest sense of both natural and sociocultural entities) can be understood as temporal relations. Dispersal in
space reflects directly, which is not to say simply or in obvious ways, sequence in Time. Given the sociopolitical context of these axiomatic truths in the industrializing and col-
onizing West, it seems almost inevitable that social theorists
would begin to look for scientific frames in which to place
ideas of progress, improvement, and development they had
inherited from the *philosophes*. This is the straightforward
story as it is most often told. In reality, the history of early
evolutionism is replete with puzzles, paradoxes, and incon-
sequential reasoning.

Theories of social evolution and *vague* ideas of biological evolution were around before Darwin proposed his specific theories of the origin of species. Once his theory gained
popular acceptance it, or elements of it, were incorporated
in views of social evolution even by those who, like Spencer,
had formed their basic convictions independently of Darwin. What they did was to redistill from Darwin's theory of
biological evolution those doctrines that were social to begin
with (Malthusianism, utilitarianism). Paradoxically, the uti-
lization of Darwin became possible only on the condition
that a revolutionary insight that had been absolutely crucial
to his views, namely a new conception of Time, had to be,
if not eliminated, then altered and emasculated. Only then
could it be applied to various pseudoscientific projects supposed to demonstrate the operation of evolutionary laws in
the history of mankind.

Numerous   developmental   and   protoevolutionary
schemes had been tried before; and there was Vico, a disturbing figure when it comes to periodizations of modernity.[14] But the qualitative step from medieval to modern time
conceptions could not have been made without a breakthrough based essentially on a *quantitative* change. This was
the demise of Bishop Ussher's biblical chronology, prepared
by earlier skeptics by fully established only when Charles
Lyell published his *Principles of Geology* (1830).[15] Its importance is stated by Darwin in a passage "On the lapse of Time"
in *The Origin of Species:* "He who can read Sir Charles Lyell's
grand work on the Principles of Geology, which the future

historian will recognize as having produced a revolution in the natural sciences, yet does not admit how incomprehensibly vast have been the past periods of time, may at once close this volume" (1861 [Third Edition]:111). Lyell's concern was with *uniformitarianism*, a theory which was to account for the present shape of the world without recourse to unique, simultaneous creation or to repeated acts of divine intervention ("catastrophes"). As summarized by him, it posited that "all former changes of the organic and physical creation are referable to one uninterrupted succession of physical events, governed by laws now in operation" (quoted in Peel 1971:293n9).

That was the basis for nineteenth-century attempts to formulate specific theories of evolution. Geological Time endowed them with a plausibility and a scope which their eighteenth century predecessors could not have had. Furthermore, while it is true that the new conception provided first of all a vast quantitative expansion of Time, its real significance was of a qualitative nature. The problem with calculations based on the Bible was not only that they did not contain enough time for natural history. That sort of problem could have been dealt with (and is dealt with, I imagine, by present-day fundamentalists) by redoing the calculations and extending the chronology. The true reason why biblical chronology had to be abandoned was that it did not contain the *right kind of Time*. Being calculated as the Time after creation as it was revealed in the Scriptures, this was Bossuet's Time of salvation. It was Time relaying significant events, mythical and historical, and as such it was chronicle as well as chronology. As a sequence of events it was linear rather than tabular, i.e., it did not allow for Time to be a variable independent of the events it marks. Hence it could not become part of a Cartesian system of time-space coordinates allowing the scientist to plot a multitude of *uneventful* data over neutral time, unless it was first naturalized, i.e., separated from events meaningful to mankind.[16]

Let us for a moment return to Darwin in order to clarify two further issues. One is Darwin's own keen awareness that Time, once it was naturalized, could and should not be rehistorized (which was precisely what the social evolutionists would try to do). He could not have been clearer than in the following passage in which he rejects tendencies to read some sort of inner necessity or meaning into the temporal dimension of evolution:

The mere lapse of time by itself does nothing either for or against natural selection. I state this because it has been erroneously asserted that the element of time is assumed by me to play an all-important part in natural selection, as if all species were necessarily undergoing slow modification from some innate law. (1861:110 f)

Second, Darwin had more than a first inkling of the epistemological status of scientific chronologies as a sort of language or code (an idea we will encounter later on in its Lévi-Straussian version):

For my part, following Lyell's metaphor, I look at the natural geological record, as a history of the world imperfectly kept, and written in a changing dialect; of this history we possess the last volume alone, relating only to two or three countries. Of this volume, only here and there a short chapter has been preserved; and of each page, only here and there a few lines. Each word of the slowly-changing language, in which the history is written, being more or less different in the successive chapters, may represent the apparently abruptly changed forms of life, entombed in our consecutive, but widely separated formations. (1861:336 f)

Unlike old sacred Time, or even its secularized form in the "myth-history of reason," the new naturalized Time was no longer the vehicle of a continuous, meaningful story; it was a way to order an essentially discontinuous and fragmentary geological and paleontological record. The social evolutionists, as I mentioned before, had to emasculate the new vision on all the three accounts in which it differed from earlier conceptions. They could not use its vastness because the history of mankind, recorded or reconstructed, occupied a negligible span on the scale of natural evolution (and I am not sure whether this has changed now that we count human time in millions rather than thousands of years). Nor could the social evolutionists accept the stark meaningless-ness of mere physical duration. They were too full of the conviction that Time "accomplished" or brought about things in the course of evolution. And finally, they had, as yet, no use for a purely abstract methodological chronology; theirs was a preoccupation with stages leading to civilization, each of them as meaningful as a sentence leading toward the conclusion of a story.

Because they had no use for the positive implications of naturalized Time, the social evolutionists accepted it in the end as a mere presupposition of natural history. In fact, some took the consequences and discarded Time altogether from their speculations about human social evolution. For instance, Morgan stated: "It does not affect the main result that different tribes and nations on the same continent, and even of the same linguistic family, are in different condi-tions at the same time, the *condition* of each is the material fact, the *time* being immaterial" (1877:13). From Morgan's timeless "condition" to the later topos of cultural "config-urations" was but a small logical step. In postulating the radical irreducibility of "superorganic" history, militant an-tievolutionists such as A. Kroeber in his "Eighteen Profes-sions" became executors of the legacy of naturalized Time.[17]

After all these observations on what evolutionist an-thropologists did *not do* with Time we can now state what they did do to it: they *spatialized* Time. We may illustrate this by going back to Spencer. J. D. Y. Peel notes that Spen-cer visualized evolution, not as a *chain* of being, but as a *tree:* "That this image holds true for societies as well as organ-isms, and for between them as well as for social groupings within them, is clear from the opening to the final volume of the Sociology where he says 'social progress is not linear but divergent and redivergent' and speaks of species and genera of societies" (1971:157). What this describes (a point not developed by Peel who in this context gets bogged down in the spurious issue of unilinear vs. multilinear evolution) is a taxonomic approach to socio-cultural reality. The tree has always been one of the simplest forms of constructing clas-sificatory schemes based on subsumption and hierarchy. We are back to Linnaeus and eighteenth-century natural history. In other words, the socio-cultural evolutionists accomplished a major feat of scientific conservatism by saving an older paradigm from what M. Foucault called "the irruptive violence of time" (1973:132). The implications of this will be spelled out at length in the chapters that follow. Let us retain at this point that the temporal discourse of anthropology as it was formed decisively under the paradigm of evolutionism rested on a conception of Time that was not only secularized and naturalized but also thoroughly spatialized. Ever since, I shall argue, anthropology's efforts to construct relations with its Other by means of temporal devices implied affirmation of difference as *distance*.

The ingredients of evolutionist naturalization of Time were Newton's physicalism as well as Lyell's (and to a lesser extent Darwin's) uniformitarianism. In the historiography of anthropology things are usually left at that. Tylor or Morgan are for many anthropologists still the uncontested founders of their discipline and, while most of their "artificial constructs" may now be rejected, the naturalization of Time which was evolutionism's crucial epistemological stance remains by and large unquestioned. That, I submit, betrays a good measure of naiveté. The use of Time in evolutionary anthropology, modeled on that of natural history, undoubtedly was a step beyond premodern conceptions. But it can now be argued that wholesale adoption of models (and of their rhetorical expressions in anthropological discourse) from physics and geology was, for a science of man, sadly regressive intellectually, and quite reactionary politically.

Let me explain. I consider regressive the fact that anthropology achieved its scientific respectability by adopting an essentially Newtonian physicalism (Time being a universal variable in equations describing nature in motion) at a moment near the end of the nineteenth century when the outlines of post-Newtonian physics (and post-"natural history" history) were clearly visible. Radical naturalization of Time (i.e., its radical dehistorization) was of course central to the most celebrated scientific achievement of that period, the comparative method, that omnivorous intellectual machine permitting the "equal" treatment of human culture at

all times and in all places. The enthusiasm and euphoria
generated by this toy made it easy to overlook that, while
the data fed into the machine might have been selected with
positivist neutrality and detachment, its products—the evolutionary sequences—were *anything but* historically or politically neutral. By claiming to make sense of contemporary
society in terms of evolutionary stages, the natural histories
of evolutionism reintroduced a kind of specificity of time
and place—in fact a history of retroactive salvation—that has
its closest counterpart in the Christian-medieval vision con-
tested by the Enlightenment.

This was politically all the more reactionary because it
pretended to rest on strictly scientific hence universally valid
principles. In fact little more had been done than to replace
faith in salvation by faith in progress and industry, and the
Mediterranean as the hub of history by Victorian England.
The cultural evolutionists became the Bossuets of Western
imperialism.

For better or worse, these were the epistemological conditions under which ethnography and ethnology took shape;
and they were also the conditions under which an emerging
anthropological praxis (research, writing, teaching) came to
be linked to colonialism and imperialism. One cannot insist
too much that these links were epistemological, not just
moral or ethical. Anthropology contributed above all to the
intellectual justification of the colonial enterprise. It gave to
politics and economics—both concerned with human Time—
a firm belief in "natural," i.e., evolutionary Time. It pro-
moted a scheme in terms of which not only past cultures,
but all living societies were irrevocably placed on a temporal
slope, a stream of Time—some upstream, others downstream. Civilization, evolution, development, acculturation,
modernization (and their cousins, industrialization, urbani-
zation) are all terms whose conceptual content derives, in
ways that can be specified, from evolutionary Time. They
all have an epistemological dimension apart from whatever
ethical, or unethical, intentions they may express. A discourse employing terms such as primitive, savage (but also
tribal, traditional, Third World, or whatever euphemism is
current) does not think, or observe, or critically study, the

"primitive"; it thinks, observes, studies *in terms* of the primitive. *Primitive* being essentially a temporal concept, is a category, not an object, of Western thought.

One last point needs to be made before we consider Time in the context of modern anthropology. Evolutionism, the very paradigm that made of anthropology a science worthy of academic recognition, was soon violently rejected on both sides of the Atlantic. One might be tempted to assume that this rejection included its use of Time. This, however, was not the case. Little needs to be said in this regard about the diffusionist opponents of evolutionism. Superficially at least, their basic assumptions were so much like those of evolutionism that their disputes could not have resulted in any major reorientation. The categorical frame of naturalized Time had become so powerful by the end of the nineteenth century that it easily absorbed ideas which the *Kulturkreis* people had inherited from the romantics.

This applies, for instance, to Graebner's textbook diffusionism. Throughout his *Methode der Ethnologie* (1911) "culture history" is predominantly construed from spatial distribution. That he accepted the evolutionist equation of time and change is implied in the following example of his reasoning: "If I can demonstrate that the total culture, in a given span of time, did not change at all, or only in minor aspects, then I am entitled to interpret dates which fall into this period more or less as if they were contemporaneous" (1911:62). In other words, in the study of "unchanging" primitive culture, temporal relations can be disregarded in favor of spatial relations. When Graebner frequently talks about temporal sequence (*Zeitfolge*), or temporal depth (*Zeittiefe*) this expresses an Aristotelian notion of effective causality; temporal sequence was indispensible for arguments concerning cultural causation. Still, diffusionism amounted to a project of writing a history without Time of peoples "without history." [18]

On the other hand, Graebner and other theoreticians of diffusionism should be read against the background of earlier culture-historical and culture-geographical writing, whose intellectual substance had not yet been diluted by postivist methodologization. A document for that period is an extraordinary essay by Friedrich Ratzel, "History, Ethnology and Historical Perspective" (1904). Half of the paper is addressed to questions of Time and temporal sequences and, in this case, romantic historism and natural history produce arguments that seem to run side by side. Ratzel begins with remarks on the theory of science, *rejecting* the evolutionist metaphor of a developmental tree. Such a taxonomic and hierarchical view obscures the radical commonality and equality of all sciences. Because all disciplines ultimately study phenomena that are on and of the earth they all are earth sciences (see 1904:488). With acknowledgements to Herder, Ratzel makes it clear that this geographism assumes a cotemporal community of mankind. Priority was given to the study of specific cultural identities understood as the outcome of processes of interaction between a population and its environment. Emphasis on real space (ecology) precluded concern with temporal grading of societies on evolutionary scales according to postulated general laws.

Nevertheless, in the century between Herder and Ratzel the episteme of natural history had established a hold on ethnology. When Ratzel turns to the question of "facts and temporal sequence" he advocates a "genetic" interpretation of cultural facts but affirms that the foundation of such an approach must be (natural-historical) collection, description, and classification of culture traits (see 1904:507). Imperceptibly, real ecological space is being replaced by classificatory, tabular space: distribution wins over growth and process. Ratzel is aware of this and describes contemporary infatuation with conjectural history, somewhat ironically, as follows: "It sounds very simple: Since all historical events occur in space, we must be able to measure the time they needed to spread by the distances that were covered: a reading of time on the clock of the globe" (1904:521). Almost immediately he doubts that in the realm of human history such simple translation of distribution in space into sequence in time will ever be "scientifically" possible. Especially, the determination of origins in developmental sequences is a matter of "practical" rather than scientific solutions (I hear in *practical* at least a connotation of *political*).

Within the human community (*Ökumene*) it is impossible to decree a specific period or area of cultural origins. Being situated on one and same earth, "no country is privileged over another" (1904:523).

The reason and excuse for this digression is to register at least one instance of anthropological uses of Time which hesitated to follow the main line of naturalization and temporal distancing. Its failure to influence mainstream anthropology in the twentieth century certainly was in part self-inflicted. It is hard to recognize Herder in Graebner's pedantry. The deeper reason, however, might be that the dominant trends in anthropology could not accommodate the anti-Enlightenment heritage that was at the roots of the culture-historical orientation.

Several discernible paradigms succeeded the evolutionist and diffusionist *Gründerzeit*. For the sake of brevity let us refer to them as (British) functionalism, (American) culturalism, and (French) structuralism. The early functionalists, notably Malinowski, simply rejected evolutionism on the grounds that it was armchair historical speculation. Notice however that he objected, not to its being too naturalist or rationalist in dealing with human society, but rather to its not being naturalist enough. Functionalism, in its fervor to explore the mechanisms of living societies, simply put on ice the problem of Time. Synchronic analysis, after all, presupposes a freezing of the time frame. Similar postulates were formulated by de Saussure and French sociologists such as Mauss and Durkheim. Eventually this made possible the rise of hyphenated functionalism-structuralism whose powerful hold on social anthropology, and, indeed, on sociology testifies to the unbroken reign of evolutionist epistemology. Its open, explicit revival in the later writings of Talcott Parsons, in debates on the history of science (Kuhn, Toulmin, Campbell, and others), and even in the latest twist of critical theory (Habermas and his opponent Luhmann), shows that it has not lost its attraction among Western intellectuals.[19]

Ironically, the supposedly radical break with evolutionism propagated by Boasian and Kroeberian cultural anthropology had little or no effect on these epistemological presuppositions. True, culturalism proclaimed "history" a domain irreducible to natural history. It relativized human, cultural time and left universal time to biological evolution. With that the Enlightenment project was in fact ignored and relegated to the natural sciences. Practically, concentration on cultural configurations and patterns resulted in such overwhelming concern with the description of states (albeit "dynamic" states) that the eighteenth-century élan in the search for a theory of universal human progress was all but abandoned.[20] In sum, functionalism, culturalism, and structuralism did not solve the problem of universal human Time; they ignored it at best, and denied its significance at worst.

Some Uses of Time in Anthropological Discourse

One might be tempted to conclude from all this that not much has changed since anthropology first emerged. Yet in at least one respect contemporary anthropology differs from its eighteenth and nineteenth century predecessors. Irrespective of theoretical orientation, field research has been established as the practical basis of theoretical discourse. That fact alone makes the problem of Time in modern anthropology complex and interesting.

If one compares uses of Time in anthropological *writing* with the ones in ethnographic *research* he discovers remarkable divergence. I will refer to this as the schizogenic use of Time. I believe it can be shown that the anthropologist in the field often employs conceptions of Time quite different from those that inform reports on his findings. Furthermore, I will argue that a critical analysis of the role Time is allowed to play as a condition for producing ethnographic knowledge in the practice of fieldwork may serve as a starting point for a critique of anthropological discourse in general. But before that argument can be developed we should be more specific about the notions of Time whose use in anthropological discourse we want to criticize. We must briefly survey uses of Time as they appear in anthropological discourse, i.e., in the writing of monographs; in synthetic and analytical works covering different ethnographic areas, or different aspects of culture and society over

several areas; and, finally, in textbooks presenting the sum
of our present knowledge. To shorten that task I propose
to distinguish three major uses of Time, each characteristic
of a genre of discourse, keeping in mind, however, that these
distinctions are not mutually exclusive.

Let us call the first one *Physical Time.* It serves as a sort
of parameter or vector in describing sociocultural process.
It appears in evolutionary, prehistorical reconstruction over
vast spans but also in "objective" or "neutral" time scales
used to measure demographic or ecological changes or the
recurrence of various social events (economic, ritual, and so
forth). The assumption is (and this is why we may call it
physical) that this kind of Time, while it is a parameter of
cultural process, is itself not subject to cultural variation. At
times, the nature of our evidence forces us to acknowledge
that a given chronology might be "relative"; but that means:
relative to chosen points within a sequence, not culturally
relative. Relativity of this kind is considered a flaw, which is
why carbon 14 and a host of other physical methods of dating caused so much enthusiasm when they first appeared.[21]
Not only were these thought to provide better, more correct
placement of human developments in Time; as far as human evolution is concerned they lead to a temporal explosion comparable to the one that did away with biblical chronology. Most importantly, though, these methods of dating
appeared to anchor human evolution and a vast amount of
cultural material once and forever in objective, natural, i.e.,
noncultural Time. To a great deal of anthropological writing they conveyed an aura of scientific rigor and trustwor-
thiness that previously was reserved to well-documented
histories of the recent past.

Of course, neither evolutionary theory, nor prehistory,
nor archaeology are confined to plotting data on temporal
scales. This leads us to considering a second use of Time in
anthropological discourse which makes its appearance in two
related forms. One I will call *Mundane Time,* the other *Typological Time. Mundane* connotes to me a kind of world-wise
relation to Time which, while resting assured of the workings of Physical Time in natural laws governing the uni-

verse, has no taste for petty chronologizing. Instead, it indulges in grand-scale periodizing. It likes to devise ages and stages. But unlike belief in the Millennium or the Golden Age, it keeps a cool distance to *all* times. The rhetoric of its discourse can therefore serve equally well the construction of imposing visions of the "human career" and the maintenance of cocktail talk about primitive mentality.

In another, more serious form this stance manifests itself as *Typological Time*. It signals a use of Time which is measured, not as time elapsed, nor by reference to points on a (linear) scale, but in terms of socioculturally meaningful events or, more precisely, intervals between such events. Typological Time underlies such qualifications as preliterate vs. literate, traditional vs. modern, peasant vs. industrial, and a host of permutations which include pairs such as tribal vs. feudal, rural vs. urban. In this use, Time may almost totally be divested of its vectorial, physical connotations. Instead of being a measure of movement it may appear as a quality of states; a quality, however, that is unequally distributed among human populations of this world. Earlier talk about peoples without history belongs here, as do more sophisticated distinctions such as the one between "hot" and "cold" societies.

In fact, constructs which appear (and often are proclaimed by their authors and users) to be purely "systematic" do in fact generate discourse on Time and temporal relations. This is obvious in the case of *class* (see, e.g., its use in the nineteenth century; Peel 1971:60 f); it is central in Max Weber's typology of authority. Systematizers such as Talcott Parsons did not succeed—and, God knows, they tried—in purifying Weber's brilliantly condensed analytical categories and type-constructs from their historical, temporal substance. After all, Weber cannot be read as if his central concern, the process of rationalization, did not exist. Rationalization clearly is a close relative of the Enlightenment idea of philosophical history. At any rate, not even the tightest formalizations of the "social system" were able to stop the logical leak kept open by the concept of charisma. In Weber's own writings about it temporal references abound: The notion of *Alltag* is used to define, by contrast, the nature of charismatic authority. As a process, charisma undergoes "routinization" (*Veralltäglichung*). Duration (*Dauer, dauerhaft*, 1964:182), emergence (*entstehen, in statu nascendi* 182, 184), flow (*münden*, 186), succession (passim), are all temporal, directional qualifications which signal fundamental links between typologizing and temporalizing. These connections were quite apparent to Weber's contemporaries. Hans Freyer noted in 1931: "Sociology grew out of the philosophy of history. Almost all of its founders regarded sociology as the legitimate heir to historical-philosophical speculations. . . . Not only historically, but with logical necessity, sociology includes problems of types and stages of culture; at least, it always leads up to that problem" (1959:294 f).

Inasmuch as some kind of typologizing is part of almost any anthropological discourse I can think of, notions of Typological Time are all-pervasive.

Finally, time has informed anthropological discourse in a third sense. For lack of a better label, I shall speak of it as *Intersubjective Time*. The term points back to one of its philosophical sources in phenomenological thought, as exemplified in Alfred Schutz's analyses of intersubjective time and in a few applications to anthropology, such as in Geertz's *Person, Time and Conduct in Bali*.[22] More importantly, the attribute *intersubjective* signals a current emphasis on the communicative nature of human action and interaction. As soon as culture is no longer primarily conceived as a set of rules to be enacted by individual members of distinct groups, but as the specific way in which actors create and produce beliefs, values, and other means of social life, it has to be recognized that Time is a constitutive dimension of social reality. No matter whether one chooses to stress "diachronic" or "synchronic," historical or systematic approaches, they all are *chronic*, unthinkable without reference to Time. Once Time is recognized as a dimension, not just a measure, of human activity, any attempt to eliminate it from interpretive discourse can only result in distorted and largely meaningless representations. The irony is that formal models, which are

often presented as the most "scientific" form of anthropological discourse, try in fact to ignore the one problem, Time,
which has been recognized as the greatest challenge by
modern natural science.

Taking Stock: Anthropological Discourse
and the Denial of Coevalness

This sketch of major ways in which conceptualizations of
Time inform anthropological thought and discourse shows
how enormously complicated our topic could get, especially
if we would now go into further differentiations and into the
many combinations in which Physical, Typological, and Intersubjective Time may be used. However, even if it were
possible to write something like a complete "grammar of
Time" for anthropological discourse, it would only show us
how anthropologists use Time in constructing their theories
and composing their writings. Findings from such analyses
would ultimately pertain to questions of style and literary
form; they are of great interest but do not as such raise the
epistemological question which must ask whether and how
a body of knowledge is validated or invalidated by the use
of temporal categorizations.

We must ask *what* it is that anthropologists try to catch
with their manifold and muddled uses of Time. (Or, which
is the same, what they are trying to escape from by employing a given temporal device). Let me indicate the direction
of my argument by formulating the following thesis: It is
not the dispersal of human cultures in space that leads anthropology to "temporalize" (something that is maintained
in the image of the "philosophical traveler" whose roaming
in space leads to the discovery of "ages"); it is naturalized-
spatialized Time which gives meaning (in fact a variety of
specific meanings) to the distribution of humanity in space.
The history of our discipline reveals that such use of Time
almost invariably is made for the purpose of distancing those
who are observed from the Time of the observer. I will illustrate this first by taking another look at the historical

break we attributed to Enlightenment thought. Then I will give a more detailed account of how distancing works in current anthropological discourse.

Enlightenment thought marks a break with an essentially medieval, Christian (or Judeo-Christian) vision of Time. That break was from a conception of time/space in terms of a history of salvation to one that ultimately resulted in the secularization of Time as natural history. For the present argument it is important to realize that this not only entailed a change in the quality of Time (sacred vs. secular) but also an important transformation as regards the nature of temporal *relations*. In the medieval paradigm, the Time of Salvation was conceived as inclusive or incorporative:[23] The Others, pagans and infidels (rather than savages and primitives), were viewed as candidates for salvation. Even the conquista, certainly a form of spatial expansion, needed to be propped up by an ideology of conversion. One of its persistent myths, the search for Prester John, suggests that the explorers were expected to round up, so to speak, the pagan world between the center of Christianity and its lost periphery in order to bring it back into the confines of the flock guarded by the Divine Shepherd.[24]

The naturalization of Time which succeeded to that view defines temporal relations as exclusive and expansive. The pagan was always *already* marked for salvation, the savage is *not yet* ready for civilization. Graphically (see figures 1.1 and 1.2) the difference between these views can be illustrated by contrasting two models. One consists of concentric circles of proximity to a center in real space and mythical Time, symbolized by the cities of Jerusalem and Rome. The other is constructed as a system of coordinates (emanating of course also from a real center—the Western metropolis) in which given societies of all times and places may be plotted in terms of relative distance from the present.

To anticipate an objection: evolutionary sequences and their concomitant political practice of colonialism and imperialism may *look* incorporative; after all, they create a universal frame of reference able to accommodate all societies. But being based on the episteme of natural history, they are founded on distancing and separation. There would be no

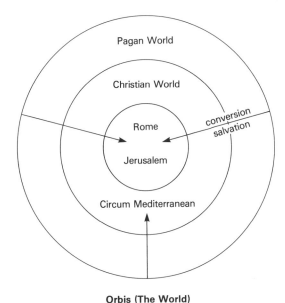

Orbis (The World)

Figure 1.1. Premodern time/space: incorporation

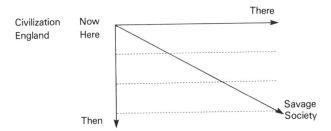

Figure 1.2. Modern time/space: distancing

raison d'être for the comparative method if it was not the classification of entities or traits which first have to be separate and distinct before their similarities can be used to establish taxonomies and developmental sequences. To put this more concretely: What makes the savage significant to the evolutionist's Time is that he lives in another Time. Little needs to be said, I assume, about separation and distancing in colonialist praxis which drew its ideological justification from Enlightenment thought and later evolutionism.

We can now examine how Time is used to create distance in contemporary anthropology. But before we get to distancing itself we should note that anthropology, like all scientific discourse, inevitably involves *temporalization* (an insight which will be developed in chapter 3). We must necessarily express whatever knowledge we have of an object in terms of temporal categorization. This is emphatically not only the case when we give "historical" accounts; Time is involved in any possible relationship between anthropological discourse and its referents. The referent shared by various subdisciplines of anthropology is strictly speaking not an object, or a class of objects, but a relationship. This is a cautious, insufficient term (I would prefer *contradiction*). In any *given* piece of anthropological writing the referent usually is a particular aspect of the relationship between elements or aspects of a culture or society; but all particular ethnography is ultimately about general relationships between cultures and societies. In fact, if we remember the history of our discipline, it is in the end about the relationship between the West and the Rest.[25]

By now it is generally admitted that all particular ethnographic knowledge we may have acquired is affected by historically established relations of power and domination between the anthropologist's society and the one he studies. In that sense, all anthropological knowledge is political in nature. However, it seems possible to me to carry our self-questioning further by focusing on Time as a key category with which we conceptualize relationships between us (or our theoretical constructs) and our objects (the Other). How exactly temporal categorizations contribute to defining and, in fact, constituting our object depends on the kind of time-use in a given anthropological discourse.

Physical Time may define seemingly objective distance between the researcher's culture and, say, the findings from an archaeological excavation or a record reconstructed from oral tradition. If an object can be located in 2000 b.c., or an event in 1865, they are definitely, irrevocably past. Such definitive anchoring in the past gives logical and psychological firmness to the standpoint of the researcher; this is why chronological dating, in itself purely mechanical and quantitative, can bestow scientific significance on a vast array of particular data. To be sure, chronology is only a means to an ulterior end. The temporal distancing it involves is needed to show that natural laws or law-like regularities operate in the development of human society and culture.

It may seem that the use of Physical Time is politically innocuous. If anything is "value-free" in science it should be the measurement of physical duration. On the other hand, one is tempted to invoke relativity theory as evidence for the inescapably positional relativity (*Standpunktbezogenheit*) of the experience of Time. Physicists commenting on the wider implications of relativity theory have done this; occasionally, social philosophers have attempted to relate their arguments for a multiplicity of cultural times to relativity theory.[26] I doubt that these connections can amount to much more than analogies or metaphors. After all, relativity theory is called for only in the realm of extremely high velocities. It is hard to see how it could be directly relevant on the level of culturally shared experiences. It might even be said that relativity theory is aiming too low in that it theorizes from the reference point of individual observers. Socially mediated "relativity" of Physical Time would have to be identified, rather, in historical processes of mechanization (the technology of clocks) and standardization (the acceptance of universally recognized units of measuring). In this latter sense of Western clock time, anthropologists have used Physical Time as a distancing device. In most ethnographic studies of other time conceptions the difference between standardized clock time and other methods of measuring provides the puzzle to be resolved.

Furthermore, the idea of Physical Time is part of a system of ideas which include space, bodies, and motion. In the hands of ideologues such a time concept is easily transformed into a kind of political physics. After all, it is not difficult to transpose from physics to politics one of the most ancient rules which states that it is impossible for two bodies to occupy the same space at the same time. When in the course of colonial expansion a Western body politic came to occupy, literally, the space of an autochthonous body, several alternatives were conceived to deal with that violation of the rule. The simplest one, if we think of North America and Australia, was of course to move or remove the other body. Another one is to pretend that space is being divided and allocated to separate bodies. South Africa's rulers cling to that solution. Most often the preferred strategy has been simply to manipulate the other variable—Time. With the help of various devices of sequencing and distancing one assigns to the conquered populations a *different* Time. A good deal of such Aristotelean political physics is reflected in the schemes of evolutionists and their cousins, the diffusionists.[27]

Physical Time is seldom used in its naked, chronological form. More often than not, chronologies shade into *Mundane* or *Typological Time*. As distancing devices, categorizations of this kind are used, for instance, when we are told that certain elements in our culture are "neolithic" or "archaic"; or when certain living societies are said to practice "stone age economics"; or when certain styles of thought are identified as "savage" or "primitive." Labels that connote temporal distancing need not have explicitly temporal references (such as *cyclical* or *repetitive*). Adjectives like *mythical*, *ritual*, or even *tribal*, will serve the same function. They, too, connote temporal distancing as a way of creating the objects or referents of anthropological discourse. To use an extreme formulation: temporal distance *is* objectivity in the minds of many practitioners. This, by the way, is reflected with great accuracy and exasperating predictability in the popular image of our discipline. I am surely not the only anthropologist who, when he identifies himself as such to his neighbor, barber, or physician, conjures up visions of a distant past. When popular opinion identifies all anthropologists as handlers of bones and stones it is not in error; it grasps the essential role of anthropology as a provider of temporal distance.

To recognize *Intersubjective Time* would seem to preclude any sort of distancing almost by definition. After all, phenomenologists tried to demonstrate with their analyses that social interaction presupposes intersubjectivity, which in turn is inconceivable without assuming that the participants involved are coeval, i.e. share the same Time. In fact, further conclusions can be drawn from this basic postulate to the point of realizing that for human communication to occur, coevalness has to be *created*. Communication is, ultimately, about creating shared Time. Such a view is not all that outlandish to anthropologists who, following Durkheim's lead, have probed into the significance of ritual and the creation of sacred Time. One could also point to an increased recognition of intersubjectivity in such new disciplines as ethnomethodology and the ethnography of speaking. But, on the whole, the dominant communication model remains one in which objectivity is still tied to (temporal) distancing between the participants. At least, I believe this is implied in the widely accepted distinctions between sender, message, and receiver. Leaving aside the problem of the message (and the code), these models project, between sender and receiver, a temporal distance (or slope). Otherwise communication could not be conceptualized as the *transfer* of information. In sum, even in communication-centered approaches that seem to recognize shared Time we can expect to find devices of temporal distancing.

These examples all lead up to the crucial point of our argument: Beneath their bewildering variety, the distancing devices that we can identify produce a global result. I will call it *denial of coevalness*. By that I mean *a persistent and systematic tendency to place the referent(s) of anthropology in a Time other than the present of the producer of anthropological discourse.*

What I am aiming at is covered by the German terms *gleichzeitig* and *Gleichzeitigkeit*. The unusual *coeval*, and especially the noun coevalness, express a need to steer between such closely related notions as *synchronous/simultaneous* and *contemporary*. I take *synchronous* to refere to events occurring at the same physical time; *contemporary* asserts co-occurrence in what I called typological time. *Coeval*, according to my pocket Oxford dictionary, covers both ("of same age, duration, or epoch"). Beyond that, it is to connote a common, active "occupation," or sharing, of time. But that is only a starting point; it will be elaborated as I proceed with my argument.

That coevalness may be denied with the figures of Physical and Typological Time needs, in my mind, no further elaboration. But there remains the difficulty we noted in regard to Intersubjective Time. It might be argued that this temporal category precludes the kind of ideological manipulation suggested by the notion that anthropologists "make use" of Time. If coevalness, sharing of present Time, is a condition of communication, and anthropological knowledge has its sources in ethnography, clearly a kind of communication, then the anthropologist *qua* ethnographer is not free to "grant" or "deny" coevalness to his interlocutors. Either he submits to the condition of coevalness and produces ethnographic knowledge, or he deludes himself into temporal distance and misses the object of his search.

This is the reasoning that underlies some of the most radical critiques of anthropology. It is implied when we are told that all anthropological knowledge is dubious because it is gained under the conditions of colonialism, imperialism, and oppression (views that were forcefully expressed in Dell Hymes' *Reinventing Anthropology*, 1974, and more thoroughly explored in a volume edited by Huizer and Mannheim, 1979).

Maxwell Owusu, in an essay "Ethnography in Africa" (1978) argues, on the basis of evidence contained in writings considered exemplary, that almost all the "classical" ethnographers failed to meet one basic condition: command of the language of the peoples they studied. As far as I can see, Owusu does not draw an explicit connection between communicative deficiencies and the denial of coevalness. He does, however, denounce the "essential anachronism" (1978:321, 322, 326) of ethnographic data collection aimed at savage society in its original state, but carried out under the political economy of colonialism. Our analysis of time distancing in anthropological discourse will reveal that this is perhaps not going far enough. Anachronism signifies a fact, or statement of fact, that is out of tune with a given time frame; it is a mistake, perhaps an accident. I am trying to show that we are facing, not mistakes, but *devices* (existential, rhetoric, political). To signal that difference I will refer to the denial of coevalness as the *allochronism* of anthropology.

The critique of anthropology is too easily mistaken for moral condemnation. But at least the more clearheaded radical critics know that bad intentions alone do not invalidate knowledge. For that to happen it takes bad epistemology which advances cognitive interests without regard for their ideological presuppositions. At any rate, what is interesting (and hope-inspiring) about ideological uses of Time is that they have not, or not yet, led our discipline into total self-delusion. To insist on field research as the fundamental source of anthropological knowledge has served as a powerful practical corrective, in fact a contradiction, which, philosophically speaking, makes anthropology on the whole an aporetic enterprise.

Let me explain. On the one hand, ethnographers, especially those who have taken communicative approaches (and that includes most ethnographers of value) have always acknowledged coevalness as a condition without which hardly anything could ever be learned about another culture. Some have struggled consciously with the categories our discourse uses to remove other peoples from *our* Time. Some needed breaks in that struggle—see Malinowski's diary;[28] some gave poetic expression to what is essentially an epistemological act—see the type of anthropological writing exemplified by Turnbull's *Forest People* and the Lévi-Strauss of *Tristes Tropiques*. But when it comes to producing anthropological discourse in the forms of description, analysis, and theoretical conclusions, the same ethnographers will often forget or disavow their experiences of coevalness with the people they studied. Worse, they will talk their experiences away with ritualistic invocations of "participant observation" and the "ethnographic present." In the end, they will organize their writing in terms of the categories of Physical or Typological Time, if only for fear that their reports might otherwise be disqualified as poetry, fiction, or political propaganda. These disjunctions between experience and science, research and writing, will continue to be a festering epistemological sore in a discipline whose self-image—and that is another heritage from the Enlightenment philosophes—is one of aggressive health and optimism.

Having diagnosed the illness as the denial of coevalness, or allochronism, we can begin asking ourselves what might be done about it. This will not be easy. An entrenched vocabulary and obstinate literary conventions alone are formidable obstacles. Moreover, coevalness is a mode of temporal relations. It cannot be defined as a thing or state with certain properties. It is not "there" and cannot be put there; it must be created or at least approached. As an epistemological condition it can only be inferred from results, i.e., from the different ways in which recognition or denial of coevalness inform anthropological theory and writing. A Kantian category of thought, or even a Durkheimian collective representation, are by definition "necessary" (otherwise they could not be categorical). As such, it would seem that the category of shared Time cannot be questioned; it is not subject to choice between recognition and denial, at least not within the frame which produces and uses it. Here is a dilemma with which we must struggle and I see no other way out of it but to focus on ideological mediations of scientific discourse such as the uses of Time we have examined here.

First of all, that it *seems possible* to refuse coevalness to another person or another people suggests that coevalness is neither a transcultural fact nor a transcendental condition of knowledge. The term *coevalness* was chosen to mark a central assumption, namely that all temporal relations, and therefore also contemporaneity, are embedded in culturally organized praxis. Anthropologists have little difficulty admitting this as long as it is predicated on a specific culture, usually one that is not their own. To cite but two examples, relationships between the living and the dead, or relationships between the agent and object of magic operations, presuppose cultural conceptions of contemporaneity. To a large extent, Western rational disbelief in the presence of ancestors and the efficacy of magic rest on the rejection of ideas of temporal coexistence implied in these ideas and practices. So much is obvious. It is less clear that in order to study and understand ancestor cult and magic we need to establish relations of coevalness with the cultures that are studied. In that form, coevalness becomes the ultimate assault on the protective walls of cultural relativism. To put it bluntly, there is an internal connection (one of logical equivalence and of practical necessity) between ancestor cult or magic and anthropological research *qua* conceptualizations of shared Time or coevalness. Paraphrasing an observation by Owusu, I am tempted to say that the Western anthropologist must be haunted by the African's "capricious ancestors" as much as the African anthropologist is "daunted" by "Malinowski, Evans-Pritchard, Fortes, Mair, Gluckman, Forde, Kabbery [sic], Turner, Schapera, and the Wilsons, among others" (1978:326).

Obviously, we are now getting into deep philosophical waters. Our examination of the uses of Time in anthropological discourse has led us to state their general effect or thrust as the denial of coevalness to the cultures that are studied. The most interesting finding, however, was one that precludes a simple, overall indictment of our discipline. This was the discovery of an aporetic split between recognition of coevalness in some ethnographic research and denial of coevalness in most anthropological theorizing and writing. There is a split between a recognizable cognitive necessity and a murky, ultimately political practice. That is, however, not an accident or simply a theoretical weakness. Such schizogenic use of Time can be traced to certain choices that were made at a time when anthropology emerged as a science. There is nowadays much talk about the political and moral complicity of our discipline with the colonial enterprise. Much remains to be said about cognitive complicity. To be sure, the logical connections between, say, British evolutionism and the establishment of the British Empire are obvious. But our critique of these connections is bound to miss its mark as long as it does not unearth some of the deeper links. The distance between the West and the Rest on which all classical anthropological theories have been predicated is by now being disputed in regard to almost every conceivable aspect (moral, aesthetic, intellectual, political). Little more than technology and sheer economic exploitation seem to be left over for the purposes of "explaining" Western superiority. It has become foreseeable that even those prerogatives may either disappear or no longer be claimed. There remains "only" the all-pervading denial of coevalness which ultimately is expressive of a cosmological myth of frightening magnitude and persistency. It takes imagination and courage to picture what would happen to the West (and to anthropology) if its temporal fortress were suddenly invaded by the Time of its Other.

Chapter Two / Our Time, Their Time, No Time: Coevalness Denied

At any rate, the primacy of space over time is an infallible sign of reactionary language.

Ernst Bloch [1]

It was then that I learnt, perhaps for the first time, how thoroughly the notion of travel has become corrupted by the notion of power.

Claude Lévi-Strauss [2]

COEVALNESS IS ANTHROPOLOGY'S problem with Time. Trying to bring that idea into focus, I have pushed the argument to a point where the next step would be to formulate a theory of coevalness. This will be a difficult task because the problem is not just "there"; it is continuously generated at the intersection of contradictions in anthropological praxis. As a project, a theory of coevalness must therefore be conceived in constant confrontation with anthropological discourse and its claims. Above all, we must seek to clarify the terms and purpose of the project by examining more closely "uses of Time" in the contexts of fully developed anthropology. For the past history of allochronic discourse is not the only obstacle on the road toward a theory of coevalness.

What was asserted about the allochronic, or schizochronic tendencies of emerging anthropology will now be extended to an analysis of two major strategies that have been employed by the established discipline. One is to *cir-cumvent* the question of coevalness through the uses of cultural relativity; the other *preempts* that question with the help of a radically taxonomic approach. Each strategy will be documented from the writings of anthropologists (especially M. Mead, E. T. Hall, and C. Lévi-Strauss) whose claims to speak for established anthropology are widely accepted. The mode of presentation will be polemical, that is, one whose primary objective is to advance or expound an argument. Such a mode must respect historical accuracy in the choice and interpretation of sources but it does not seek historio-graphic completeness. In no way is this chapter to be mistaken as an historical account of the schools it touches upon. The evidence for allochronism I am going to assemble should, therefore, be read as reasons *for* a thesis and not so much (at least not yet) as evidence against an adversary.

At any rate, the polemic will become accentuated as I move on in later chapters. In the end, I cannot accept what I appear to be granting now: that anthropology could ever legitimately or even just factually circumvent or preempt the challenges of coevalness.

To oppose relativity to taxonomy may cause a logical brow to rise. In what sense are the two opposed? Here the terms are taken merely as convenient labels evoking distinctive orientations toward culture and knowledge. The trends they designate correspond roughly to the Anglo-American and French "epistemic paradigms" analyzed by B. Scholte (1966). These paradigms are undoubtedly in practical opposition (and competition) even though, or perhaps because, they share a common ancestry. But it is of course possible to combine a relativist outlook on culture with a taxonomic approach to it. This is the case with various eth-noscientific or ethnosemantic schools to which, for practical reasons, we will not pay much attention in these essays.[3]

Circumventing Coevalness: Cultural Relativity

In *Thought and Change,* a book which treats explicitly of the uses of Time in anthropological theory, Ernest Gellner comments on the critique of evolutionism. As a theory, incidentally, he considers it "quite dead in academic philosophy, which is now superbly timeless . . . [and] virtually dead in sociology . . . [while] in formal thought only defended by very occasional biologists and historians" (1964:11). Noting that the conflict between evolutionary-genetic (time-centered) and structural (timeless) theories of explanation was fought out most dramatically in British social anthropology, he observes:

Systematic study of "primitive" tribes begun first in the hope of utilizing them as a kind of time-machine, as a peep into our own historic past, as providing closer evidence about the early links in the great Series. But real progress was achieved when this supposed time-machine was used with redoubled vigour but *without* any concern for reconstructing the past: when the tribal groupings were studied for their own sakes and explained in terms of themselves, and not as 'survivals' from a past supposedly even further back. (Gellner 1964:18 f)

If structuralism-functionalism showed disregard for Time (i.e., for Time as past) this does not mean that anthropology ceased to serve as a time-machine. Just because one condemns the time-distancing discourse of evolutionism he does not abandon the allochronic understanding of such terms as *primitive*. On the contrary, the time-machine, freed of the wheels and gears of the historical method, now works with "redoubled vigour." The denial of coevalness becomes intensified as time-distancing turns from an explicit concern into an implicit theoretical assumption.

What happened, and how did it happen? The celebrated progress of anthropology from Enlightenment cultural chauvinism toward treating other societies "in their own terms" (notice: not *on* their own terms) was made possible theoretically by logical and sociological positivism and its radical rejection of "historicism." As regards anthropology, this meant above all that the task of our discipline was decreed to be the "explanation" of systems or "structures" (in Radcliffe-Brown's use of the term). Explanation was said to be possible only within the frame of a present, synchronic set of relationships. It matters little whether that frame is metaphorized as a logical arrangement of structures, a mechanical or biological coordination of elements in an organism, or, somewhat later, as Popper's "logic of the situation."[4] We know now that extreme antihistorism has been difficult to maintain. Malinowski himself was led to concede that the functional method must admit the "time element"[5] and Evans-Pritchard was eventually moved to formulate a full rehabilitation in his essay "Anthropology and History" (1962 [1961]). British functionalist anthropology is quite interesting in this respect because it shows that to get rid of Time as "past" (theoretically) is not equal to conquering Time altogether. Even if these thinkers could convince themselves that temporal relations between a given sociocultural order or system and its antecedent forms have no explanatory value they could not ignore the problem of Time and temporal relations within a given order.

Talcott Parsons was aware of that in *The Social System:* Social action and interaction crucially involve "time relations" in such forms as time of action, "location in time" of actors, and "interpersonal time" (1963 [1951]:91 f.). Concerned as he was to show the social system as equilibrium maintaining, he links Time to the problem of deviance. He speaks of "time allocation" in the form of time schedules for certain kinds of action (251), "time off" for others (see 254n2, 302). Time is internally connected to deviance by virtue of the fact that Time is a "possession" (120), i.e., an inherently limited resource for an actor or a society. Time being an essential condition for "goal attainment," misallocation of time is at the bottom of most deviant behavior. Properly allocated, Time is a means to keep out conflict and interference. But then Parsons notes, cranking up the time machine, while time allocation is a task for all societies (relative to each society) it is more crucial in our own complex industrial world (which makes Time more relative to our society). After all, "we know that in many societies the motivational prerequisites for fitting into such a time orientation do not exist."[6]

Parsons illustrates the effect which the logic of functionalism had on thought about culture and Time: Time was encapsulated in given social systems. This made possible or, at any rate, reflected an ethnograpic praxis which asserted the importance of studying Time within cultures, while it virtually *exorcised Time from the study of relations between cultures.* "Theories of Time" held by various cultures could now be studied with "timeless" theory and method. This is what I mean by circumventing coevalness: Time as a dimension of intercultural study (and praxis) was "bracketed out" of the anthropological discourse.

To be exact, functionalist encapsulation of Time had two effects, and critical analysis must focus on the relationship between the two.

First, in the view of its adherents, the functionalist-structuralist approach actually favored ethnographic study of Time. To be sure, culturally different conceptualizations of Time, recognizable in language, symbols, and norms of behavior and in material culture had been studied for a long time (not only by anthropologists but also by classicists, historians of religion, and psychologists). Yet to the extent that their perspective was "comparative," these studies were out to establish "contrast"—between, say, Western linear Time and primitive cyclical Time, or between modern Time-centeredness and archaic timelessness. Functionalism made it possible to avoid these stereotypes of comparative discourse and to examine instead the specific, often contradictory uses of Time by a given society or culture. Even when the notion of Time is not explicitly discussed it clearly is touched upon in such classics as Malinowski's *Dynamics of Culture Change,* Leach's *Political Systems of Highland Burma,* Gluckman's *Order and Rebellion in Tribal Africa,* as well as in much of the work of Evans-Pritchard, M. Fortes, the Wilsons, Mary Douglas, and especially in Victor Turner's analyses of ritual process.[7]

Liberating and productive as it may have been ethnographically, functionalist emphasis on system-internal Time stood on questionable theoretical ground. This brings us to the second effect of "encapsulating" Time. As it turns out, the richness of relativistic ethnography of Time has its price. It must apparently be paid for with epistemological naïveté and logical inconsistency on a higher theoretical level. Naïveté often characterizes talk about the "cultural construc-

tion" of Time. The very notion of cultural construction (unless it is backed up by a theory of symbolization, which it
was not in classical functionalism) implies that cultural encoding works on some precultural, i.e., "natural" or "real"
experience of Time. By relegating *that* problem to philosophy
or to the psychology of perception, cultural relativism not
only does not solve the question of human time experience; it does not even raise it. Much of the study of "cultural transformation" of human experience remains sterile
because it is not capable (or unwilling) to relate cultural variation to fundamental processes that must be presumed to
be *constitutive* of human Time experience.

In that respect the problem with Time resembles, and
bears on, the problem with language and communication.
This was observed recently by Maurice Bloch in an essay
critical of structuralist-functionalist presuppositions about the
relativity of Time experience. Taking note of debates involving British anthropologists and philosophers, Bloch rejects the arguments for relativity, all of which ultimately
break down in the face of two facts: 1) "Anthropology itself
bears witness to the fact that it is possible, within certain
limits, to communicate with all other human beings, however different their culture" and 2) "If other people really
had different concepts of Time we could not do what we
patently do, that is to communicate with them" (1977:283).

The first observation is the weaker one. It either rests
on an equivocal use of *communication* (one that would have
to accommodate such instances of patent noncommunica-
tion as the denial of coevalness in anthropological discourse); or it is naively positivistic in that it tries to convince
us that the success of a project legitimizes the means or even
explains how it works. But I do believe that Bloch touches
the heart of the matter in his second observation. Time, in
the sense of shared, intersubjective Time, is a necessary
condition of communication.[8] As such it is the inescapable
counterpole to any investigation into culturally different notions of time, not only logically but also practically.

Bloch came to his position by way of analyzing the logical difficulties structuralist-functionalist theory had with explaining *change*. Radical functionalism in the line of Durk-

heim and Radcliffe-Brown asserts the essentially social, that is, system-relative nature of categories of thought. If followed through to its ultimate consequences, this means that social theory can account neither for new rules nor for new concepts; because "if all concepts and categories are determined by the social system a fresh look is impossible since all cognition is already moulded to fit what is to be criticized." Or, "if we believe in the social determination of concepts . . . this leaves the actors with no language to talk *about* their society and so change it, since they can talk only within it" (Bloch 1977:281). Paraphrasing that last statement, one might continue to reason that the anthropologist, inasmuch as he succeeds in entering another society/culture and comprehending it from *within* (which is the avowed ideal of cultural relativists), would be incapable of saying anything *about* it. Such *reductio ad absurdum* has of course always been countered by insisting on "universal translatability." But unless one can come up with a theory of translatability, all talk about it is just begging the question.

Bloch's own way out of the dilemma does not offer a viable solution either. His attempt is unsuccessful because he formulates a critique that accepts the terms of his adversaries. Not surprisingly, this leads him ultimately back to the same empiricism and naive realism we identified earlier as the hidden assumption of cultural relativism. If I understand him correctly, his argument can be summarized as follows: If conceptions and categories of Time are socially determined we must ask how it is possible to study them critically. We can avoid the logical impasse if we insist, first of all, that the problem with Time is a problem with *perception* of Time. Bloch then postulates two types of time perception (using, it seems to me, *perception* almost synonymously for *conceptualization*) There are perceptions of Time that are close to nature and others that are removed from it. He then asserts (criticizing but in fact reaffirming Durkheim's distinction of profane and sacred reality) that Time-close-to-nature is found in one kind of cultural knowledge, that which serves in "the organization of practical activities, especially, productive activities." Time-removed-from-nature is involved in "ritual communication." It is in practical contexts that we find universal categories of Time, while in ritual contexts we can expect to encounter the kind of relative conceptualizations studied by the structuralist-functionalist (see 1977:285, 287). That, I fear, will not do. Bloch's solution does accommodate universality and relativity but only at the price of compartmentalizing human praxis. Granted, his intention is to contribute a critique of ideological uses (that is, misuses) of Time, something, as he observes correctly, that was precluded by structuralist-functionalist theory. But by aligning rational use with practical activities and nonrational use with ritual he in fact seems to relapse into a Comtean sequence of developmental stages, a device whose Time-distancing function is obvious. These consequences cannot be avoided by insisting that *praxis* is here invoked in the Marxist sense. Marx was keenly aware that to oppose religious or ideological appearance (*Schein*) to socioeconomic and political reality (*Wirklichkeit*) is in itself a practical act of revolutionary emancipation. Hence, the temporal conditions of critically understanding "ritual" and "practical" conceptions of Time are essentially the same. It is a positivist strategy to make of religion and ideology objects *sui generis*, epistemologically, while at the same time reducing them to their social functions, ontologically.

Appeals to basic, universal human needs not withstanding, structuralism-functionalism promotes a kind of relativism whose neglect for the epistemological significance of Time becomes visible in unsurmountable logical inconsistencies. These have been demonstrated over and over.[9] In fact little could be added to a much earlier incisive critique by another Bloch, Ernst, of another relativism, Spengler's. Here we find in one condensed passage all the major elements that should make us anthropologists constantly reconsider our allegiance to a doctrine which we know to be untenable in our heads even if we continue to cling to it with our hearts. This is how E. Bloch summarizes the effects of relativism:

The very process of history is broken up into Gardens of Culture or "Culture Souls." These are as unrelated to each other as they are without connec-

tion to Man and human labor (which is the pervading matter of history) or to nature. . . . Quite artfully, historical relativism is here turned into
something static; it is being caught in cultural mo-
nads, that is, culture souls without windows, with no
links among each other, yet full of mirrors facing
inside. (1962 [1932]:326)

Bloch's critique is aimed at Spengler, but it does hit much
closer to home. There is now an anthropology which is fascinated with "symbolic" mirrors (signs, signifiers, symbols)
lining the inside walls of "cultures" and reflecting all interpretive discourse inside the confines of the chosen object.
These reflections give to an anthropological observer the illusion of objectivity, coherence, and density (perhaps echoed
in Geertz' "thick description"); in short, they account for
much of the pride anthropology takes in its "classical" ethnographies. One is tempted to continue Bloch's metaphorical reverie and to muse over the fact that such mirrors, if
placed at propitious angles, also have the miraculous power
to make real objects disappear—the analyst of strange cultures as magician or sideshow operator, a role that is not
entirely foreign to many a practitioner of anthropology and
one that is most easily assumed under the cover of cultural
relativism.

A critique of relativism could of course easily take up
most of this book, especially if we were to pay closer attention to its crucial role in the development of American anthropology. Such is not the purpose of these essays. But before we turn to another form of denying coevalness the point
needs to be made that relativistic circumvention of the
problem on a *theoretical* level did by no means lead its proponents to ignore Time and temporal relations as they affect *practical* relations between cultures.

So far we have commented on forms of cultural relativism whose roots must be sought in theories of sociocultural
integration stressing the social origins of cognitive categories (the Durkheimian approach in French and British anthropology). E. Bloch's critique of Spengler points to other
sources in romanticism and Nietzschean ideas, and numerous influences from Gestalt psychology to linguistics. This

second trend, exemplified and popularized by Ruth Benedict's *Patterns of Culture* (1934) proposed to study culture
with the help of aesthetic concepts such as pattern, style,
and configuration. Both movements, however, converged in
their intense concern for the unifying *ethos,* the common
morality that accounts for regularities in the behavior of the
members of a culture. In the United States, these research
efforts found their conceptual focus in such notions as "national character" and in the debates about "values." Insti-
tutes and programs (for instance at Columbia and Harvard)
brought anthropologists together with psychologists, sociologists, and political scientists and spawned unprecedented
interdisciplinary efforts.

To assess their bearing on the problem of coevalness,
we must recall for a moment the political context of these
studies, situated as they were during and soon after World
War II. Because intellectual-scientific and political preoccupations were so intimately connected in the minds and daily
activities of these researchers, much of the work of that period now seems dated and destined for oblivion. Yet, many
of the senior anthropologists who continue to influence and
shape the discipline today (and who are by no means to be
found in the same theoretical or political corners) spent their
formative years with culture-and-personality, national-char-
acter, and value studies. Taking into account the usual de-
lay of one generation it takes for scientific insights and concerns to percolate to the level of popular consciousness, one
realizes that a particular brand of wartime cultural relativism continues to inform the outlook of a good deal of anthropology.[10] It certainly cannot be overlooked in this critical examination of anthropological uses of Time.

Of special interest in this context is the clash between
extreme value-relativism in anthropological theory and the
perceived necessity to pass value judgments in political
practice. Perhaps there was never a stronger methodological emphasis on explaining entire nations in terms of their
basic values and patterns of socialization and institutionali-
zation than during that period of war against Germany and
Japan and in the cold war against the Soviet block which
followed victory over the enemy of mankind. With historical

hindsight we note the paradoxical nature of an enterprise in which relativistic studies of values were to produce knowledge that would help to bring the enemy down and, soon after, establish effective control and assure transformation of these values toward the model of the anthropologist's society.

Such an alliance between theoretical relativism and fight for a cause perceived as just and necessary was neither new (it resembles formally, if not historically, the links between colonial expansion and functionalist anthropology), nor was it much of a logical problem. To see this we need only be aware of an obvious implication of all cultural relativism: Once other cultures are fenced off as culture gardens or, in the terminology of sociological jargon, as boundary-maintaining systems based on shared values; once each culture is perceived as living its Time, it becomes possible and indeed necessary to elevate the interstices between cultures to a methodological status. At that moment the study of cultures "from a distance," clearly a vice in terms of the injunction demanding empirical research through participant observation, may turn into a theoretical virtue. A situation of political antagonism may then be rationalized epistemologically as the kind of objective distance that allows the anthropologist to view another culture in its entirety. A cultural holism is born which, in spite of terminological similarities, has little in common with the emphasis on totality that originates in dialectical thought (whose constituting acts are *negations* of cultural distance and of concomitant notions of scientistic objectivity). It is therefore not at all surprising to find relativistic and holistic orientations in the service of methodological projects which spurn time-consuming descriptive and comparative study in favor of projects designed to get at the jugular of other cultures, that is, at their central values and vital characteristics.[11] The spirit of the times is aptly expressed in "Assignment: Japan," the introductory chapter in Ruth Benedict's *The Chrysanthemum and the Sword*. "Tough-minded" acceptance of radical cultural difference is there opposed to soft sentiments about One World and Universal Brotherhood (see 1967 [1946]:14 f). Benedict fully realizes that pursuit of national identity may be intimately connected with the exercise of power over others, but that does not cause her to question the legitimacy of "being American to the hilt" (see 1967:12, 15), let alone consider the epistemological implications of a nation-centered theory of culture.

National character was one of the unifying concepts in these endeavors. The scholars who under the early leadership of Ruth Benedict participated in studies of national character eventually produced a manual significantly titled *The Study of Culture at a Distance* (Mead and Métreaux 1953). The book is a document for an important period in the history of anthropology. Its purpose is stated in the first paragraph of Margaret Mead's introduction:

This Manual is concerned with methods that have been developed during the last decade for analyzing the cultural regularities in the characters of individuals who are members of societies which are inaccessible to direct observations. This inaccessibility may be spatial because a state of active warfare exists—as was the case with Japan and Germany in the early 1940s; or it may be—as is now the case with the Soviet Union and Communist China—due to barriers to travel and research. Or the inaccessibility may be temporal, since the society we wish to study may no longer exist. (1953:3)

In another contribution to the volume, M. Mead speaks of the political applications of studies of culture at a distance:

The approach described in this Manual has been used for a variety of political purposes: to implement particular governmental programs within a country, to facilitate relationships with allies, to guide relationships with partisan groups in countries under enemy control, to assist in estimating enemy strengths and weaknesses, and to provide a rationale for the preparation of documents at the international level. All these uses involve diagnosing the cultural regularities in the behavior of a particular group or groups of people that are relevant to the proposed action—whether this be the dissemination of a propaganda statement, issuing an order against fraternization, a threat of a certain type of reprisal, an introduction of a new international regulation, or a like matter. The diagnosis is made for the purpose of facilitating some specific plan or policy, and at least implicitly, includes predictions of expected behavior that may make such a plan or policy successful or unsuccessful. (*Ibid.* 397)

It would be fascinating to subject this and similar passages to closer conceptual analysis. They illustrate the contention that anthropological approaches based on cultural relativism are easily put to work for such nonrelativist purposes as national defense, political propaganda, and outright manipulation and control of other societies. Having made that much clear, we must now ask a more pointed question: How does this particular amalgam of science and politics illuminate conditions and motives responsible for that affliction of anthropology we called allochronic discourse?

The mechanisms that translate relativistic studies of other cultures *in their terms* (and, incidentally, the ease with which theories and methods developed for the study of "primitive" culture are transferred to investigations of "developed" nations and to groups and classes within our own society) are subtle and not always obvious. Reading, for instance, through Mead's introduction one cannot help but be impressed by the intelligence and differentiated views she brings to her task, especially when she comments on concrete problems encountered in the practice of anthropological research. In this she is representative of her generation of eminent ethnographers. One gets the distinct impression of a decline toward crudeness and simplification in much of what is currently written about ethnographic method, even, and sometimes especially, by those who rightly criticize the ethical, political, and intellectual presuppositions of their predecessors.

Awareness of problems with Time could be a case in point. To begin with, M. Mead makes it clear that cultural distance is a problem of Time as well as space. In the brief statement on political applications she notes the importance of Time and timing in relations between cultures, cognitive or political. The passages where she makes recommendations for fieldworkers contain numerous observations on the importance of native attitudes toward Time which must be matched by the researchers's temporal awareness. After all, if the aim of such research is to observe "regularities" of behavior exhibited by individual members of a culture, some notion of Time and temporal sequence and, consequently, some methodological consideration of these temporal aspects must be an integral part of the approach. The pioneering work of Mead and Bateson (the latter also contributed to the manual) on the use of ethnographic film certainly gives evidence for a keen awareness of the temporal flow of human action.

In sum, the sort of cultural relativism which guided American anthropologists involved in the study of culture at a distance seems to put to a test our global thesis that anthropology has been constructing its object—the Other—by employing various devices of temporal distancing, negating the coeval existence of the object and subject of its discourse.[12] At the very least, we would have to credit numerous cultural relativists with awareness of the role of Time in shaping cultural behavior and, consequently, interaction between cultures (including field research).

This is the moment when a brief look at E. T. Hall's *The Silent Language* will show that ethnographic sensitivity to Time alone does not at all guarantee awareness of the problem of coevalness. The opening paragraph of chapter 1, ("The Voices of Time") exemplifies the rhetorical appeal of Hall's writing. It also manages to pack numerous theoretical assumptions into a few lapidary sentences: "Time talks. It speaks more plainly than words. The message it conveys comes through loud and clear. Because it is manipulated less consciously, it is subject to less distortion than the spoken language. It can shout the truth where words lie" (1959:15). Read in the light of elaborations in the later chapters, this opening statement describes Hall's position as follows: Time is not a mere measure, or vector, of culture; it is one of its constituents. Time contributes to the makeup of a culture because it is one of the most important means of communication. Conceptualizations of Time belong to the core of beliefs and values which account for the identity of a culture.

Taken at face value, such could indeed be the starting point for a theory of culture that would assign crucial epistemological significance to temporal relations. But closer analysis soon reveals that Hall is not concerned with epistemology. He does not raise the problem of *knowledge in terms of Time;* nor does he ask how temporal relations and conditions affect the validity of anthropological findings. His interest is in methodology and leads him to examine cultural "use" of Time. The book is replete with examples and comparisons between how *we* use time and how *they* use time.

Hall's opening statement also contains a theoretical assumption about culture in general, namely that it shapes and regulates behavior through unconscious mechanisms or rules. That implies in turn the methodological axiom that anthropology's major task is to reveal the unconscious forces by cutting through the layers of deceptive conscious behavior. In short, the study of Time in culture is valuable because it reveals what is hidden beneath the "lies" of spoken words. Truth and conscious awareness are here aligned with the knower, the anthropologist; dissimulation and submission to unconscious powers are on the side of the Other. No wonder that the theoretical notion of an unconscious culture and the methodological prescriptions that go with it easily turn into schemes to influence, control, and direct others; the anthropology of Time becomes the politics of Time. As one reads through *The Silent Language* one realizes that the many perceptive observations and examples illustrating how *they* use Time turn into so many recipes for how to use that knowledge so that *their* behavior can be tricked into serving *our* goals. Hall's frequent criticism of American boorishness and intransigence in dealing with other cultures cannot hide the fact that his book, too, is a "manual" for people who want to get things done (diplomats, expatriate managers and supervisors, salesmen and economic advisors).[13] Nowhere does his awareness of the role of Time in communication lead him to question the premises of cultural relativism. Because Hall holds an instrumental view of communication, *The Silent Language* is about temporal strategies, not about the role of Time in processes of cultural creation. Nor can it be said that Hall's persuasive and influential treatment of the subject is merely a political extension, or perhaps perversion, of anthropological insights. The political act is built into the very theory. The axiomatic assumption that much of culture is inaccessible to the consciousness of the "average member"[14] is already expressive of a political praxis where true knowledge about the workings of society is the privilege of an elite. The point of that observation is not to deny the existence of unconscious motives but to question the strategy of a discourse which, with the help of distancing devices, places the threat of the unconscious somewhere outside its own present.

Preempting Coevalness: Cultural Taxonomy

As Ernst Bloch observed, cultural gardens lie behind the walls of relativism. The anthropologist may watch them grow and change but whatever happens behind the walls occurs in a Time other than his. Whether he moves, temporarily, inside the walls, or whether he considers a culture garden from afar, the very notion of containing walls and boundaries creates order and sense based on discontinuity and distance. But this sort of relativism which circumvents the problem of common Time by postulating a multiplicity of times and spatial coexistence is not the only way of avoiding the question of coevalness and temporal coexistence. We will now consider a trend or paradigm which goes much farther. Rather than walling-in the Time of others so that it cannot spill over into ours, this school simply preempts the question of coevalness. Its strategy is to eliminate Time as a significant dimension of either cultural integration or ethnography. To this trend we usually affix the label of *structuralism* and we see it exemplified in the work of Lévi-Strauss. For the sake of simplicity I will follow that practice, fully realizing, however, that structuralism is at best a crude index of a highly complex intellectual tradition whose worldwide success became paradoxically linked to the idiosyncrasies of the intelligentsia of one country and, for all that matters, of one city.

By now numerous critical readings and appraisals of Lévi-Strauss's work are available.[15] The only excuse for adding my own observations to this literature is that no critique of the uses of Time in anthropology can ignore a movement whose proponents like to point out that they have no use for Time.

To begin with, I do not think that musings about the notion of structure are helpful in approaching structuralism. The term simply has too wide a currency in anthropology, especially in the kind of relativist discourse we discussed in the preceding section. Lévi-Strauss has taken great pains to set himself apart from these approaches on the grounds that they are guilty of too much empiricism, i.e. naïve trust in that which is immediately observable. Following Durkheim's and de Saussure's leads he disdains search for connections between cultural isolates and a reality outside. As a science of culture, anthropology is for him the study of relations *between* cultural isolates and of the rules or laws governing these relations. In such an enterprise it is futile to expect explanations either from history (asking how a given isolate came about) or from psychology (asking what a given isolate means to members of a culture, or how it motivates their behavior).

The fundamental assumptions of structuralism are best understood as a radically *taxonomic* approach to culture.[16] An analysis of the temporal aspects of structuralist discourse must therefore concentrate on the problem of Time and taxonomy. Among the many possible points of departure in Lévi-Strauss' writings I have chosen the following remarks, which are part of his famous attack on Sartre's idea of history in *The Savage Mind*. Nothing illustrates better the peculiar mixture of lucidity and duplicity characteristic of structuralist talk about Time.[17]

In style with his fundamental convictions regarding the binary organization of all knowledge, Lévi-Strauss begins by positing a "symmetry" between the preoccupations of the historian and those of the anthropologist: "The anthropologist respects history, but he does not accord it a special value. He conceives it as a study complementary to his own: one of the them unfurls the range of human societies in time, the other in space." He asserts that "distribution in space and succession in time afford equivalent perspectives" and rejects the claims of those who posit that history constitutes an irreducible and indeed privileged approach "as if diachrony were to establish a kind of intelligibility not merely superior to that provided by synchrony, but above all more specifically human" (see 1966:256).

An unattentive reader may be lulled into taking this for a conciliatory view, emphasizing complementariness, symmetry, and even equivalence (Which? None of these terms simply implies the others). Such is not at all Lévi-Strauss' intention. His structuralist duplicity rests on a not-so-subtle trick he operates in these passages. Ostensibly he sets up an argument with an opponent holding a view different from his own. In reality he has already reduced the opponent's position to his and from then on his argument is nothing but an elaboration of his own views. His ruse is to substitute diachrony for history. That sleight of hand is supported, much like the diversions all illusionists try to create while operating their magic, by directing the reader's attention to something else, in this case to the "opposition" of Space and Time.

Lévi-Strauss leads us to believe that *space* here could mean real space, perhaps the space of the human geographers who became the ancestors of anthropological schools that define themselves as historical. He permits the *sous-entendu* that his concern with space is expressive of attempts to understand human distribution in space as a reflex of ecological variation, of the emergence of different modes of production, or of geopolitical arrangements. In fact, he has little interest in understanding the role of real space in the genesis of human differences and conflict. Space for Lévi-Strauss is what M. Foucault likes to call "tabular" space, i.e., the kind of taxonomic space that must be postulated if cultural differences are to be conceived as a system of semiological constructs, organized by a logic of oppositions. Lévi-Strauss' thought does not inhabit a world; it lives in a matrix

that allows him, not just to place, but to *plot* any and all
cultural isolates in a logical grid.

At this point, those who are familiar with Lévi-Strauss'
writings might object that he constantly sets his structural
analysis of myth against the background of the spatial dis-
tributions of variants. But the point is that he perceived his
work as a radical break with "historical" reconstruction based
on the geographic distribution of culture traits. Even when
he ostensibly uses hard data on the ecology of the honeybee
or of the porcupine, his ultimate goal remains to show that
structural analysis of bee and porcupine tales can establish
connections of which historical-geographic research knows
nothing. Often one cannot help but feel that he deliberately
creates confusion between structural and ecological and historical arguments because that confusion works in his favor.
It makes him, at first, appear to take ethnographic accounts
on the location of variants in space seriously so that, later,
he can show the irrelevance of such information to a deeper
understanding. All along, he knows that the distribution
maps on which culture historians and folklorists locate variants in the hope of translating spatial relations into historical sequences are just that—maps. Maps are devices to classify data. Like tables and diagrams they are taxonomic ways
of ordering cultural isolates with the help of categories of
contrast and opposition: source vs. variant, center vs. periphery, pure form vs. mixed variant, displaying criteria of
quality vs. those of quantity, or whatever else diffusionists
use to map the traits of cultures. All of them are as taxonomic as the oppositions used in structural analysis, the difference being in whether or not one attributes the location
of an isolate to conscious activities and historical events (such
as borrowing, migration, and diffusion) or whether one accounts for it in terms of the operation of unconscious rules
or laws.

Diachrony serves a similar strategy. In the context of
Lévi-Strauss' attacks on Sartre one is led to believe that
diachrony could mean the same as history. This is manifestly not the case. Ever since de Saussure canonized the
opposition between synchrony and diachrony it served, not
as a distinction *of* temporal relations (as one might expect

from the presence of the component *chrony* in both terms), but as a distinction *against* Time.[18] The possibility of identifying and analyzing semiological systems is unequivocally said to rest on the elimination of Time and, by implication, of such notions as process, genesis, emergence, production, and other concepts bound up with "history." Diachrony does not refer to a temporal mode of existence but to the mere succession of semiological systems one upon another. Succession, strictly speaking, presupposes Time only in the sense of an extraneous condition affecting neither their synchronic nor their diachronic constitution. Thus structuralism, while accusing its opponents of reifying Time as a sort of mythical power, is guilty of ultimate reification. Time is removed from the realms of cultural praxis and given its place in that of pure logical forms. Of course, he who exorcises the devil must somehow believe in him, which is why structuralist exorcism of Time deserves serious attention.[19]

For a radical structural anthropology, Time (as Physical Time?) is a mere prerequisite of sign systems; its real existence, if any, must be sought where Lévi-Strauss likes to locate the "real:" in the neural organization of the human brain being part of nature. Structuralism thus illustrates one of the ideological uses of Time I identified in chapter 1: it *naturalizes* Time by removing it from the sphere of conscious cultural production. Lévi-Strauss, quoting Engels in support of his position, maintains that forms of thought reflect natural laws. Consequently, it is futile to use our (cultural) conceptions of temporal relation for the purpose of explaining relationships between things (see 1969:451). To expect meaning from Time would be Hegelian idealism; at any rate, it would run against the Saussurean principles on which structural anthropology is based. In *L'Origine des manières de table* Lévi-Strauss gives a succinct summary of the differences between the historical and his own approach. Where the former seeks "to make out contingent links and the traces of a diachronic evolution," the structuralist discovers "a system that is synchronically intelligible":

In doing this we have merely put into practice a lesson by Ferdinand de Saussure . . . : As one considers the subject matter of linguistics more deeply

one gets more and more convinced . . . of a truth
which gives us much to think, namely that the link
one establishes between things pre-exists . . . the
things themselves and serves to determine them.
(1968:216)

This is clear enough. If the proper subject matter of anthropology is the study of relationships between cultural
isolates, and if these relationships rest on principles or laws
that pre-exist their actualization in "contingent" history, then
Time is effectively removed from anthropological consideration.[20] Lévi-Strauss' attitude toward Time is firmly rooted
in nineteenth-century notions of natural history, a fact which
casts considerable doubt on his claim to be the legitimate
heir of the eighteenth century. Admittedly, Enlightenment
thinkers were interested in history for "philosophical" reasons. Above all they saw history as the theater of moral
principles ultimately traceable to "constant laws of nature."
But nature was decidedly *human* nature and the challenge
of the historian was to show the temporal unfolding of its
principles. The radical distinction between contingent human history and necessary natural history was drawn in the
nineteenth century. To maintain, as Lévi-Strauss does, that
anthropology *tout court* belongs to natural history is to deny
the Enlightenment origin of our discipline.

    As if it were not clear enough that the equivocation of
history and diachrony implies the rejection of historical
Time, Lévi-Strauss seems to feel the need to rub this in, so
to speak. He sets out to demonstrate that even *chronology—*
a conceptualization of Time one might accept as the objective residue after all the mystifications of the historical school
have been cleared away—is nothing but a classificatory, taxonomic device. "History," we are told, "does not . . . escape
the common obligation of all knowledge, to employ a code
to analyse its object, even (and especially) if a continuous
reality is attributed to that object." For history, "the code
consists in a chronology" (1966:258). Predictably, this view
of the conceptualization of Time leads straight back to its
reduction to taxonomic space:

Given that the general code consists not in dates
which can be ordered as a linear series but in

classes of dates each furnishing an autonomous system of reference, the discontinuous and classificatory nature of historical knowledge emerges clearly.
It operates by means of a rectangular matrix . . .
where each line represents classes of dates, which
may be called hourly, daily, annual, secular, millen-
ial for the purposes of schematization and which together make up a discontinuous set. In a system of
this type, alleged historical continuity is secured
only by dint of fraudulent outlines. (1966:260 f)

One cannot help but be astounded by the temerity of this
argument. A banal fact, that classification is one of the tools
of knowledge, perhaps even a tool of all knowledge at some
point of its production, is made into a transcendental rule.
Structuralism's own creature, the code, is promulgated as a
standard, in fact a "common obligation" of all knowledge (a
formula that rings with Durkheimian assumptions). This is
metaphysics of the worst sort, the one which is mixed with
moralism. So paralyzing is this self-righteousness of the taxonomist that one almost forgets to question the insinuation
that history of any kind could ever amount to chronology—
as if historians of all persuasions, at least since the eighteenth century, had not always insisted that chronology is
but a scaffold or tool for ordering what remains to be
understood. The same goes for history's alleged fixation on
continuity. Where is the historian after Hegel and Marx who
would dare to think continuity without discontinuity? Certainly Lévi-Strauss cannot find him in Sartre, against whom
he argues in this context.

But let us for a moment grant Lévi-Strauss his peculiar
view of history and admit that historians are indeed concerned with establishing chronologies and determining continuities. Such continuities, we are given to understand, are
fabricated by a deceptive use of Time. The remedy Lévi-
Strauss prescribes is to concentrate on space and discontinuous distribution. If the historian's use of Time may be a
deception—and it is the argument of this book that such is
the case in much of anthropology—then Lévi-Strauss' use
of space is a deception upon a deception. As we have just
seen, he himself has no difficulty packing chronological Time

into a spatial matrix. But as one need not accept the claim that a temporalizing usage, such as talk about the primitive, is innocent of spatialization (in the form of distancing) so it would be naïve to believe that when setting up a spatial taxonomic matrix of human culture one does not temporalize. At any rate, structuralism, to my knowledge, does not provide us with criteria to choose between a deception that imposes continuity on the discontinuous and one that cuts up the continuous into discontinuous isolates. Worse, by virtue of its self-assurance and faith that, with its own advent, such criteria are no longer needed, structuralism has in effect functioned to freeze and thereby preserve earlier historical and temporalizing ethnology. It is in such ethnology, after all, where Lévi-Strauss mines the building blocks for his monumental edifices. Behind the structural ramparts of his *mythologiques* he peruses and digests enormous amounts of ethnography without showing signs of being disturbed by the possibility that most of it might be corrupted to the core by the temporalizing ideological interests for which he has so much contempt. Why is he so impatient with Sartre when he has so much tolerance for the histories told by his anthropological forerunners and colleagues? He assures us that it "is not a bad thing . . . to borrow a quotation from a writer [W. J. Perry] whose work is generally denounced as an extravagant abuse of this historical method" (1969:122 f). He is, as I said, safe and does not need a true critique of bourgeois historism because "luckily, structural analysis makes up for the dubiousness of historical reconstructions" (1969:169).

In the end, one comes to suspect that Lévi-Strauss' flailing attack on history might really be instigated by his difficulties with another problem. He is troubled by the role of subjectivity in the production of both culture and knowledge about culture. In *The Savage Mind,* from which I have been quoting, this shows up repeatedly. Sartre, the existentialist, obviously irritates him more than Sartre, the Marxist. Lévi-Strauss' position on history and subjectivity, I believe, can be read in two ways: either as a rejection of history qua ideological prop for a misconceived subjectivity; or as a rejection of subjectivity for fear that history—and with it

Time— might pierce the armor of scientific anthropology. Be that as it may, it is important for our larger argument that structuralism's problem with Time is in various ways linked up with a reluctance to admit conscious, intentional, and therefore subjective activity as a source of knowledge, native or anthropological. Perhaps one needs to be reminded constantly that this position grew out of a critique of a rival camp on the French intellectual scene; otherwise one fails to appreciate the urgency with which it is advanced. But it is truly intriguing in the international context of anthropology that rejection of subjectivity did not lead to contempt for ethnographic "observation," to use Lévi-Strauss' favorite term for fieldwork. The structuralists, at least those who practice anthropology, do not escape the aporia arising from the conflicting demands of coeval research and allochronic discourse any more than their historical and relativist predecessors and contemporaries.

Having outlined ways in which structuralism contributes to the Time-distancing conventions of anthropological theorizing and writing, we must now briefly examine its struggle with the other horn of the dilemma, the temporal demands on personal, participant research. Once again, Lévi-Strauss likes to confuse us. He may ridicule dogmatic fixation on fieldwork *in situ* as when he declares futile the hope of the ethnographer in the Malinowskian tradition "to grasp eternal truths on the nature and function of social institutions through an abstract dialogue with his little tribe" (1967:12). But he never discards ethnography as a basis of all anthropological knowledge, neither explicitly (as we will see presently from a number of statements regarding the role and importance of fieldwork) nor implicitly (as is clear from his untiring use of ethnography, his own and that of other anthropologists). Furthermore, he is aware of intimate links between the praxis of fieldwork and what we called anthropology's problem with Time.

On at least one occasion, Lévi-Strauss invokes fieldwork precisely in the problematic sense I try to explore in this book. A chapter in *The Elementary Structures of Kinship* is titled "The Archaic Illusion." In it he criticizes the widespread tendency, especially among psychologists, to draw parallels between the minds of children and lunatics and

the "primitive mind." This old evolutionist strategy of arguing from ontogeny to phylogeny (and back) is of course
a classical example for "methodological" abuses of Time:
Primitive thought illuminates the thought of Western children because the two are equidistant from Western adult
thought. Both represent early stages in a developmental sequence. Lévi-Strauss is quick to denounce this as an insult
to both, our children and primitive adults, and he calls on
the ethnographer as a witness. He especially rejects ontogenetic-phylogenetic arguments which would make primitive children even more infantile than our own: "Every
fieldworker who has had concrete experience of primitive
children will undoubtedly agree that the opposite is more
likely to be true and that in many regards the primitive child
appears far more mature and positive than a child in our
own society, and is to be compared more with a civilized
adult." (1969:92)

Even more important than the specific context of this
remark is the strategy of invoking the fieldworker and his
"concrete experience" as an instance from which to judge
the claims of a temporalizing discourse. Unfortunately, it
soon turns out that a critique of temporal distancing is by
no means central to his argument. Foremost in Lévi-Strauss'
mind is the role of fieldwork in distinguishing the anthropologist from the historian (it being understood that for him
the latter is always the "culture historian" fascinated by culture traits and their spatial distribution). He must, therefore, find a rationale for fieldwork which not only asserts
the ethnographer's subjective experience as the ultimate instance of anthropology but also claims superior objectivity
for such knowledge. Somehow there must be a way of showing that one person's immersion in the concrete world of
another culture accomplishes the scientific feat of reducing
that concrete world to its most general and universal principles. Living in the Time of the primitives, the ethnographer will be an ethnographer only if he outlives them, i.e.,
if he moves *through* the Time he may have shared with them
onto a level on which he finds anthropology:

Indeed, such is the way the ethnographer proceeds
when he goes into the field, for however scrupulous

and objective he may want to be, it is never himself,
nor is it the other person, whom he encounters at
the end of his investigation. By superimposing
himself on the other, he can at most claim to extri-
cate what Mauss called facts of general functioning,
which he showed to be more universal and to have
more reality. (1976:8 f)

Such feats of transcendence as Lévi-Strauss expects from
the ethnographer turn out to be variously linked to the
achievement of "distance" conceived, not as a mere fact, but
as a methodological tool in a manner that reminds us of its
uses in relativist discourse. Much like American culturalism,
French structuralism manages to turn denial of coevalness
into a positive tool of scientific knowledge. A few examples
will show this.

Let us return, first, to Lévi-Strauss' critique of the "archaic illusion" in *The Elementary Structures of Kinship*. Drawing parallels between Western children and primitives, he
argues, is an insult to all involved except, as it turns out, to
the Western adult mind (which is responsible for drawing
those parallels in the first place). To our surprise, Western
thought is in the end acquitted of the crime of ideological
Time distancing which ontogenetic-phylogenetic arguments
seem to perpetrate on the primitive. The reasoning is as
follows: We do have a valid point after all when we observe
that the primitives appear to think like (our) children. Calling the primitive childlike is to "generalize" him as someone
with whom we share a common transcultural basis. Analogies between socialization into a culture and learning a language supposedly demonstrate this.

Lévi-Strauss assumes (much like the American cultural
relativists) that a culture takes shape and identity by select-
ing a few among a practically infinite number of possibilities
(as a language selects its significant sounds from an infinite
number of possible sounds). Such a view is not just methodological—proposing that culture is best *described* taxo-
nomically—it is also ontological when it maintains that culture is *created* by selection and classification. It is a concept
of culture devoid of a theory of creativity or production,
because in a radically taxonomic frame it makes no sense to
raise the question of production. By extension, we never

appreciate the primitive as a producer; or, which is the same, in comparing ourselves to the primitive we do not pronounce judgment on what he thinks and does, we merely classify ways *how* he thinks and acts.[21] When Western man calls the primitive childlike, this is for the structuralist not a statement on the nature of primitive man. That particular conceptualization of a relationship between us and the Other, we are assured, is merely taxonomic. All we do in calling primitives infantile is class perceived similarities: The choices primitive societies have not yet made are analogous to the choices children in our societies have not yet made (see 1969:92 f).

Lévi-Strauss' demonstration of taxonomic innocence leaves us with questions that must be asked. Are we to accept his contention that in our own society relations between adults and children merely reflect different degrees of "extension" of knowledge? Are we to overlook that adult-child relations are also, and sometimes primarily, fraught with barely disguised attitudes of power and practices of repression and abuse? Even worse, are we to forget that talk about the childlike nature of the primitive has never been just a neutral classificatory act, but a powerful rhetorical figure and motive, informing colonial practice in every aspect from religious indoctrination to labor laws and the granting of basic political rights? Is apartheid, one might ask, tendentiously but not without justification, only a classificatory scheme? Aside from the evolutionist figure of the savage there has been no conception more obviously implicated in political and cultural oppression than that of the childlike native. Moreover, what could be clearer evidence of temporal distancing than placing the Now of the primitive in the Then of the Western adult?

My comment on these passages from *The Elementary Structures of Kinship* was occasioned by Lévi-Strauss' invoking the fieldworker as a witness against Time-distancing. What became of that testimony in the course of a few pages of structuralist argument? With remarkable ease, fieldwork experience was neutralized by an overriding taxonomic concern to justify one of the more despicable devices of anthropological and Western political discourse.

So that it may not appear as if the only objection to

taxonomic subterfuge was a political one (although in the end all objections are political, even those that are made on "logical" grounds) let us take a look at another example. Once again the issue appears to be the role of fieldwork. Twice in his essay "History and Anthropology" Lévi-Strauss is impelled to note the paradoxical nature of their relationship. Commenting on Boas' valuation of fieldwork he states:

> Knowledge of social facts must be based on induction from individualized and concrete knowledge of social groups localized in time and space. Such specific knowledge, in turn, can be acquired only from the history of each group. Yet such is the nature of the subject-matter of ethnographic studies that in the vast majority of cases history lies beyond reach. (1967:9)

Later on he sums up the struggle of anthropology with history in this paradoxical formula:

> The criticism of evolutionist and diffusionist interpretations showed us that when the anthropologist believes he is doing historical research, he is doing the opposite; it is when he thinks that he is not doing historical research that he operates like a good historian, who could be limited by the same lack of documents. (1967:16 f)

To solve that paradox one must first realize that the "good historian" and the anthropologist are really concerned with one and the same problem: otherness (see 1967:17). It is a secondary matter that for the historian otherness normally means remoteness in Time, whereas the anthropologist is concerned with cultural difference as it appears in spatial distance and distribution. The historian finds his sources of knowledge in documents which he uses as best he can to understand the actual, specific genesis of an institution or society. The anthropologist relies on fieldwork instead of historical documents which are lacking for most of the societies he studies. But there is more to fieldwork than its being a substitute for lacking documents. Nor is it adequate to think of fieldwork as piecemeal induction: "forms of social existence cannot be apprehended simply from the out-

side—the investigator must be able to make a personal reconstruction of the synthesis characterizing them, he must
not merely analyze their elements, but apprehend them as
a whole in the form of a personal experience—his own"
(1967:370 f).

So we are back to personal experience, and one begins
to wonder how the same scholar who shows such relentless
contempt for subjectivity in his attacks on Sartre could assign epistemological significance to fieldwork as a subjective
activity. Our doubts are soon put to rest when we discover
that, once again, in affirming fieldwork, Lévi-Strauss gets
around the problem with Time. As expected, he posits that
the fieldworker's personal, concrete encounter with another
culture is of a taxonomic nature. This is how the argument
runs: The researcher's task is to make the otherness of the
societies he studied available to his own *as experience*. He
achieves this by enlarging "a specific experience to the dimensions of a more general one" (1967:17). Most important, a "transition from the conscious to unconscious is associated with progression from the specific to the general"
(*ibid.* 21). The fieldworker's experience, while personal and
concrete, is not subjective but objective, inasmuch as he reasons

on the basis of concepts which are valid not merely
for an honest and objective observer, but for all
possible observers. Thus the anthropologist does
not simply set aside his own feelings; he creates new
mental categories and helps to introduce notions of
space and time, opposition and contradiction, which
are as foreign to traditional thought as the concepts
met with today in certain branches of the natural
sciences. (1967:361)

The key to understanding this view of empirical objectivity is its glorification of distance based on a denial of the
conditions of shared Time. The structuralist can continue
to insist on the importance of concrete experience without
much of a problem because personal experience is in this
view nothing but the vehicle or medium for the epiphany
of the "general" and "unconscious." [22] Like rays focused by

a lens, like the spirit's voice speaking through the medium, objective knowledge of the unconscious appears *through* the ethnographer's (conscious) activity, but it is not a result of it. Anthropological knowledge, like myth, thinks the anthropologist, not the other way round. He takes on his role as the priest and missionary of the transsubjective, scientific, speak taxonomic, structures that govern the universe.

The most disconcerting fact about such a view of field research is that it leaves no instance for appeal or critique. There may be bad anthropologists (as there are bad priests) but, structuralism seems to hold, that does not affect the role and validity of the discipline they celebrate. Being the apprehension of the general and unconscious, anthropology is once and forever removed from the lowly regions of political struggle, from intellectual contestation, and from outright abuse, in short, from the dialectic of repression and revolt that makes up the real context in which it appeared as an academic discipline.

Still, as if unable to find acquiescence in the exorcism of the subjective, concrete, and conscious, Lévi-Strauss appears to struggle with a recalcitrant residue in his theory of ethnographic objectivity. He is, after all, not only a theoretician but also a practitioner of anthropology as an ethnographer and teacher. He recognizes that fieldwork experience involves in many cases a conversion, an "inner revolution that will really make [the ethnographer] into a new man" (1967:371). But apparently he has no difficulty at all in separating the effects of field experience from their significance. The fact of personal conversion does not cause him to reconsider his epistemological stance. He takes the easy way out, which is to insist on the social function of the personal experience. With disarming frankness he qualifies it as a kind of initiation whose function it is to admit adepts to the discipline and to provide a selected few with legitimacy and a license to practice. In fact, he compares the ethnographers' field experience to training analysis among psychoanalysts and goes on to recommend "personal" supervision in the training of the novice, suggesting that close contact with someone who has had the experience before might expedite conversion in the apprentice.

The observation that notions such as conversion and initiation smack of religio-mystical thought is easily made but perhaps not quite so easily understood.[23] In pointing out these resemblances I have no interest in joining the chorus of critics who claim to recognize in that monumental inkblot which is Lévi-Strauss' *oeuvre* almost every major intellectual movement in history (including gnosis, the Kabala, and similar esoteric pursuits). But there are serious reasons for dwelling on his way of turning apparent emphasis on the personal into affirmations of the trans-subjective, the ritual and institutional: The researcher's personal encounter, we are told, *is* the objective working of science because it is posited as a sort of pure channel through which ethnography passes into ethnology and anthropology. Closer examination of the many statements Lévi-Strauss makes about the nature of fieldwork reveals that the one notion which for him characterizes this activity more than any other is *observation*. He does not seem to have much use for the qualifier *participant*, customarily attached to the term. Even less does he consider communicative interaction, an idea currently much discussed in theories of fieldwork. For Lévi-Strauss the ethnographer is first and foremost a viewer (and perhaps voyeur). Observation conceived as the essence of fieldwork implies, on the side of the ethnographer, a contemplative stance. It invokes the "naturalist" watching an experiment. It also calls for a native society that would, ideally at least, hold still like a *tableau vivant*. Both images are ultimately linked up with a visual root metaphor of knowledge. In this, structuralism rejoins the aestheticizing attitudes of the cultural relativists. In both movements, the illusion of simultaneity (as between the elements of a picture that is contemplated, or between the visual object and the act of its contemplation) may lead to utter disregard for the active, productive nature of field-*work* and its inevitable implication in historical situations and real, political contradictions.

Another strategy of escape from Time and history common to both movements has been to declare the unconscious the true object of anthropological research. But nowhere are these convergences clearer and more directly significant for the problem of Time-distancing and the denial of coevalness than in the valuation of cultural difference as *distance*. In the Mead-Métreaux volume this remained rather implicit and vague; it is spelled out clearly by Lévi-Strauss: Social anthropology "apprehends" its objects, i.e., semiological facts as defined by de Saussure, "either in their most remote manifestations or from the angle of their most general expression" (1976:10). The point is, as could be shown from other contexts, that the two are interchangeable. Distance is the prerequisite for generality as the study of primitive society is the road toward uncovering the universal structures of the human mind.

It is insofar as so-called primitive societies are far distant from our own that we can grasp in them those "facts of general functioning" of which Mauss spoke, and which stand a chance of being "more universal" and having "more reality." . . . This observation which has the privilege of being distant, no doubt implies some differences of nature between these societies and our own. Astronomy not only demands that celestial bodies be far away but also that the passage of time have a different rhythm there, otherwise the earth would have ceased to exist long before astronomy was born. (1976:28)

Statements like this leave little room for speculation. Distance in space and time and, in fact, a different Time are made the prerequisites not only for certain ways of doing anthropology but for its very existence. With that, the temporal is finally and totally removed to the level of metaphysical presuppositions; it no longer can be a problem in the exercise of anthropology as a "science."

The pains taken by structuralism to remove Time and the problem of coevalness from anthropological praxis and discourse should of course be evaluated historically; its allochronic escape is a response to its own social and political context. Far from expressing the coming-to-rest of a troubled discipline on a solid scientific basis and an unassailable logic, structuralism indicates (by virtue of opposition) that something might be basically wrong with Western conceptions of scientific rationality. Politically, Lévi-Strauss' rise to prominence and the quantitative explosion of anthropology in the United States coincide with the period of "decolonization" i.e., the demise of direct colonization demanding personal and direct involvement in the *oeuvre civilisatrice*. American anthropology and French structuralism, each having developed ways to circumvent or preempt coevalness, are potential and actual contributors to ideologies apt to sustain the new, vast, anonymous, but terribly effective regimen of absentee colonialism.[24]

Chapter Three / Time
and Writing About the Other

Even if [an observer] is in communication with other observers, he can only hear what they have seen in their *absolute pasts, at times which are also* his *absolute past. So whether knowledge originates in the experience of a group of people or of a society, it must always be based on what is past and gone, at the moment when it is under consideration.*

David Bohm [1]

La raison du plus fort est toujours la meilleure: Nous l'allons montrer tout à l'heure.

La Fontaine [2]

SO FAR, EXAMPLES of temporal distancing between the subject and the object of anthropology were invoked to support the argument that the temporal conditions experienced in fieldwork and those expressed in writing (and teaching) usually contradict each other. Productive empirical research, we hold, is possible only when researcher and researched share Time. Only as communicative praxis does ethnography carry the promise of yielding new knowledge about another culture. Yet the discourse that pretends to interpret, analyze, and communicate ethnographic knowledge to the researcher's society is pronounced from a "distance," that is, from a position which denies coevalness to the object of inquiry. Is this contradiction real or only apparent? To make sure that we are not losing our time with a false problem we must name the conditions under which, in our understanding of the term, a real contradiction arises.

Contradiction: Real or Apparent

First, the two activites under examination—field research and the communication of findings in writing and teaching—must in fact be part of a discipline claiming a unified existence. This was certainly not always the case. After all, travelogues and armchair syntheses coexisted side by side during most of the early history of anthropology without being practically united in the same person or institution.[3] Even today the degree to which empirical research is emphasized over theoretical and synthetic work varies from country to country and from practitioner to practitioner. But wherever anthropology presently is recognized as an academic discipline (albeit often under different names, or in conjunction with qualifiers indicating specialization within the field) its representatives insist on the necessity of both empirical research and theoretical interpretation of some sort.[4]

Second, for a contradiction to arise between two activities there must be an issue, a problem with regard to which contradictory attitudes or effects can be identified. We found such an issue in the contradictory uses of Time. But there remains a question that will need much further thought and clarification. It could be argued that to accept shared Time in personal fieldwork is a matter of convenience, something that goes with the prevalent lore of our discipline. Denying coevalness need not affect in principle the production of ethnographic knowledge. Or one might posit that because prose narrative is the literary genre of most anthropological writing, devices of temporal sequencing and distancing are simply inevitable aspects of literary expression.

If the first objection holds, our contention that there is a contradictory, indeed schizoid and often hypocritical practice in need of careful analysis and critique would be seriously weakened. Many anthropologists insist that there is nothing to the mystique of fieldwork. All it does, and it matters little how, is to produce *data*. Data may be used, selected, and manipulated to verify the theories formulated in anthropological discourse in any shape and manner the theoretician sees fit. The conditions under which data were

obtained, as long as certain basic rules were followed, neither validate nor invalidate theories. Validity rests on logical
criteria of consistency, parsimony, elegance, and so forth.
In fact, to be at all admissible as evidence, data are required
by some canons of scientific inquiry (those that rule quantitative approaches and certain structural methods) to come
in bits and pieces, preferably selected at random and
cleansed from possible contamination by lived experience
and the personal bias such experience might introduce. Such
a view of social scientific inquiry could not possibly admit a
contradiction between the temporal conditions of research
and writing. The only thing that could contradict the propositions formulated in writing would be contrary evidence.
Such counterevidence, however, would not in principle be
different from evidence supporting the explanations that
would have to be dismissed. It, too, results from the manipulation of data, not from contradictions between insights
gained in lived experience and those reached by the operations of a method. If coevalness were recognized by the positivist, he would presumably relegate the problem to psychology or philosophy.

Communicative and dialogic alternatives to positivist and
empiricist ethnography have been widely discussed in recent years.[5] Here I want to concentrate on the argument
that the idea of a contradiction between research and writing might raise a spurious problem. Could it be that temporal distancing and denial of coevalness are not faults, but
conditions of possibility of anthropological discourse? Anthropologists, like other scientists, are expected to produce
a discourse of facts and not of fiction. The *factum* is that
which *was* made or done, something that inevitably is "past"
in relation to the acts of recording, interpreting, and writing. In view of its obligations to facticity, how could there be
any claims on anthropological discourse to heed the demands of coevalness qua copresence of talk and of that which
is talked about?

Because these questions bear on the theory of literary
production in general they may lead us into an area too vast
to be adequately covered in these essays. Yet if we continue
to identify (and denounce) denial of coevalness in anthro-

pological discourse we must at some point ask how such denial can be identified on the level of texts. We should be
able to adduce semantic, syntactic, and stylistic examples of
allochronism. As will be seen presently, it is not difficult to
point out the workings of such devices here and there.
However, to do this in a systematic fashion one would have
to submit the *oeuvre* of a number of representative anthropologists to linguistic and literary analysis, a task of vast
proportions and one for which no single critic can claim
adequate competence. We must settle here for something
more modest and more general. I will first ask to what extent anthropological discourse actually rests on temporalization and whether such temporalization inevitably results
in temporal distancing. Following that, I will take up a more
specific problem, namely, the inherently autobiographic nature of much anthropological writing. Finally, I will once
more confront the claims of "taxonomic" discourse with respect to temporalization.

Temporalization, being an object of inquiry in these essays, cannot be defined axiomatically at the outset. In my
understanding, it connotes an activity, a complex praxis of
encoding Time. Linguistically, temporalization refers to the
various means a language has to express time relations. Semiotically, it designates the constitution of sign relations with
temporal referents. Ideologically, temporalization has the
effect of putting an object of discourse into a cosmological
frame such that the temporal relation becomes central and
topical (e.g., over and against spatial relations). Finally, temporalizing, like other instances of speech, may be a deictic
function. In that case a temporal "reference" may not be
identifiable except in the intention and circumstances of a
speech-act.

Temporalization: Means or End?

A rapid review of the most common temporal operators in
anthropological prose could follow customary (but somewhat questionable) distinctions between lexical, (morpho-)
syntactic, and stylistic levels of discourse. On the level of the

lexicon, anthropological language is of course crowded with expressions which in one way or another signal conceptualization of Time and temporal relations (such as sequence, duration, interval or period, origins, and development). We already commented on some of these terms, as well as on the fact that a term need not be manifestly "temporal" in order to serve as a Time-distancing device. In fact, expressions that have a clear temporal referent (a date, a time span, an indication of past, present, or future) are probably less important, quantitatively as well as qualitatively, than those whose temporalizing function derives from the context in which they are used. With regard to our special interest in the critique of allochronic discourse we would have to concentrate, in semiological parlance, on connotation rather than denotation. The Time-distancing effect may, for instance, be achieved by the moral-political connotations of ostensibly pure temporal terms, or by the temporal connotations of "strictly technical," classificatory terms.

Take a word like *savagery*. As a technical term in evolutionary discourse it denotes a stage in a developmental sequence. But no degree of nominalist technicality can purge the term of its moral, aesthetic, and political connotations. Cumulatively, these result in a semantic function that is everything but purely technical. As an indication of relationship between the subject and the object of anthropological discourse, it clearly expresses temporal distancing: *Savagery* is a marker of the past, and if ethnographic evidence compels the anthropologist to state that savagery exists in contemporary societies then it will be located, by dint of some sort of horizontal stratigraphy, in *their* Time, not ours.

Kinship, on the surface one of the most innocent descriptive terms one could imagine, is fraught with temporal connotations. From the early debates on "classificatory" kinship systems to current studies of its *continued* importance in Western society, *kinship* connoted "primoridal" ties and origins, hence the special strength, persistence, and meaning attributed to this type of social relation. Views of kinship relations can easily serve to measure degrees of advancement or modernization. By comparing the relative importance of kinship bonds in different societies or groups one can construct developmental, i.e., temporal scales. In this context of connotative, symbolic function one would also have to examine the use of metaphors and other tropes.[6] Lévi-Strauss' distinction between hot and cold societies belongs here (see 1966:232 f) as do observations such as the one where he aligns the synchronic with the diurnal and the diachronic with the nocturnal (see 1968:156).

We need not go into further detail to make the point that counts: An examination of the temporal lexicon inevitably leads critical analysis beyond the lexicon, to higher levels of discourse and to wider contexts. In the words of Roland Barthes: "As for the signified of connotation, its character is at once general, global and diffuse; it is, if you like, a fragment of ideology" (1970:91).

One would come to similar conclusions if one were to examine the syntactic means by which anthropological discourse signifies temporal aspects and relations. Verbal and adverbial temporal markers abound in ethnographic accounts and theoretical syntheses. As we shall see, studies of the use of tense soon converge on such conventions as the "ethnographic present" which, although achieved by syntactic means, is evidently used to stylistic ends. In other words, the "meaning" of the ethnographic present cannot be ascertained simply from the ways in which the present tense expresses conceptions of Time and temporal relations through the construction of sentences. Rather, it must be derived from the intentions and functions of a total discourse of which sentences are parts. In sum, a critique of allochronic discourse needs to be carried out from top to bottom, so to speak, although it may involve constant checks and reflections in the other direction.

There is, for instance, one kind of anthropological discourse which understands itself as historical. Unless one rejects the legitimacy of such an understanding, it would seem that, in all fairness, one cannot hold the use of temporal devices against it. That some or all of these devices not only indicate, refer to, or measure Time, but also signify temporal distance between the writer and the object, would then be a problem internal to the production of anthropological discourse and would have no bearing on relationships between anthropologists and their "informants" as moral and political agents.

Such a view would have to be taken if one chooses to approach a given social-scientific discourse as a self-contained sign system. In that case, temporalization would have to be evaluated strictly with respect to its semiotic function.[7] One assumes that temporal signs, like all signs, are constituted as signifiers and signifieds, keeping in mind that according to semiotic theory the referent (or object) of a discourse is part of a sign relation; it is constituted, so to speak, inside the discourse. Expressions and content are but two aspects of one and the same semiotic system (or semiotic process, depending on which aspect one wishes to stress). Above all, the semioticians tell us, one must avoid confusing "content" with the real world. Accordingly, anthropological discourse about the "primitive" or "savage" is not about peoples in a real world, at least not directly. First and immediately, it is about the primitive as internal referent of a discourse or as a scientifically constituted object of a discipline. The articulation of such a semiotic system with the real world (with its "external referent") is a different matter altogether.

We will ask later whether such a position is tenable. At this point I want to follow the semiotic view and pursue its implications for the problem of temporalization. In his essay about scientific discourse in the social sciences, A. J. Greimas contrasts historical discourse with an "ideological humanistic discourse." The latter projects its referent on an "a-temporal mythical plane of eternal presence" (1976:29). Anthropology, we may extrapolate, differs from such an achronic humanism in that its discourse refers to, speaks about, human culture and society as it exists and develops in Time (and space). In this sense all anthropology is historical (but not to be confused with the discourse of a discipline called *history*). Greimas goes on to state:

Now, historical discourse introduces two new presuppositions in that it, first, replaces the concept of achronicity with that of temporality. At the same time it assumes that the signifier of the text which is

in the present has a signified in the past. Then it
reifies its signified semantically and takes it for a referent external to the discourse. (1976:29)

In other words, temporalization is not an incidental
property of historical discourse; *temporality* constitutes such
a semiotic system by providing its signifiers with a signified.
According to Greimas, this works "through the mechanism
of *temporal uncoupling*, which mechanism consists of stipulat-
ing present statements (*énoncés*) as being situated in the past,
thus creating a *temporal illusion*. In its turn, the reification of
the signified is recognized as a procedure producing the *referential illusion* (ibid.)."

In this sense, Time is used to create an object. The consequence of that "positivist illusion" is a naïve realism expressing the unfounded claim that "the lexemes and phrases
of historical texts really represent the objects of the world
and their interrelationships." Furthermore, because of this
sort of realism the positivist illusion leads to relativism: "The
best historical discourse which has as its 'referent' a given
society can, through the lexicological interpretation of its
sources, only reproduce the 'categorizations of the world'
proper to that society as they manifest themselves in the
way the society covers its universe with lexemes" (1976:30).[8]

Once again, and in an unsuspected context, we find that
relativism in anthropological discourse and temporal distancing are internally connected. Moreover, it is now possible to read that connection in both directions: Historical discourse (of the positivist variety) is incapable of giving more
than relativistic reproductions of the societies and cultures
that are its referents. Conversely, relativistic discourse (such
as structuralism-functionalism or American culturalism, or,
for that matter, remote descendants such as "ethnoscience")
can always be expected to rest, epistemologically, on temporalizations, even if it professes a lack of interest in history.

How can temporal, positivist illusions be shattered? In-
terestingly enough, Greimas proposes that this can only be
achieved by anthropology (see 1976:30). To understand him

one has to realize that his "anthropological discourse" is identical to French structuralist anthropology. He can therefore postulate that

only a structural comparative method (*comparatisme*) is capable of giving historical science a *taxonomic model* of human societies or, which comes to the same, of providing the methodological tools for a taxonomic enterprise (*faire taxinomique*) which history could employ to construct its semiotic objects, after which it would be free to relegate them to the past. (1976:30)

A truly elegant solution (one that echoes Lévi-Strauss'): *Taxonomy* purifies historical discourse from its illusionary uses of Time. But is the "ideological machine" (Greimas 1976:31) of historical discourse as simple as that? What, apart from the taxonomic satisfaction of having classed away historical discourse, is accomplished by showing that temporalizing is a form of signifying? Greimas himself insists that sign relationships should be considered as processes and action, not only as systems. Even a strictly "linguistic" approach to social scientific discourse cannot ignore its subject, the "producer of discourse," a notion which would seem to anchor a discourse in the real world (even if its referent is merely semiotic). I am not sure, however, that *production* means to Greimas more than an "ensemble of mechanisms by which language is made into discourse" (1976:11). In that case, his "producer" would be but a concept strictly within the system of sign relations, a mere auxiliary notion permitting to speak of process even if the system "proceeds" nowhere in the real world. Be it as it may, to me production signals the necessity to go beyond the confines of established sign systems; it evokes the labor involved in creating knowledge and the elements of a discourse capable of conveying knowledge. From that perspective, semiotic analysis of temporalization can do little more than prepare the ground for a critique of its epistemological and political implications.[9]

Time and Tense: The Ethnographic Present

In conversations about the planning of this book, the "ethnographic present" was often brought up as an example for the uses of Time in anthropological discourse. To my knowledge, there does not exist a well-documented history of this literary convention. If it were to be written, such a study would probably retrace the use of the present to the very first instances of *ethnography*. Herodotus gave his accounts of strange peoples in the present tense. In recent times, however, anthropologists appear to have been troubled by this venerable tradition.[10] The ethnographic present certainly should be an issue of debate as soon as *the act of writing* ethnography is perceived to have temporal implications. Yet neither the exact problem with the use of the present tense in ethnographic accounts nor its bearing on temporalization are easy to define. One needs to take a considerable detour through linguistics and epistemology if one wants to get a grip on the problem.

In simple terms, the ethnographic present is the practice of giving accounts of other cultures and societies in the present tense. A custom, a ritual, even an entire system of exchange or a world view are thus predicated on a group or tribe, or whatever unit the ethnographer happens to choose. Intradisciplinary critique of that practice may aim at two implications, one logical, the other ontological, both bearing on the referential validity of statements in the present tense.

In the sentence 'The X are matrilineal,' the present tense copula *are* (especially if taken in conjunction with the definite article *the*) may give rise to doubts concerning the statistical validity of the assertion. To be sure, the present is the proper tense in which to report the results of counts or the value of correlations. But without qualifying or quantifying modifiers ("most X," or "70 percent of all X questioned"), the present unduly magnifies the claim of a statement to general validity. In principle, the same criticism could of course be raised if the statement were in the past tense ("The X were matrilineal"). But in that form it appears less offensive to empirically or statistically minded readers because the stated fact would no longer be subject to direct verification or falsification. It now poses a problem of historical accuracy and would have to be judged by criteria which by their nature are indirect. Historical accuracy is a matter of the "critique of sources." Furthermore, historical accuracy no longer is a strictly referential criterion. It is a quality of metastatements about statements and accounts. Certainly, these few remarks hardly scratch the surface of the logical problems of historical inquiry; but they may help us understand why the present tense in ethnographic accounts is troubling in ways in which the past tense is not.

Another type of objection to the use of the ethnographic present may identify itself as *historical* but in fact it reprimands the ethnographer for ontological reasons. In that case, the statement "the X are matrilineal" is taken to imply a static view of society, one that is unattentive to the fact that all cultures are constantly changing. What is objected to is not so much that the X may no longer be matrilineal by the time their ethnography is published; rather the charge is one of projecting a categorical view on their society. At the very least, say these critics, the present tense "freezes" a society at the time of observation; at worst, it contains assumptions about the repetitiveness, predictability, and conservatism of primitives.

Both objections, logical-statistical and ontological, are easily met by disclaimers. The ethnographic present may be declared a mere literary device, used to avoid the awkwardness of the past tense and of constant doubling up in the form of numeric or temporal qualifiers; that sort of problem can be dealt with once and for all in a methodological appendix. In this way, intradisciplinary critique of the ethnographic present quickly completes a full circle: something bothers us about a literary practice and we alleviate our doubts by finding out that it is "just" a literary practice.

That will not do for the critique of one of the most pervasive characteristics of anthropological discourse. As we turn to linguistics for illumination we find that matters are much more complicated and also more interesting. In the preceding sections on temporalization in social-scientific discourse we came to an important conclusion: Relations between a given type of temporal discourse and its referent as well as relations between specific temporal operators and their signifieds are seldom, if ever, plainly referential. What temporalizing discourse and temporal devices have to say about Time and temporal relations must almost always be ascertained in a context that is wider, and on a level that is higher than the one in which uses of Time can first be identified. The term *primitive,* for instance, is not (only) temporalizing qua lexical item. It is the key term of a temporalizing discourse.[11]

If the devices of temporalizing discourse have little referential value—i.e., say little or nothing about real Time or real temporal relations—this may appear to weaken the case against allochronism in anthropology. Allochronic expressions might "for all practical purposes" be neglected; *practical* being what anthropology "really" does by way of manipulating concepts of Time in setting up relations between Us and Them. The contrary is the case. If any, there is an inverse relationship between referential function and practical importance. The power of language to guide practical-political action seems to increase as its referential function decreases.

Does this also hold true for the use of tense? Following a ground-breaking essay by E. Benveniste (1971 [1956]:205–222) and a thorough study by H. Weinrich (1973[1964]) we may retain these crucial findings before we focus again on the problem of the ethnographic present: Neither semantically (regarding their conceptual "content") nor syntactically (regarding their function in structuring utterances) can temporal verb forms be adequately understood. Linguistic analysis must concentrate on their role in constituting communicative situations whose objectified products are texts, not words or sentences (see Weinrich 1973:25 f). Temporal forms are one of the ways in which a speaker (writer) communicates with a hearer (reader); they are signals exchanged between the participants in complex situations and "it would be wrong to reduce [temporal forms] to simple informations about Time" (Weinrich 1973:60).

If we examine occurrence of temporal forms in given texts we discover that certain among them are infrequent (e.g., dates, adverbial expressions) while others occur at a rate of about one per line of written text. The latter are the verb forms. Exactly what kind of verb form is used varies to some extent from language to language but in the texts of any language one may expect that the distribution of temporal verb forms—tense—is not random. Benveniste writing only, and Weinrich mainly, about the French verb found that certain tenses tend to be associated with each other, forming "groups," and these groups appear to correspond to two fundamental categories of speaking/writing: discourse vs. history (Benveniste), or commentary vs. story (Weinrich). Dominance of a certain tense in a text signals directly the "locutionary attitude" (or the rhetorical intent) of the speaker/author.Tense only has indirect reference to Time in the "real world" outside the communicative situation of the text. Hence, to write ethnography in the present tense despite the fact that it is descriptive of experiences and observations that lie in the author's past, would be indifferent because tense does not locate the content of an account in Time. All the same, the present tense does signal the writer's intent (at least in French and related languages) to give a *discourse* or *commentary* on the world. Ethnographic accounts in the past tense would prima facie situate a text in the category of *history* or *story,* indicating perhaps a humanistic rather than scientific intent on the part of the writer. That, however, is not a satisfying solution. It could be easily shown that anthropologists of a scientific bent may write ethnography in the past tense while others who profess a humanistic-historical orientation may write in the present.

There remains ambiguity even if one accepts the basic distinctions of locutionary attitude discovered by Benveniste and Weinrich because—as these authors point out—temporal verb forms are *verb* forms. Their temporal significance must not be separated from other types of information carried by, or associated with, verb forms, such as *person.* The occurrence of pronouns and person markers is as *obstinate,* a term Weinrich borrows from music (*ostinato*) to designate both frequency and repetitiveness, as that of verb forms. Person and pronouns may have important temporal functions. Ideally and typically, the first person singular *I* should co-occur with tenses marking the genre discourse/commentary, e.g., the present. This would reflect the locutionary attitude or communicative situation where a speaker conveys directly and purposefully to a listener what he believes to be the case or what he can report as a fact. In contrast to this, history/story would be

> the mode of utterance that excludes every "autobiographical" linguistic form. The historian will never say *je* or *tu* or *maintenant,* because he will never make use of the formal apparatus of discourse [or "commentary,"] which resides primarily in the relationship of the persons *je:tu.* Hence we shall find only the forms of the "third person" in a historical narrative strictly followed. (Benveniste 1971:206 f)

Now if this is so, a good deal of anthropological discourse confronts us with a paradox in the form of an anomalous association of the present tense and the third person: "they are (do, have, etc.)" is the obstinate form of ethnographic accounts.

There are at least two ways to explain such co-occurrence. One is to probe more deeply into the significance of verb person and pronouns; the other is to trace the locutionary function of the present tense in ethnographic accounts beyond the confines of its immediate communicative situation, revealing its roots in certain fundamental assumptions regarding the nature of knowledge.

For the first argument we draw again on Benveniste's observations contained in his essays on relations of person in the verb and on subjectivity in language. Philosophically, his findings are not new but they are of special interest because they are derived from linguistic analyses of the ways of speaking (and writing) rather than from abstract speculation. Keep in mind that our problem is to understand the obstinate use of the third person in a genre which, by the dominance of the present tense, is clearly marked as discourse/commentary pronounced by an *I*, first person singular. As it turns out, the problem may not be one of contradiction but of confusion. The fundamental communicative situation which encompasses the genres of discourse/commentary is dialogical: An *I* addresses (reports to) a *you*. But only the first and second persons are distinguished along the axis of personness. The grammarian's "third person" is opposed to the first and second person as a nonparticipant in the dialogue. The " 'third person' is not a 'person'; it is really the verbal form whose function is to express the *non-person*" (Benveniste 1971:198). The connection between the first two and the third persons is a "correlation of personality." First and second person are in a "correlation of subjectivity" (1971:201 f):

What differentiates "I" from "you" is first of all the fact of being, in the case of "I," *internal* to the statement and external to "you"; but external in a manner that does not suppress the human reality of dialogue. . . . One could thus define "you" as the *non-subjective* person, in contrast to the *subjective* person that "I" represents; and these two "persons" are together opposed to the "non-person" form (= he). (1971:201)

Then what does the obstinate use of the nonperson "third person" in ethnographic accounts whose present tense signals that they are dialogical tell us about the relationship between the subject and object of anthropological discourse? If we go along with Benveniste we must conclude that the use of the third person marks anthropological discourse in terms of the "correlation of personality" (person vs. nonperson). The ethnographer does not address a *you* except, presumably, in the situation of fieldwork when he asks questions or otherwise participates in the life of his subjects. He need not explicitly address his ethnographic *account* to a *you* because, as discourse/commentary it is already sufficiently placed in a dialogic situation; ethnography addresses a reader. The dialogic Other (second person, the other anthropologist, the scientific community) is marked by the present tense; *pronouns and verb forms in the third person mark an Other outside the dialogue.* He (or she or it) is not spoken to but posited (predicated) as that which contrasts with the personness of the participants in the dialogue.

"Removal from the dialogic situation" is, in my view, another way to describe denial of coevalness, a conclusion which, however, could not be drawn if we were to follow Benveniste's linguistic theory of subjectivity to the end. To declare, as he does, that the dialogic situation is a mere pragmatic consequence of certain fundamental linguistic oppositions (see 1971:224, 225) amounts to making both the participants and the events of communication epiphenomenal to language; personal consciousness and social praxis are reduced to linguistic phenomena. I agree with Benveniste when he rejects the notion that language is only an instrument (see 1971:223 f) but I cannot go along with his blatant idealism, which would have us conclude that the opposition of Self and Other and the preference for a certain tense in anthropological discourse are but general facts of language. On the contrary, these facts of language are but special instances in which self-assertion, imposition, subjugation and other forms of human alienation manifest themselves. Because Benveniste (with de Saussure) is convinced of the "immaterial nature" of language (1971:224) he is incapable of relating a certain discursive practice to political praxis. His (and Weinrich's) detailed and ingenious analyses of the workings of tense and person constantly rebound from the inner walls of language qua system (or of speaking qua locutionary situation).

Much as we can learn from linguistics about the intricate workings of tense, in the end we must leave the confines of linguistic analysis, especially if we take language seriously. The ethnographic present represents a choice of expression which is determined by an epistemological position and cannot be derived from, or explained by, linguistic rules alone. Anticipating an argument to be developed in the next chapter, the following hypothesis may be advanced: The use of the present tense in anthropological discourse not only marks a literary genre (*ethnography*) through the locutionary attitude of discourse/commentary; it also reveals a specific cognitive stance toward its object, the *monde commenté* (Weinrich). It presupposes the givenness of the object of anthropology as something to be *observed*. *The present tense is a signal identifying a discourse as an observer's language.*

Such a language provides glosses on the world as *seen*. It depicts and re-presents another culture; it is its re-production by linguistic (symbolic) means. All this corresponds to a theory of knowledge construed around a visual root metaphor. Historically, anthropology has been linked up with the tradition of "natural history," with its ethos of detached observation and its fervor to make visible the hidden relations between things. It is in that direction that we will have to probe further. To remonstrate that the ethnographic present is an inappropriate temporal form is beside the point. We accept the linguist's verdict that tense in itself has no temporal reference. What must be critically investigated is the peculiar incidence of atemporal modes of expression in a discourse which, on the whole, is clearly temporalizing. Putting it bluntly, we must attempt to discover the deeper connections between a certain type of political cosmology (defining relations with the Other in temporal terms) and a certain type of epistemology (conceiving of knowledge as the reproduction of an observed world).

In My Time: Ethnography and the Autobiographic Past

Anthropological discourse often exhibits (or hides, which is the same) conflict between theoretical-methodological conventions and lived experience. Anthropological writing may be scientific; it is also inherently autobiographic. This is not limited to the trivial observation that ethnographic reports are sometimes cluttered with anecdotes, personal asides, and other devices apt to enliven an otherwise dull prose. In fact, until recently anthropologists were anxious to keep autobiography separate from scientific writing. The strictures of positivism account for this, although they may have been operating indirectly. Somehow the discipline "remembers" that it acquired its scientific and academic status by climbing on the shoulders of adventurers and using their travelogues, which for centuries had been the appropriate literary genre in which to report knowledge of the Other. In many ways this collective memory of a scientifically doubtful past acts as a trauma, blocking serious reflection on the epis-

temological significance of lived experience and its autobiographic expressions. How would such reflection have to
proceed?

Once more we begin with the supposition that anthropology is based on ethnography. All anthropological writing
must draw on reports resulting from some sort of concrete
encounter between individual ethnographers and members
of other cultures and societies. The anthropologist who does
not draw on his own experience will use accounts by others.
Directly or vicariously, anthropological discourse formulates
knowledge that is rooted in an author's autobiography. If
this is seen together with the convention that fieldwork
comes first and analysis later, we begin to realize that the
Other as object or content of anthropological knowledge is
necessarily part of the knowing subject's past. So we find
Time and temporal distance once again linked up with the
constitution of the referent of our discourse. Only now temporalization clearly is an aspect of a praxis, not just a mechanism in a system of signification. That praxis includes all
the phases of the production of anthropological knowledge;
Time is not just a device but a necessary condition for that
process to occur. In a general way, the same holds true, of
course, for any type of literary production. The writer of a
novel uses his or her past experiences as "material" for the
literary project. However, the anthropologist makes the peculiar claim that certain experiences or events in his past
constitute facts, not fiction. What else could be the sense of
invoking ethnographic accounts as "data"?

Our inevitably temporal relation to the Other as object
of knowledge is by no means a simple one. In a most basic
sense (one that is, I suspect, quite acceptable to the positivist) temporal distance might be a sort of minimal condition
for accepting any kind of observation as a fact. A frame for
such a view was sketched out in a note on "co-apperception
of time" by C. F. von Weizsäcker. His reflection is all the
more interesting because it comes from a natural scientist
and philosopher venturing to make a contribution to "historical anthropology." Von Weizsäcker states:

That which is past is stored in facts. Facts are the
possibilities of the appearance of that which is past.

Possibilities are founded on facts. . . . One could
say that the present is the one-ness [*Einheit*] of
time. But here the concept of the present does not
explain the one-ness of time, rather it is the other
way round. Similarly, the concept of past does not
explain facticity . . . rather, that which is past is the
presently factual (1977:315).

Fact and *past* are not interchangeable, nor is their relationship primarily one that points from the writer's present
into the object's past. As I understand him, von Weizsäcker
asserts the inverse: The object's present is founded in the
writer's past. In that sense, facticity itself, that cornerstone
of scientific thought, is autobiographic.[12] This, incidentally,
is why in anthropology objectivity can never be defined in
opposition to subjectivity, especially if one does not want to
abandon the notion of facts.

Against the background of these abstract and difficult
thoughts about Time and facticity we may now consider
temporal distancing in a more concrete, hermeneutic frame.
Hermeneutic signals a self-understanding of anthropology as
interpretive (rather than naïvely inductive or rigorously deductive).[13] No experience can simply be "used" as naked
data. All personal experience is produced under historical
conditions, in historical contexts; it must be used with critical awareness and with constant attention to its authoritative
claims. The hermeneutic stance presupposes a degree of
distancing, an objectification of our experiences. That the
anthropologist's experienced Other is necessarily part of his
past may therefore not be an impediment, but a condition
of an interpretive approach.[14] This is true on several levels.

Fieldwork, demanding personal presence and involving
several learning processes, has a certain time-economy. The
anthropological rule of thumb—one full cycle of seasons—
may not be its exact measure but it recognizes at least that
a certain passage of time is a necessary prerequisite, not just
an annoying expenditure. More time, often much more time,
is necessary to analyze and interpret experience recorded in
texts. In sum, doing anthropology needs distance, temporal
and often also spatial.

At this point, after all the critical remarks we addressed
to positive valuation of "distance" in relativist and structur-

alist anthropology, a warning signal should go off. Are we not admitting now, by a detour through hermeneutics, what we found questionable earlier? Not at all. In the first place, the distance just invoked is essentially temporal. It is, so to speak, only supplemented by spatial distance. Moving from one living context to another in the course of anthropological work merely underscores the necessity of objectifying our experiences. However, it is imaginable that an ethnographer *constantly* "on the move" may lose his ability to make worthwhile ethnographic experiences altogether, for the simple reason that the Other would *never have the time* to become part of the ethnographer's past. Time is also needed for the ethnographer to become part of his interlocutor's past. Many anthropologists have noted and reported dramatic changes in the attitudes of their "informants" on second or subsequent visits to the field. Often these are interpreted in psychological or moral terms of increased trust, deepened friendship, or plain getting used to each other. If it is true that ethnography, in order to be productive, must be dialogical and therefore to a certain degree reciprocal, then we begin to appreciate the epistemological significance of Time.

Secondly, hermeneutic distance is called for by the ideal of reflexivity which is always also self-reflexivity. Affirmation of distance is in this case but a way of underlining the importance of subjectivity in the process of knowledge. Hermeneutic distance is an act, not a fact. It has nothing in common with the notion (such as Lévi-Strauss', see above, chapter 2) that distance be somehow the source of more general, hence more "real" knowledge. It may be useful to introduce a convention which distinguishes between *reflexion* qua subjective activity carried out by and revealing, the ethnographer, and *reflection*, as a sort of objective reflex (like the image in a mirror) which hides the observer by axiomatically eliminating subjectivity.

I can think of at least two reasons for advocating a reflexive over a reflective stance. First, attempts to eliminate or hide the subject in anthropological discourse too often result in epistemological hypocrisy. Consider, for instance, the following innocuous looking statement in *The Savage Mind*.

The context is Lévi-Strauss' assertion that primitives, much like ourselves, rely on observation and interpretation of natural phenomena: "The procedure of the American Indian who follows a trail by means of imperceptible clues . . . is no different from our procedure when we drive a car. . . . (1966:222)

Now, it seems to me, that the qualifier *imperceptible* here has an intriguing function. Upon closer examination it turns out that it cannot possibly be used in a denotative, referential manner; an *imperceptible* clue is a logical impossibility. But perhaps that is being too rigorous. Imperceptible may be a manner of speaking and a reader familiar with the language can be expected to correct *nonperceptible* as *scarcely perceptible*. But that way out is too easy. I would argue that *imperceptible* here functions as an index revealing (or hiding) the fact that not one but two subjects inhabit the semantic space of the statement. One is the Indian who "follows a procedure," the other is the ethnographer to whom the Indian's clues are imperceptible. Such literary sleight-of-hand camouflages the second subject *in order to* mark the observation as objective fact.

The "imperceptible clue" is only one example for the many conventionalized figures and images that pervade ethnographic and popular reports on encounters with Others. When it is said that primitives are *stolid* this translates as "I never got close enough to see them excited, enthusiastic, or perturbed." When we say that "they are born with rhythm" we mean "we never saw them grow, practice, learn." And so on and so forth. All statements about others are paired with the observer's experience. But why would hiding the Self in statements about the Other make ethnography more objective?

There is another reason for preferring reflexion over reflection. Reflexivity asks that we "look back" and thereby let our experiences "come back" to us. Reflexivity is based on memory, i.e., on the fact that the location of experience in our past is not irreversible. We have the ability to present (make present) our past experiences to ourselves. More than that, this reflexive ability enables us to be in the presence of others precisely inasmuch as the Other has become content of our experience. This brings us to the conditions of possibility of intersubjective knowledge. *Somehow we must be able to share each other's past in order to be knowingly in each other's present.* If our experience of Time were nonreflexive, unidirectional, we would not have anything but tangential knowledge of each other, on the level of interpersonal communication as well as on the collective level of social and political interaction. When much or most of anthropology is indeed perceived as tangential (beside the point, irrelevant) by those who have been its objects, this points to a severe breakdown of "collective reflexivity"; it is yet another symptom of the denial of coevalness.

Needless to say, these thoughts about reflexive distance would not be universally accepted. Some social scientists want to measure the reactions of experimental subjects, or the distribution and frequency of certain kinds of quantifiable behavior. They could in principle work without temporal distance, *as soon as* data are fed into the analytical machine. At any rate, the time which even the most operationally minded social scientist must spend on devising his "instruments" (e.g. questionnaires), on collecting, coding, and counting responses and then often on "cleaning up" his data, is to him a practical nuisance, not an epistemological necessity. More sophisticated techniques and faster computers offer the prospect of cutting down on time to the point where we can conceive research setups (such as used to determine television ratings) where large numbers of subjects are hooked up directly to analytical machinery—the statistician's dream, perhaps, but our nightmare.

In this context one should also examine the temporal implications of data storage, a notion that tempts many anthropologists who seem to be troubled by the burden of accumulated ethnography. Are our data banks simply more sophisticated archives of the kind societies have kept from the beginning of historical times? Is the term *bank* really just an innocent metaphor for a depository? Not at all. Data banks are banks, not only because things of value are stored in them, but because they are institutions which make possible the circulation of information.[15]

So far, anthropology has done little more than toy

around with such crude data banks as the *Human Relations Area File* and with low-power statistical operations on doubtful samples. There is no sign that operationalism will determine a significant part of the discipline in the near future. If machine time were, at some point, to replace (not just assist) human time, and if our observations on the role of Time in constituting the object of our discourse are correct, we would expect anthropology to disappear. For the time being, ethnographic objectivity remains bound up with reflexion, an activity which will call for Time as long as it involves human subjects.

To say that reflexive distance is necessary to achieve objectification does not mean that the Other, by virtue of being located in our past, becomes thinglike, or abstract and general. On the contrary, an ethnographic past can become the most vivid part of our present existence. Persons, events, puzzlements, and discoveries encountered during fieldwork may continue to occupy our thoughts and fantasies for many years. This is probably not just because our work in ethnography constantly turns us toward the past; rather it is because our past is present in us as a *project,* hence as our future. In fact, we would not have a present to look back from at our past if it was not for that constant passage of our experience from past to future. Past ethnography is the present of anthropological discourse inasmuch as it is on the way to become its future.

Such are the general outlines of the processes in which anthropological consciousness emerges. In any concrete case, however, consciousness of the ethnographic past may be as deformed and alienated as other types of consciousness. Take, for example, one of the most irritating of our professional habits which I will call the possessive past. There is a trivial and probably harmless form of that affliction. Those who suffer from it show the symptoms of an irrepressible urge to recall, refer to, cite, and recount experiences with "their natives." Sometimes they are just conversational bores; they often resemble former soldiers who are unable to separate their present lives from memories of "their war." For many anthropologists, fieldwork obviously has this effect of an intensified, traumatic period which remains an intellectual and emotional reference point throughout their lives. Whenever experience becomes so much part of an individual's psychological history that a reflexive distance can no longer be generated, neither the person involved nor those to whom he reports his experiences can be sure of the nature and validity of his accounts and insights. To some extent, such psychological ingestion and appropriation (Lévi-Strauss would call it *cannibalism*) of the Other may be a normal and inevitable condition for the production of ethnographic knowledge, but it may verge on the pathological (as there are indeed links between psychopathology and an exaggerated exoticism).

Such 'allophagy' is seldom critically analyzed or even noted because of an institutionalized fear of being accused of unscientific autobiographic divagation. Intellectual dishonesty may then take its revenge in the form of utter confusion when it comes to taking a stand on such disturbing cases as Père Trilles or Carlos Castaneda. I doubt that the experts on American Indian religion who have all but dismantled Castaneda's credibility as an ethnographer realize that he probably parodied and exaggerated (with enviable commercial success) the little disputed privilege of the possessive past which the conventions of anthropological discourse grant to all practitioners.[16] How many are the anthropologists for whom the aura of "empirical research" has served to legitimize as fieldwork varying periods spent on getting over culture shock, fighting loneliness and some humiliating tropical illness, coping with the claims of the local expatriate community, and learning about corruption in the local bureaucracy—all this before finally getting together some meager, secondhand information? Or what about those who quite simply invented or faked their ethnographies, perhaps because that was the only way in which they could live up to the expectations of degree-granting departments and funding agencies to "deliver" within the time allotted for research in the field? One shudders at the thought of what time pressure may have done to the vast body of ethnography produced in the most expansive period of our discipline.

The point of these questions is not to cast vague suspicion on moral integrity. More insidious than individual moral failure is a collective failure to consider the intellectual effects of scientific conventions which, by censoring reflexions on the autobiographic conditions of anthropological knowledge, remove an important part of the knowledge process from the arena of criticism.

To make it clear that moral indignation at the sins of ethnographers is not enough, one only needs to consider another aspect of what we called the possessive past. Figures of speech—the use of possessive pronouns, first person singular or plural, in reports on informants, groups, or tribes— are the signs in anthropological discourse of relations that ultimately belong to political economy, not to psychology or ethics. After all, dogmatic insistence on fieldwork, personal and participative, coincides with the virulent period of colonization. Participant observation, however, was not canonized to promote participation but to improve observation. Personal presence was required for the collecting and recording of data prior to their being deposited and processed in Western institutions of learning. In structure and intent these conventions of our discipline have been analogous to the exploitation of natural resources found in colonized countries. Talk of "geopolitics" and the predominance of *spatial* images such as Western "expansion" cloud the fact that our exploitative relations also had *temporal* aspects. Resources have been transported from the past of their "backward" locations to the present of an industrial, capitalist economy. A temporal conception of movement has always served to legitimize the colonial enterprise on all levels. Temporalizations expressed as passage from savagery to civilization, from peasant to industrial society, have long served an ideology whose ultimate purpose has been to justify the procurement of commodities for our markets. African copper becomes a commodity only when it is taken possession of by removing it from its geological context, placing it into the history of Western commerce and industrial production. Something analogous happens with "primitive art."[17]

The idea of a commodification of knowledge owes much of its conceptual clarity to Marx. But the basic insight on

which it rests is by no means a recent one. When Georg
Forster, one of the founders of modern anthropology, once
contemplated the hustle and bustle of Amsterdam harbor
he was moved to the following meditation:

> The eagerness of greed was the origin of mathe-
> matics, mechanics, physics, astronomy and geog-
> raphy. Reason paid back with interest the effort in-
> vested in its formation. It linked faraway continents,
> brought nations together, accumulated the products
> of all the different regions—and all the while its
> wealth of concepts increased. They circulated faster
> and faster and became more and more refined.
> New ideas which could not be processed locally
> went as raw material to neighboring countries.
> There they were woven into the mass of already ex-
> istent and applied knowledge, and sooner or later
> the new product of reason returns to the shores of
> the Amstel. (1968: [1791] :386)

If analogies (or homologies) between the colonial enterprise and anthropology hold, one would have to admit that
ethnography, too, may become a commodity. Its commodification would require a similar temporal passage of data
(the goods) from their historical context in societies considered primitive to the present of Western science. In the
idiom of our economic philosophies, anthropology is an "industry" with the peculiar trait that anthropologists are both
workers who produce commodities, and entrepreneurs who
market them, albeit in most cases at the modest profit of
academic salaries.[18]
    This is a disquieting conclusion indeed, one that could
hardly be expected from a review of some of the literary
conventions of anthropological discourse. If it is correct it
would mean that precisely the autobiographic origins of the
ethnographer's possessive past link his praxis to the political
economy of Western domination and exploitation. That link
is by no means just one of moral complicity, easily dis-
avowed by repenting on the ways of our colonialist predecessors. The connection is ideological and even epistemological; it regards conceptions of the nature of
anthropological knowledge, not just of its use. Most impor-

tantly it confirms that temporal manipulations are involved in working out our relationship to the Other.

Politics of Time: The Temporal Wolf
in Taxonomic Sheep's Clothing

We have examined temporalizing in anthropological discourse as it manifests itself in the ethnographic present and the autobiographic past. Now we must face once more the claims of "timeless" structuralism. After all, in his semiotic analysis of social scientific discourse, Greimas promised salvation from the evils of temporalizing in the form of a *faire taxinomique* which is (Lévi-Straussian) anthropology. Any invocation of anthropology as a savior or *deus ex machina* should make us suspicious. It only makes more urgent the task of examing how Time is used in defining relations with the referent of our discourse.

In an attempt to understand what exactly taxonomy does we may begin by considering the following proposition: Whether taxonomy is carried out in the structuralist vein or in more modest varieties (such as in ethnoscience and various structural approaches to folklore) taxonomic description always consists of rewriting our ethnographic notes or texts. At the very least (and leaving aside its technical understanding propagated by N. Chomsky) the project of rewriting rests on two presuppositions, one being a presumption of fact, the other amounting to a kind of judgment. The presumption of fact holds that there *is* a text to be *rewritten*. This is ultimately an ontological statement, one that anchors the taxonomic enterprise in a real world of texts and writers. Even the most abstract logico-mathematical reduction of an ethnographic text is still writing. It remains within the confines of discourse qua activity carried out by a subject. Being produced by a subject (and granting that "production" often is nothing but reproduction of cognitive templates and literary conventions) taxonomic discourse stays linked with other forms of discursive expression. Taxonomic description is therefore not a revolutionary alternative to other forms of anthropological discourse. It is but a taxon, a class of writings in a taxonomy, a view we encountered earlier as Lévi-Strauss' way of "reconciling" anthropology and history.

However there is, secondly, a suggestion of judgment in the idea of rewriting—as if taxonomic description were to make up for deficiencies in the original text, it being perhaps too confused, too cryptic, too exotic or simply too long to surrender its meaning upon simple inspection. In this respect, "scientific" structuralism is undoubtedly akin to hermeneutic and historical philology which it wishes to surpass and replace. Both are pervaded by an urge to restore, to provide a better reading of, the original text. It makes little difference whether the aim is the philologist's *Urform,* or the structuralist's form *tout court,* both traditions are shaped by an ethos developed in the course of searching for the "authentic" meaning of the sacred texts of our tradition.[19] Lévi-Strauss obviously sensed this. Because he wanted to dissociate himself at all cost from the enterprise of a historical hermeneutic he took his famous escape when he pronounced that anthropological discourse is but a myth upon a myth (1969b:6). He can feel free of the burden of having to justify his own rewriting of myth as a (judgmental) act of liberating the original from its existence in obscurity. Of course, he also leaves unanswered the question why anthropology needs to write *over* its ethnographic texts at all. If the hermeneutic stance is to *extract* meaning from a text, structuralist construction of a myth upon a myth appears to work by *imposition*. Models that map basic and derived relationships are laid upon the native text. Where the hermeneutic approach envisages its task as work, structuralism sees it as play, as a game whose rules are the elegance and parsimony displayed in "matching" text and model.

But this is only part of the story. Taxonomic rewriting never is just a purely contemplative, aesthetic game of reducing messy data to elegant models. It is a drawn-out, serious game in the course of which pieces of ethnography, isolated and displaced from their historical context, are used in a series of moves and countermoves, following certain basic rules (those of binary opposition, for example) until a point is reached where the pieces fall into place. The game is over when the solitary player, the anthropologist, has exhausted the moves permitted by the rules. Now one may invoke (following Lévi-Strauss' example) the analogy of the game in order to characterize the playfulness of taxonomic description. But one should not forget that behind the mask of the modest, candid, and tentative *bricoleur* hides a player *who is out to win.*

Winning the taxonomic game consists of demonstrating synchronic relations of order beneath the flux and confusion of historical events and the expressions of personal experience. The temporally contingent is made to reveal underlying logical necessity. The Now and Then is absorbed by the Always of the rules of the game. And one must never forget that structuralist discourse accomplishing these feats is not just a discourse which has taxonomies as its referent. It defines itself as a taxonomic *faire.* Far from merely reflecting relations of order, it creates them. The founding classificatory act, the first binary opposition (or in Bateson's famous terms, the difference that makes the difference) is the one between the native text and the taxonomic discourse about that text. Two steps follow: one is to declare the native text itself taxonomic (by opposing its constituent classificatory relationships to real relations, culture vs. nature); the other is to posit the taxonomic, speak scientific, nature of anthropological discourse as being opposed to the humanistic, speak hermeneutic-historical, approach.

The outcome of all this is not at all a structural arrangement of oppositions suspended in an equilibrium, nor is it just a classificatory schema innocently construed in a game of imposing arbitrary models on reality. What we get is a *hierarchy* made up of relationships of order which are sequential and irreversible; hence the seriousness of the taxonomic game. If we take Lévi-Strauss (and for that matter, the cognitive anthropologists) seriously we find that their theory of science is out to integrate anthropology itself at some point in the sequence of "transformations" to be derived from certain basic oppositions such as nature and culture, form and content, sign and reality, and so forth. A way to visualize this in a taxonomic idiom would be figure 3.1.

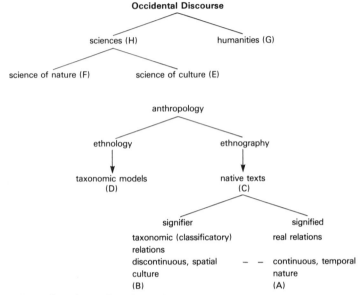

Figure 3.1: The place of anthropology in a taxonomy of relations

Undoubtedly this is not the only way to draw the diagram; another form could include different kinds of science or humanities, kinds of native texts, and even different ways to set up the oppositions on the lowest level. But even in its fragmentary form it illustrates the crucial point; because the nodes are arranged hierarchically, the relationships that constitute taxonomic discourse are sequential and can also be presented as a string of points (steps, stages) on a line or arrow:

x   x   x   x   x   x   x   x   x

A   B   C   D   E   F   G   H   I

or as two strings emanating from an opposition:

H/G

E   F

C   D

A   B

Because the arrangement is hierarchical, movement within the parallel/opposed strings is always either ascent or descent. This would seemingly not affect relations of opposition. But that is not really the case as soon as one takes into account the ontological assumptions of taxonomic approaches in anthropology. The "oppositions" *AB, CD, EF* (*and HG,* for that matter) are expressive of evolutionary development; they are directional, in fact one-way relations: Nature precedes Culture (at least in the minimal sense that it was there before people existed); ethnography precedes ethnology (according to the canons of anthropological praxis); and the humanities precede the sciences (in the history of Western thought). Again, it matters little that any of those assumptions might be debated as soon as a context is specified. The point is that a taxonomic conception of them cannot but present them in chains and, in the words of M. Serres, none of these chains "can be thought without time" (1977:91).[20] The logic of these relationships of opposition and inclusion generates the rules of the game which is a *faire taxinomique.* If that game is, according to Greimas and Lévi-Strauss, the "constitution of the semiotic object" then it is clear that such constitution is arrived at in a sequence of temporally ordered steps. Viewed from that angle, taxonomic anthropology is indistinguishable from approaches it dismisses as historical and subjective.

Following Serres (who in turn follows mathematical notions regarding "relations of order") we can now more accurately characterize the nature of relations which taxonomic discourse attempts to establish between the subject and object of its discourse.

The relationships whose concatenation amounts to a taxonomy of anthropological knowledge are *nonreflexive.* None of the members in the chain that makes up the structure represented in our diagram can precede or succeed itself; it is always predecessor or successor of another member in the chain. For example, a discourse having posited that the lexicon for a certain cognitive domain consists of arbitrary labels for things, and that the object of taxonomic analysis is the ordered system of relationships between *labels,* will not go back on itself and reexamine the assumption that the imposition of labels is indeed arbitrary. Similarly, the structural analysis of pieces of ethnography (myths, kinship systems) will proceed by reducing them to models. There it will either come to rest, or it will seek further refinements, or more encompassing models, until it comes to rest. But it will not, at the same time, question the method it employs. Science, as T. S. Kuhn and many others seem to tell us, cannot be done critically, that is, reflexively *when* and *while* it is being done. Critique needs the extraordinary time of crisis—*extraordinary* meaning outside the established relationships of order.

Implied in the chainlike arrangement is also that relationships between any two members *cannot be symmetrical.* If *A* precedes *B*, *B* cannot precede *A*. One might object that this neglects the possibility that, within the two parallel chains, movement may be either ascending or descending. For instance, ethnological theory may, depending on circumstances, precede as well as succeed ethnography. Or events in nature such as ecological and demographic changes may precede as well as succeed cultural change. Nevertheless, the rule demands that no two members of the chain can precede and succeed each other at the same time. Therefore it is ruled out that taxonomic discourse could ascend and descend the relations of order in the same act. This does not mean that in taxonomic anthropology ethnography should not be "mixed" with ethnology, or autobiography not with scientific analysis, or structural analysis not with history. Any given instance of taxonomic discourse may contain juxtapositions of all of those "opposed" elements. But the rule of nonsymmetry does carry an injunction against reciprocal and dialectical conceptions, both of which would presuppose that two members of the chain coexist in Time.

Finally, the chain of relationships of order implies that if *A* precedes *B* and *B* precedes *C* then *A* precedes *C*. In other words, the entire structure is *transitive.* If culture masters nature, and if the anthropologists master culture, then science, through anthropology, masters nature. Perhaps it is the other way round; but never both at the same time or, in analogy to the game, never in the same move.

To object that such an interpretation of relations of order confuses logical sequences with temporal sequences is gratuitous unless one deludes oneself into accepting the untenable position that taxonomic discourse is outside the realm of human action. The demonstrable fact that discourse qua spatiotemporal action can be described in purely logical-taxonomic terms in no way justifies the belief that it *consists* of logical relations. A theory that holds this is guilty of the same confusion of method and substance, means and ends, which Greimas found to be the fallacy of historical discourse unredeemed by taxonomy (1976:30). Marx, whom structuralists now like to claim as their ancestor, saw and avoided the fallacy when he criticized Hegel and Feuerbach: To be able to distill from history the "logic" of the process or to find the "law" that the dominating class will inevitably be overthrown by the oppressed class does not absolve the analyst (as spokesman for "history") from the necessity to translate logic into revolutionary projects. To take a position on "logical relations" is always also a political act.

Which finally brings us to the moment when the wolf enters the story. In La Fontaine's fable he comes to a river to drink and accuses the lamb of troubling the water. But the lamb is positioned downstream. In M. Serres' interpretation of the "game of the wolf," the wolf is the scientist, in our case the taxonomic anthropologist. In the story, much as in our diagram, he is placed in a chain of relations of order in such a way that he is upstream, up the temporal slope. Yet his posture is to accuse the lamb, that is, to question the "lamb"—the primitive or the native text which he takes as his "problem"—as if the two were engaged in a game allowing moves in both directions. He acts as if there were a give and take; as if what is valid in the time of the lamb (there and then) could be made visible in the time of the wolf (here and now). As it is the avowed aim of taxonomic discourse to establish relations that are always and everywhere valid, the story must end with the wolf absorbing historical time into his time—he will eat the lamb. This fable is an "operational definition of hypocrisy" (Serres 1977:94) because the wolf appears placed in the middle of the chain. The anthropologist proclaims himself to be in the service of

science, to be nothing but an executor of the laws of nature
or reason. He uses the taxonomic cover to hide his relentless appetite for the Time of the Other, a Time to be in-
gested and transformed into his own: "He has taken the
place of the wolf, his true place. Western man is the wolf of
science' (Serres 1977:104).

What we take the fable to illustrate is an *ideology* of relations, a game that defines its own rules. A crucial strategy
in this game is to place the players on a temporal slope.
That the time of the lamb is not the time of the wolf is
postulated, not demonstrated. An evolutionary view of relations between Us and the Other is the point of departure,
not the result of anthropology. A taxonomic approach inserts itself effortlessly into that perspective. Its ostensibly
achronic stance turns out to be a flagrant example of allochronic discourse.

Chapter Four / The Other and the Eye: Time and the Rhetoric of Vision

Singly [the thoughts of man] are everyone a representation *or* appearance *of some quality, or other accident of a
body without us, which is commonly called an* object.
Thomas Hobbes [1]

*The major defect of materialism up to this day . . . has
been to conceive the object, reality, sensuousness, only in the
form of an object of contemplation, not as sensuous-human
activity, praxis, not subjectively.*
Karl Marx [2]

GENERATIONS OF ANTHROPOLOGY students setting
out to do their first fieldwork have received, and followed,
advice to learn the language, if possible before beginning
with research, and to start their inquiries on the spot by
mapping settlements, counting households, and drawing up
genealogies of the inhabitants.[3] This is sensible advice. Much
time is saved if one comes to the field prepared linguistically. Maps, censuses, and kinship charts are the quickest
way to get a grip on the shape and composition of a small
community. If the society studied keeps records which can
be used for these projects, all the better. No one expects this
sort of work to be without snags and difficulties; but neither
have most anthropologists considered the possibility that
such simple and sensible methods or techniques might be
biased toward a certain theory of knowledge whose claims
to validity are not beyond questioning.

Method and Vision

These conventional prescriptions contain at least three underlying assumptions deserving critical attention:

First, they recommend the native language as a *tool,* as a means to extract information. Somehow, what one seeks is thought to exist separately from language and the activity of speaking. To be sure, anthropologists have, before and after Whorf, maintained that the language of a people offers clues, perhaps even the key, to its culture. In one respect, however, the views of those who saw in the native language a mere vehicle of research, and others, who proclaimed it the depository of culture, converged: neither considered seriously that the "usefulness" of the native language might rest on the fact that it draws the researcher into a communicative praxis as a result of which metaphors such as *tool, vehicle,* or *receptacle* might be difficult to maintain. All these images encourage a manipulative use of language derived from visual and spatial conceptualizations whose long history will occupy us throughout this chapter.

Second, the recommendations to use maps, charts, and tables signals convictions deeply ingrained in an empirical, scientific tradition. Ultimately they rest on a corpuscular, atomic theory of knowledge and information.[4] Such a theory in turn encourages quantification and diagrammatic representation so that the ability to "visualize" a culture or society almost becomes synonymous for understanding it. I shall call this tendency *visualism* and because visualism will play a role in our argument comparable to that of denial of coevalness or temporalization, some sort of descriptive statement is in order. The term is to connote a cultural, ideological bias toward vision as the "noblest sense" and toward geometry qua graphic-spatial conceptualization as the most "exact" way of communicating knowledge. Undoubtedly, the social sciences inherited that bias from rationalist thought (based on Descartes' distinction of *res cogitans* and *res extensa*) and from the empiricists (see Hobbes' fascination with geometry). However, deeper and more remote sources will be considered in the sections that follow, as well as the paradoxical possibility that visualism may be a symptom of the denaturation of visual experience.

Visualism[5] may take different directions—toward the mathematical-geometric or toward the pictorial-aesthetic. In the latter case, its idolatrous tendency is often mitigated by the precept to approach culture not as a picture but as a text. Certainly there has been progress in anthropology from mere counting and mapping of cultural traits toward accounts of culture which are attentive to context, symbols, and semantics. Still, sooner or later one will come upon syntheses of knowledge whose organizing metaphors, models, and schemes are thoroughly visual and spatial. This is obvious in such terms as trait, pattern, configuration, structure, model, cognitive map; it is presupposed in notions such as system, integration, organization, function, relation, network, exchange, transaction, and many others which cannot be purified from reference to bodies, parts of bodies, ensembles, machines, and points in space; in short, to objects of knowledge whose primary mode of perception is visual, spatial, or tangible. Therefore it is not surprising that anthropologists of all persuasions have been in overwhelming agreement that their knowledge is based upon, and validated by, *observation*.

Third, even the most simple and seemingly commonsensical recommendations of the kind which served as a point of departure for these remarks carry notions of speed, or expeditiousness of procedure. In other words, they are aimed at instituting a time-economy for anthropological research. Not only is the total time for fieldwork conventionally fixed, it is also thought (and often said) that the fieldworker "saves time" by learning the language beforehand; that he "gains time" through the use of techniques and devices. Advice may take a moral twist, when the student is told to make good use of time by never letting the sun set on untyped field notes. In all this it is *the researcher's time* which is thought to affect the production of knowledge. This observation is not invalidated by recommendations to take note of native ideas of Time, either as explicitly formulated, or as inferred from the organization of ritual and practical activities. As an object of knowledge, the Time of the natives will be processed by the visual-spatial tools and methods invoked earlier.

Anthropologists who have gone through the experience of field research, and others who are capable of imagining what happens to a stranger entering a society with the intention of learning something about it, are likely to be put off by this account. Why did extrapolations from simple and sensible advice regarding method result in a caricature of ethnography? Because these recommendations not only exaggerate (the visual), they omit dimensions of experience. No provision seems to be made for the beat of drums or the blaring of bar music that keep you awake at night; none for the strange taste and texture of food, or the smells and the stench. How does *method* deal with the hours of waiting, with maladroitness and gaffes due to confusion or bad timing? Where does it put the frustrations caused by diffidence and intransigence, where the joys of purposeless chatter and conviviality? Often all this is written off as the "human side" of our scientific activity. Method is expected to yield objective knowledge by filtering out experiential "noise" thought to impinge on the quality of information. But what makes a (reported) sight more objective than a (reported) sound, smell, or taste? Our bias for one and against the other is a matter of cultural choice rather than universal validity. It derives from a scientific tradition which was firmly established by the time J. Locke formulated the empiricist canons of modern social science. "The perception of the mind," he maintained, is "most aptly explained by words relating to the sight" (1964 [1689]:227). Among all the tenets of empiricism this one seems to have been the most tenacious.

Even if detached observation is regarded positively as a means to lift oneself above the immediacy of fleeting sounds, ineffable odors, confused emotions, and the flow of Time passing, the anthropologist so inclined should give, at the very least, some thought to the cultural determinedness of his quest for distance. Evidently, such critical reflection will have a bearing on arguments regarding anthropology's uses of Time and what I termed its denial of coevalness. For it remains to be shown what sort of theory of knowledge brought about, or facilitated, a discourse whose visual-spatial concepts, models, and type-constructs always seem to work against the grain of temporal continuity and coexistence between the Knower and the Known.

Space and Memory: Topoi of Discourse

In the *Art of Memory*, Frances Yates gives an account of the depth and complexity of Western preoccupation with visual and spatial root-metaphors of knowledge. Her findings seem to be supported by historians of science who concur with the thesis that Western science derives from an earlier art of *rhetoric*, chronologically (i.e., with regard to the sequence of developments in our tradition), as well as systematically (regarding the nature of scientific activity). Paul Feyerabend goes as far as declaring that *propaganda* belongs to the essence of science, a view also held, but less outrageously formulated, by T. S. Kuhn in his theory of scientific paradigms.[6] Far from dismissing science as mere rhetoric—a hopeless attempt in view of its practical and technological triumphs—this position states the obvious fact that all sciences, including the most abstract and mathematized disciplines, are social endeavors which must be carried out through the channels and means, and according to the rules, of communication available to a community of practitioners and to the wider society of which they are a part.

As such, the observation that all science rests on rhetoric is a very general one and would not add much to our understanding unless it is possible to show that the rhetoric invoked here is a specific product of our Western tradition as well as the principal channel through which sciences are "feeding back" into Western culture. Yates finds that tradition in the "art of memory." It began as a set of prescriptions, rules, and techniques developed by Greek and Roman rhetoricians to enable the ancient orator, who spoke without a manuscript, to recall the points and arguments of a speech. She describes in detail several sources in the Latin tradition (1966:ch. 1) whose common element was a method of joining the principal parts of a speech to objects in various places in a real or imagined building. While he delivers his oration, the speaker's mind is supposed to walk through the rooms or parts of the building, stopping to consider the things onto which he previously (and habitually) conferred the status of "places" of memory (hence the Greek term *topoi*).

Such are, in the briefest possible terms, the outlines of a conception of rhetoric which was to have consequences reaching far beyond its apparently simple, mnemotechnic function. For the theory of "places" did not merely *aid* memory and recall; as it was developed in more and more complex ways during the Middle Ages and the Renaissance, it served to *define* the nature of memory, and, through it, the nature of any kind of knowledge which is communicated with an intent to convince, to win over an audience.

Most teachers of rhetoric also prescribed techniques based on sound and hearing (such as rote learning by repetition and phonic association). Nevertheless, there seems to have developed very early a consensus that the higher and more exclusive art of memory was tied, by natural gift and training, to an ability to visualize the points of a speech, a poem, or any other text destined for rhetorical use. In the forms in which they are reported, these theories were by no means just rudimentary prephilosophical epistemologies. The classical rules of the art of memory as summarized by Yates are based on numerous philosophical assumptions, none of them simple.

First, the visualized objects (such as statues or parts of them, furnishings, and elements of architecture) were not simple images of the points to be memorized. They were assumed to work best when they were somehow "striking" and when the connection between image and point of an oration was an *arbitrary* one, decreed by the orator. "Places" were thought of as products of the *art* of memory, not as actual images of the content of a speech. What set the skillful orator apart from other mortals was precisely his ability to visualize without actually picturing the contents of his mind; the use of illustrative pictures and images belonged to delivery, not to the foundation of rhetoric. This is probably where we have to seek the roots of increasingly successful attempts to represent the parts of speeches, and later the parts of speech and the structures of propositions and arguments through "signs."

Furthermore, the rules of the art of memory did not only prescribe visualization. Inasmuch as they spoke of movements between "places" of memory they called for *spatialization of consciousness*. The rhetor's art consisted in his capacity to present to himself the temporal flux of live speech as a spatial topography of points and arguments. This, I think, entitles us to trace the spatialization of Time, of which I gave some examples in earlier chapters, to the rules of an ancient art of memory. In Bossuet's historical method, the notion of epochs ("places to stop and look around") is undoubtedly identifiable as a theory of topoi devised to give firm foundations to his discourse, i.e., his oration on history. The same holds for Enlightenment philosophical history, which prided itself in being topical and not merely chronological. Which leads us to the doorstep of modern anthropology: Culture traits and cycles, patterns and configurations, national character and evolutionary stages, but also "classical monographs," compel us to attach our arguments to the Kwakiutl, Trobriands, Nuer, or Ndembu. They are so many topoi, anchorings in real or mental space, of anthropological discourse.[7]

Finally, the art of memory not only employed "places," i.e., a topography, but also an architecture of memory. The orator's topoi were to be found in a house, preferably a large, public building. In the Renaissance this architectural conception led to actual construction of "theaters" of memory/knowledge (see Yates 1966:chs. 6 and 7). Vast projects to systematize knowledge were also based on astrological symbols and charts. The space of rhetoric was ultimately *cosmo-logical* and this may point to some of the historical roots of those uses of Space and Time in anthropology which we qualified earlier as a "political cosmology." As images, places, and spaces turn from mnemotechnic aids into topoi they become that which a discourse is about. When modern anthropology began to construct its Other in terms of topoi implying distance, difference, and opposition, its intent was above all, but at least also, to construct ordered Space and

Time—a cosmos—for Western society to inhabit, rather than "understanding other cultures," its ostensible vocation.

Among the most suggestive lessons to be learned from Yates' *The Art of Memory* is the evidence that links the prehistory of Western science to an artfully cultivated tendency to visualize the contents of consciousness. Of equal importance are some of the effects which an image-theory of knowledge may have on social practice. Stressing visualization in terms of arbitrarily chosen "reminders" makes memory an "art" and removes the foundations of rhetoric from the philosophical problematic of an accurate account of reality. The main concern is with rhetorical effectiveness and success in convincing an audience, not with abstract demonstration of "truth." This prepares the nominalist tradition in Western thought out of which empiricism was to grow.

To recognize this may help us to get away from attributing the development of the Western scientific mind mainly to literacy or, at any rate, to our kind of literacy. The arbitrariness of the memory-images was not the same as that of phonetic script. The symbols used in writing were, once they had been agreed upon, constrained in their combinations and sequence by the sounds of the spoken language. The visual images and topoi of the art of memory provided much freedom of combination and invention, precisely because their manipulation was thought of as an art quite different from the simple skill of reading and writing. Yates describes in her account successful systems of what might be called combinatorial mnemonics, up to the invention of calculus by Leibniz. Modern mathematics thus has its roots, at least some of them, in the same tradition of visualized, spatialized, and ultimately cosmological thought to which we can trace Enlightenment philosophical history and the modern origins of the social sciences.[8]

Finally, the view of memory/knowledge as an "art" favored pretentions to exclusive and arcane knowledge. As the memory images and topoi proliferated and as various kinds of gnostic, magical, and astrological schemes came to be used for the purpose of systematizing this wealth of images, the art of public orators turned into the secret posses-

sion of esoteric groups. Perhaps Yates' fascination with her-
metic-magic origins of Western science gets too close to a
conspiracy theory of intellectual history; but her findings
point to the very deep common roots of social and religious
sectarianism. Both claim to possess special and exclusive
knowledge conceived as manipulation of an apparatus of
visual-spatial symbols removed from ordinary language and
communication.[9]

Many other developments had to occur before anthropology and similar disciplines staked out their exclusive territories, devised technical languages, and gained professional recognition. These developments may be understood
sociologically and we can generalize them as instances of
functional specialization and role differentiation within
larger institutions and social systems. Only, such generali-
zations are often too abstract and at the same time naïve. In
their fixation on goal-oriented behavior and adaptive func-
tionality they tend to overlook the expressive, playful origins
of social forms and institutions. Deep historical connections
such as those between the modern sciences and the ancient
art of memory provide us with the means to correct and
counterbalance sociological utilitarianism or functionalism in
the history of science. I am convinced, and the following
section will offer further reasons, that some very important
aspects of anthropological discourse must be understood as
the continuation of a long tradition of rhetoric with a peculiar cosmological bent. Conceiving outlandish images and
moving in strange space, mostly imaginary, was a preoccupation of savants long before actual encounter with exotic
people and travel to foreign parts, and for reasons to which
actual encounter seems to have added very little. The detour through past and current concerns in anthropology
which we took in the first three chapters has shown that the
hold of a visual-spatial "logic" on our discipline is as strong
as ever; the bodies or organisms of functionalism, the culture gardens of the particularists, the tables of the quanti-
fiers, and the diagrams of the taxonomists all project conceptions of knowledge which are organized around objects,
or images of objects, in spatial relation to each other.

Logic as Arrangement: Knowledge Visible

Pierre de la Ramée, or Petrus Ramus (1515–1572), was a schoolman, a logician and dialectician who taught at the University of Paris. He is perhaps rightly forgotten as a minor philosopher. Yet, as the work of W. J. Ong has shown some time ago (1958), he was a major figure as a theoretician of the *teaching* of knowledge. His writings, which were published in many languages and countless editions, and the pedagogical movement associated with his name had an incalculable influence on Western intellectual history. The fact that his theories soon became anonymous (precisely because they were thought to be synonymous with pedagogical method) only underlines the importance of Ramism. In many circles, especially among the Protestant educators of Germany, England, and its colonies in North America, the precepts of Ramism gained such a degree of acceptance that they virtually disappeared in the undisputed practice of Normal Science, to use Kuhn's term.

The sources of Ramism were medieval "quantitative" logic and contemporary forms of the art of memory as it was expounded in the works of Renaissance and Humanist thinkers. They are far too numerous and complex even to attempt a summary. Suffice it to state that, for Ramus, the most pressing problem about knowledge—any kind of knowledge—became its teachability. This concern placed him firmly in the tradition of rhetoric to which he addressed most of his polemical disquisitions. He was to become a key figure in transmitting some of the deepest convictions of that tradition—those concerning visual images and spatial ordering—to the seventeenth- and eighteenth-century thinkers whom we recognize as immediate precursors of modern science.[10]

The outlook of Ramism is best summarized in the following passage from Ong's work:

Ramist rhetoric . . . is not a dialogue rhetoric at all,
and Ramist dialectic has lost all sense of Socratic
dialogue and even most sense of scholastic dispute.
The Ramist arts of discourse are monologue arts.

They develop the didactic, schoolroom outlook
which descends from scholasticism even more than
do non-Ramist versions of the same arts, and tend
finally even to lose the sense of monologue in pure
diagrammatics. This orientation is very profound
and of a piece with the orientation of Ramism toward an object world (associated with visual perception) rather than toward a person world (associated
with voice and auditory perception). In rhetoric,
obviously someone had to speak, but in the characteristic outlook fostered by the Ramist rhetoric, the
speaking is directed to a world where even persons
respond only as objects—that is, say nothing back.
(Ong 1958:287)

Ramus was a transitional figure in another, even more
important, respect. The beginning of his career coincided
with the period immediately preceding the invention of the
letterpress. His systems reached their maturity and had their
enormous popular success in the beginning of the Gutenberg era. Ong goes as far as depicting Ramus as one of the
ideologues whose thoroughly visualized, spatialized, and
combinatory conception of knowledge prepared the breakthrough (noting that all the technological requisites had been
available for some time before typography was finally "invented"). The connections are far reaching:

Spatial constructs and models were becoming increasingly critical in intellectual development. The
changing attitude manifested itself in the development of printing, in the new Copernican way of
thinking about space which would lead to Newtonian physics, in the evolution of the painter's vision
climaxed by Jan van Eyck's use of the picture frame
as a diaphragm, and in the topical logics of Rudolph Agricola and Ramus. (1958:83; see also 89)

Letter printing made possible mass reproduction with a
great degree of reliability; which in turn favored mass circulation of what Ramus considered his major contribution
to "method": his ambitious renditions of teaching matter
(poems, philosophical texts, biographies, and others) in the
form of diagrams based on a dichotomization of its con-

tents. These figures (some of which are reproduced by Ong) bear an uncanny resemblance to generations of visual devices used by anthropologists, from earlier evolutionary trees to contemporary ethnosemantic paradigms and structuralist arrangements of binary oppositions. If one reflects, for instance, on the nature of kinship charts (of the genealogical grid type) one finds that, ultimately, they are limited only by the size of the paper on which they are drawn or printed. Having learned more about the connections between printing and diagrammatic reduction of the contents of thought, one is tempted to consider the possibility that anthropological kinship theories (at least the ones that take off from data collected with River's chart) are actually determined by the presentability of whatever knowledge they may contain in terms of diagrams that fit onto a conventional printed page. In other words, it is the mode of storing, reproducing, and disseminating knowledge in print (in articles, monographs, and textbooks) which, in ways that may have to be specified in much more detail than it is possible here,[11] prejudge the What and How of large portions of ethnography.

Perhaps the most important lesson to be learned from the study of Ramism and from similar critical analyses of forgotten or suppressed periods in Western intellectual history is that methods, channels, and means of presenting knowledge are anything but secondary to its contents.[12] Anthropologists show varying degrees of awareness of this when they allow themselves to be drawn into debates about whether or not their formal reductions of culture reflect arrangement of ideas in "the heads of the natives." Not many realize that this question makes little sense, not so much because we cannot actually look into the heads of natives (psychologists might disagree with this) but rather because our diagrams are unquestionably artifacts of visual-spatial conventions whose function it is to give "method" to the dissemination of knowledge in *our* society.

Ramism and its belated reincarnations (did not Chomsky's trees descend, via Port Royal, from that tradition?) equate the knowable with that which can be visualized, and logic, the rules of knowledge, with orderly arrangements of pieces of knowledge in space. In that tradition, scientific objectivity was to be guaranteed by the kind of dispassionate visual inspection and measurement practiced in the sciences of nature. Once the source of any knowledge worthy of that name is thought primarily to be visual perception of objects in space, why should it be scandalous to treat the Other— other societies, other cultures, other classes within the same society—*comme des choses?* To be sure, Durkheim did not coin this famous principle because he wanted persons or the moral and spiritual aspects of society treated as things; but he did postulate in that context that the social and cultural must assume, through observation, quantification, and systematic generalization, the same facticity that is exhibited by the *choses* in our field of vision. Behind all this is what S. Moravia called a *méthodologie du regard,* which Enlightenment philosophes and their positivist successors inherited from ancient sources and which, as in these sources, remained tied to rhetoric.[13]

Later, in the nineteenth and twentieth centuries, this stance became more pedantic and more generally effective. Rhetoric developed and hardened when the pursuit of knowledge became inextricably part of its standardization, schematization, and compartmentalization in the vastly expanded rhetoric enterprise of academic teaching.

In the light of connections that are revealed by the studies of Yates and Ong our present self-understanding as anthropologists appears historically and theoretically shallow. It is all the more urgent to remedy that situation because, among the sciences that share common sources in the rhetoric of images and topoi and which employ pedagogical methods of visualizing knowledge, anthropology occupies a peculiar position. It patrols, so to speak, the frontiers of Western culture. In fact, it has always been a *Grenzwissenschaft,* concerned with boundaries: those of one race against another, those between one culture and another, and finally those between culture and nature. These liminal concerns have prevented anthropology from settling down in any one of the accepted domains of knowledge other than in the residual field of "social science." There, many of us live in hiding from biologists, paleontologists, geneticists, psychologists, philosophers, literary critics, linguists, historians and, alas, sociologists on whose territories we are inevitably led without being able to offer any excuse except that the "study of man" must embrace all these fields. That situation alone makes synopticism—the urge to visualize a great multitude of pieces of information as orderly arrangements, systems, and *tableaux*—a constant temptation. There are reasons why we should resist that temptation. Some are political, others epistemological; both kinds will direct the discussion back to the principal theme of these essays—Time and the Other.

Vide et Impera: The Other as Object

Ong's principal intent is expressed in the subtitle of his work on Ramus: "Method and the Decay of Dialogue." Throughout the book he deplores the antipersonalist orientation of visualism. In this respect he anticipated themes which were taken up in the debates of the sixties and seventies when critics of sociology and anthropology began to denounce the dehumanizing effects of overly scientistic methods. A common complaint was that social scientists treated their subjects as objects, that is, as passive targets of various structural, behaviorist, and often quantitative schemes of explanation, and this to the detriment of "understanding" the motives, values, and beliefs of their subjects as persons.

The study of Ramism reveals some deep historical reasons for linking visual-spatial reduction of knowledge with the ethos of scientific explanation. Undoubtedly, modern science progressed as a result of this alliance but, according to Ong, such progress had its price:

Ramism specialized in dichotomies, in "distribution" and "collocation" . . . , in "systems" . . . and in other diagrammatic concepts. This hints that Ramist dialectic represented a drive toward thinking not only of the universe but of thought itself in terms of spatial models apprehended by sight. In this context, the notion of knowledge as word, and the personalist orientations of cognition and of the universe which this notion implies, is due to atrophy. Dialogue itself will drop more than ever out of dialectic. Persons, who alone speak (and in whom alone knowledge and science exist), will be eclipsed insofar as the world is thought of as an assemblage of the sort of things which vision apprehends—objects and surfaces. (1958:9)

As an alternative, Ong invokes the world of the "oral and auditory" which is also "ultimately existential" (1958:110).

I have doubts about this solution. Ong (and the critics of the social sciences who echo his views) rightly denounce visualist reductions. One can only applaud his inspiring efforts to think through the consequences which conceptions of knowledge could have that are based on auditory rather than visual root metaphors.[14] But to equate the aural with the personal and to identify both with the "existential" and humane comes dangerously close to a kind of antiscientism which feeds on moral indignation and nostalgia for "dialogue," rather than on epistemological arguments.

To begin with, aural perception and oral expression neither presuppose nor guarantee a more "personal" idea or use of knowledge. That the spoken word is more fleeting, and that it lends itself less easily to apersonal forms of fixation and transmission than images or print, can no longer be held as a truism. New techniques available to record (and process) spoken language and to translate it directly into print via electronic signals rather than type and font make the old divisions harder to maintain (even if one does not care to go along with Derrida's reversal of relations between speaking and writing as he expounds it in his *Grammatology*).[15] We may be approaching the point where the exchange of spoken words will be distinguishable from the circulation of printed messages and images mainly because the time economy of the former must respond, not so much to personal, but to interpersonal conditions of communication. *Dialogue* is perhaps too weak a term to cover the nature of oral communication. The aural and oral must be invoked for epistemological reasons because they may provide a better starting point for a *dialectical* concept of communication.

Knowledge may be "depersonalized" orally as much as through visual-spatial reduction. Why should mindless oral repetitions of standardized formulae or, for that matter, skillful manipulation of a store of tautological terms as they occur in teaching, in religious sermons, or in political speeches be any less depersonalizing than the peddling of printed words, diagrams, and images? If by *personal* one means something more specific than a vague reference to humane ways; if one wants to designate with this term a greater degree of personal awareness and of individual control, a sharpened sense for authorship and for knowledge as a possession or tool, then it seems obvious to me that visualization and spatialization of knowledge signal a greater, not a lesser, emphasis on the knower as an individual.

In short, to invoke personalism in this and similar debates creates confusion. Perhaps it can be avoided if one rejects too simple an opposition between the visual and the aural. A step into that direction might be to consider Time and especially those temporal relations that must be involved in interpersonal and, *a fortiori,* in intercultural production and communication of knowledge.

Limiting ourselves to anthropology, we can link the findings of the previous chapters to the question at hand: Visualism alone is not to blame for what I called a political cosmology. That vision is the noblest, most comprehensive, and most reliable of the senses has been an article of faith since the beginning of our philosophical tradition. As 'phenomenalism,' this emphasis on vision became part of empiricist and positivist theories of knowledge. But before it could assume the political twist which we ascribe to anthropological discourse, visualism had to be expounded in spatial schemes. Empiricist phenomenalism does presuppose that Nature, at any rate experienced Nature, is atomistic and that knowledge is derived from myriads of sense impressions, especially visual impressions. Because knowledge was thought to operate by collecting, comparing, and classifying impressions, the notion of the mind as a naturalist's collection or cabinet encouraged further extension of the visual bias toward the spatial. Not only the sources of knowledge, but also its contents were imagined to be visible. Add to this the rhetorical intent of teaching such knowledge, and the transformation from visible source to visible content is completed. Taught knowledge became *arranged,* ordered knowledge, easily representable in diagrammatic or tabular form.

To use an extreme formulation, in this tradition the object of anthropology could not have gained scientific status until and unless it underwent a double visual fixation, as perceptual image and as illustration of a kind of knowledge. Both types of objectification depend on distance, spatial and temporal. In the fundamental, phenomenalist sense this means that the Other, as object of knowledge, must be separate, distinct, and preferably distant from the knower. Exotic otherness may be not so much the result as the prerequisite of anthropological inquiry. We do not "find" the savagery of the savage, or the primitivity of the primitive, we posit them, and we have seen in some detail how anthropology has managed to maintain distance, mostly by manipulating temporal coexistence through the denial of coevalness.

Visualization and spatialization have not only been points of departure for a theory of knowledge, they become a program for the new discipline of anthropology. There was a time when this meant, above all, the exhibition of the exotic in illustrated travelogues, museums, fairs, and expositions. These early ethnological practices established seldom articulated but firm convictions that presentations of knowledge through visual and spatial images, maps, diagrams, trees, and tables are particularly well suited to the description of primitive cultures which, as everyone knows, are supremely "synchronic" objects for visual-esthetic perception. Underlying this may be an even older association, to which Ong directs our attention. The rise of topical logic and the use of outlines and dichotomized tables, he points out, was a natural outcome given the necessities of teaching philosophy to teenagers (1958:136 f). It is commonly believed that the visual-spatial is more germane to the infantile and adolescent mind than to mature intelligence. Whether such is indeed the case may be for the psychologist to decide. However it is easy to see how arguing from ontogenetic to phylogenetic visualism may turn pedagogical principles into political programs. Concretely speaking, we must at least admit the possibility that striking images, simplified outlines, and overwrought tables were fed to students in order to impress them with a degree of orderliness and cohesiveness which the fields of knowledge taught by these methods never possessed. Not the students' simplicity but the teacher's determination to maintain his superior position may have to be blamed. The same goes *mutatis mutandis* for the preponderance of visual-spatial presentation of the Other in anthropology. The hegemony of the visual as a mode of knowing may thus directly be linked to the political hegemony of an age group, a class, or one society over another. The ruler's subject and the scientist's object have, in the case of anthropology (but also of sociology and psychology), an intertwined history.

If this is true, it would allow us to see the dogma of empirical fieldwork in a new light. It was already noted that, as a systematic pursuit, it emerged as a symptom of anthropology's professionalization.[16] But we can ask now, what is behind the professionalization of anthropology? In some way or other it reflects the organization of a segment of bourgeois society for the purpose of serving that society's inner continuity (through teaching and writing). Professionally required field research also contributes to maintaining the position of that society vis-a-vis other societies. It is in this role that ethnography came to be defined predominantly as *observing* and *gathering*, i.e., as a visual and spatial activity. It has been the enactment of power relations between societies that send out fieldworkers and societies that are the field. Observing reason (*Beobachtende Vernunft*) seems to be implicated in victimage, an insight which, long before Lévi-Strauss, was candidly expressed by one of the great ethnologists of the nineteenth century: "For us, primitive societies (*Naturvölker*) are ephemeral, i.e., as regards our knowledge of, and our relations with, them, in fact, inasmuch as they exist for us all. At the very instant they become known to us they are doomed" (Bastian 1881:63 f). This was said in a political treatise pleading for the recognition of ethnology as a scientific discipline and proposing to create ethnographic museums as its principal research institutions.

At the risk of repeating myself, I must insist that I have

been using "visualism" to designate an *ideological* current in Western thought. I am not trying to argue, by way of naïve reification, that vision, visual experience, and visual expressions of experience should be removed from the agenda of anthropological thought and discourse. As an ideological bent, especially if it is true that there is collusion between such a bent and allochronic tendencies, visualism functions as a cognitive style that is likely to prejudice the study of all kinds of cultural expression, *including* those that pertain to visual experience in general and to visual aesthetics in particular. The visualist bias that is brought to the visual productions of other cultures is no less in need of critique than visualist reductions of, say, language, ritual, dance and music, social relations, or ecological conditions.

All this applies, of course, to the emerging field of visual anthropology. Its evaluation in terms of the visualist and allochronic tendencies we are exploring in this chapter would require more than a note in passing. My feeling is that, paradoxically, we may have a movement here which is directed against the limiting effects of visualism on a theory of knowledge. At least some visual anthropologists affirm the importance of intersubjective experience of Time and explore hermeneutic approaches to visual data (see Ruby 1980 and further references in that article). Needless to say, visual ethnography lends itself to methodologization, in some instances of the most excessive kind (see the heroic attempts at graphic reduction and formal analysis in proxemics, kinesics, and related fields).

"The Symbol Belongs to the Orient": Symbolic Anthropology in Hegel's Aesthetic

When one criticizes epistemological and political implications of visualism and spatialism, allegations of *abuse* should, of course, be weighed in a larger context of *use*. One must ask what the convictions and reasons are that make anthropology accept visual-spatial reductions as legitimate modes of knowledge. We have done this for the periods when cultural anthropology emerged under the episteme of natural history and developed its relativist and taxonomic discourse. It would be impossible to conclude this account without considering how a trend in current anthropology which uses the notion of *symbol* as a unifying concept fits into our argument regarding allochronic discourse. Because "symbolic anthropology" is of more recent origin and an ongoing concern it defies easy summation; it also lacks a single towering figure on whose oeuvre one could concentrate as being representative of the symbolic approach. Compared to the historical and critical literature on, say, evolutionism or structuralism, there is as yet little to build on.

The notion of symbol may have to be counted among those allochronic devices whose use entails or encourages denial of coevalness between the subject and the object of anthropological discourse. This is not a verdict but a point for debate. At any rate, it would be extremely difficult to demonstrate this fully if only because the sources from which anthropologists have been borrowing their ideas are too varied. Between "symbolist" poetry and American "symbolic interactionist" sociology, a critique of symbolic anthropology would have to cover vast areas of intellectual history, not to mention further complications that arise from dissenting views within symbolic anthropology.[17]

The pragmatist heritage of symbolic anthropology has caused its best representatives to preserve a critical distrust for the kind of abstract formalizations to which French structuralists are given (even though connections between the two have by no means been severed, see Leach 1976). It has, above all, led them to recognize concrete experience and communicative interaction as principal sources of ethnographic knowledge. Still, deciding on the symbol as a key notion has far-reaching consequences and there are reasons for arguing that contemporary symbolic anthropology is part of a tradition of thought which constructs its objects with the help of a visual-spatial rhetoric. System, order, models, blueprints, and similar terms which regularly occur in these writings signal a visualist epistemology. They are characteristic of an anthropological discourse whose self-definition oscillates between semiotics (French-Saussurian) and semiology (American-Peircean). In either case, the symbolic anthropologist is inclined to "view" the Other as an object of aesthetic contemplation. "In the country of the blind," says C. Geertz, "the one-eyed is not king but spectator" (1979:228). The example of M. Sahlins will show that this may be carried to the point where the ardor to defend a symbolic approach even leads a bonafide materialist to affirm the aesthetic "autonomy" of culture. The detour through the symbolic study of primitive culture leads one to discover a universal and transhistorical mode of existence of all culture: religion, art, and even ideology will then be declared "cultural systems" and nothing should in principle prevent science, politics, and economics from being resorbed by such panculturalism.

In sum, the symbolic carries a heavy load indeed. But whose load is it? Is the subject of anthropological discourse burdened with it or is it carried by the object? When we ask these questions we note the ambiguity of *symbolic* in symbolic anthropology. Is it the primitive whose way of thinking, expressing, or being is symbolic, or is anthropology symbolic in the sense that it projects onto its Other symbolic meanings and understandings, much as the ancient artists of memory populated their consciousness with esoteric images and signs? Is the symbolic, as a mode of being, an object of inquiry or does it constitute a method? If it is a mode of cultural existence then it is a problem *for* us; if it is a mode of inquiry then it is a problem generated *by* us, a load with which we burden those whom we analyze "symbolically." These questions, to be sure, contain age-old philosophical puzzles which have eluded definitive solutions and are likely to elude them in the future. But they also touch on history and politics. It makes sense to ask them, for instance, in the light of what we called allochronic discourse. In what sense does talk of symbols and the symbolic foster a tendency in anthropological discourse to place its Other in a Time different from our own?

At the risk of incurring the wrath of both symbolic anthropologists and historians of philosophy, I will illustrate how symbol may be used as a temporalizing device by commenting briefly on some passages in the first and second parts of Hegel's *Lectures on Aesthetics*.[18] There are striking resemblances between these philosophical texts and certain positions held by contemporary analysts of cultural symbols (perhaps expressive of historical connections via Royce, Peirce, and other American pragmatists). Moreover, assumptions that are usually hidden in anthropological discourse are explicitly stated by Hegel, who was unhampered by cultural relativism and its conventions of intercultural civility.

Hegel proposes his theory of the symbol in order to distinguish between three major art forms: symbolic, classic, and romantic. As is characteristic of him, he makes these distinctions in such a way that they not only yield a systematic typology but also a developmental sequence. The symbolic mode precedes the classic and romantic forms by logical necessity, not by mere historical accident. The historical meaning of symbolism and its logical position in a system of relations are therefore interchangeable.

To analyze the logic of symbolism is the purpose of an introductory section to the second part of the *Aesthetic* with the predictable title "On the symbol as such." It begins with a statement whose temporalizing intent could not be expressed more clearly:

> In the sense in which we are using the word, symbol marks, conceptually as well as historically, the origin of art; therefore it should be, as it were, regarded only as pre-art, belonging mainly to the Orient. Only after many transitions, transformations and mediations does it lead to the authentic reality of the idea of a classical artform. (i:393)

Such is the real meaning of symbol as opposed to a secondary, "external" use according to which certain modes of presentation that can occur in any of the three art forms may also be called *symbolic*.

In these few sentences, Hegel summarized many of the assumptions that have been guiding inquiries into (temporally or spatially) remote expressions of culture. Most importantly, he sets a precedent for an extraordinary claim, namely that symbolic could be at once analytical ("logical") and historical: that it marks a type of relation between content and form, reality and expressions, presumably characteristic of all culture, as well as a specific form or a peculiar mode of expression characteristic of certain cultures. These he finds, at least in their authentic state, at the early stages of civilization, outside of his own Western world, in the "Orient." That which is past is remote, that which is remote is past: such is the tune to which figures of allochronic discourse are dancing.

Neither Hegel nor later symbologists could confine themselves to affirmations of temporal distance. They had to elaborate on the logic of distance lest placing the symbolic in the past might remove it altogether from serious consideration. Our *temporal* dismissal of the Other is always such that he remains "integrated" in our spatial concepts of logic (such as order, difference, opposition). Hegel, therefore, proceeds in his *Aesthetic* to shore up his position. Conceptually, it must be guarded against confusion of the symbolic mode of expression with other types of sign relations; historically, the symbolic must be shown to cause in the contemporary spectator reactions that are unlike those we expect from more familiar art forms.

Hegel, accordingly, first distinguishes symbols from other signs, e.g., linguistic signs. Whereas the latter are arbitrarily assigned to the sounds or meanings they represent, the relationship between symbols and what they express is not "indifferent." The symbol suggests by its external appearance that which it makes appear, not in its concrete and unique existence, however, but by expressing "a general quality of its meaning" (see 1:395). Furthermore, symbolic expression and symbolized content are not reducible to each other. They lead, so to speak, an independent existence: one symbol can have many contents, one content is capable of being expressed by different symbols. Hence symbols are essentially ambiguous; they leave the viewer necessarily "doubtful" (1:397). If and when ambiguity is removed and doubts are assuaged, then a symbolic relationship in the strict sense no longer obtains. What remains of the symbol is "a mere image" whose relation to the content it depicts is that of an analogy or simile (see 1:398; the terms are *Vergleichung* and *Gleichnis*).

Hegel insists that doubtfulness and insecurity vis-à-vis the symbolic are not limited to certain cases. Rather, they are the response

to very large areas of art; they apply to an im-
mense material at hand: the content of almost all
oriental art. Therefore, when we first enter the
world of ancient Persian, Indian, or Egyptian figures (*Gestalten*) we feel uneasy. We sense that we are
walking among *tasks;* in themselves, these forms do
not strike us; their contemplation does not immediately please or satisfy us. But they contain a challenge to go beyond their external appearance], to
their meaning, which must be something more and
something more profound than these images. (1:400)

In a manner reminiscent of relativist appeals to the unity of mankind, Hegel then notes that a symbolic interpretation is called for because we simply cannot dismiss as childish the productions of peoples who may be in their childhood, but who ask for "more essential content." Their true meaning must be "divined" beneath their "enigmatic" forms (*ibid.*).

All this sounds quite modern and is in fact ritually as-serted by contemporary anthropologists, especially the no-tion that the non-Western poses a "problem" (*eine Aufgabe*, in Hegel's words). Being alerted by the fable of the wolf and the lamb to a certain kind of hypocrisy whenever the Other is said to be problematic, one suspects Hegel of duplicity. He *seems* to be driven by an effort to give us a theory of the symbolic as a special type of sign relation. Ambiguity and doubtfulness appear to be a "logical" property of the sym-bolic. In reality, they are caused by actual historical con-frontation with non-Western forms of cultural expression. Ambiguity and doubtfulness are the primary datum; *they* are the task or problem, not the symbolic images by which they are triggered. The symbolic approach is that part of a gen-eral theory of signs which functions most directly as an anx-iety-reducing method.

One might argue that it is mere pedantry to hold Hegel (and perhaps symbolic anthropology) to the actual sequence of steps by which they arrive at a theory of symbolic expres-sion. Not at all, because sequence may make a considerable difference when one wishes to examine ideological and political implications of symbolic approaches. As is often the case (and Hegel would be the first to say so), the logical structure of an argument may contain assumptions, or decrees, of developmental, evolutionary sequence. In fact, in Hegel's case it is quite clear that he proposes his theory of the symbolic as a (part of a) theory of history. As such it is a theory about Time, one that "temporalizes" relations between Western and non-Western cultures by placing the latter in the time of origins. Given the resemblances between Hegel's views and those of present-day symbologists (not to speak of convergences between Hegel and Comte and Durkheim) one cannot help but suspect that the symbolic continues to serve essentially as a time-distancing device.

Hegel and modern symbolic anthropology part company as far as the extension of their symbol-theories are concerned. Hegel, whose dialectic thought always moves toward the concrete and who, in the *Aesthetic* as in his other works, proposes to account for specific, historical realizations of the spirit, rejects the notion that all art, and hence all culture should be approached as symbolic. He admits (in some comments on symbolic theories fashionable at his time)[19] that such a view might be construed, but his interest goes in the opposite direction. He wants to show that the symbolic was, necessarily, a historical mode of art production. As such it is part of a typology within which it contrasts with two other major forms, called classic and romantic (see 1:405).

In later sections of his *Aesthetic*, Hegel elaborates on this typology and names the grounds on which the three types are to be distinguished. The common criterion in all three forms is the relation of form and content, expression and meaning. The symbolic, "the stage of the *origin* of art" is characterized by an inherent ambiguity of that relation. Meaning and expression are, so to speak, merely juxtaposed; the human spirit is still groping for unity of substance and expression. Classic art, exemplified by Greek sculpture, achieved unity, albeit in an "external," impersonal form (see 11:13 ff). Such external unity was, to use a Hegelian term not invoked by Hegel in this context, mere antithesis to symbolic juxtaposition and ambiguity. Only Romantic art accomplishes the synthesis of form and content as inner unity, as the subjective realization of the Spirit. From it springs a new and "modern" creativity; in its

> pantheon all gods are dethroned, the flame of subjectivity has destroyed them, and instead of plastic polytheism [i.e. a multitude of symbolic figures] art now knows only *one* God, *one* Spirit, *one* absolute autonomy. Art is constituted in free unity as its own absolute knowledge and will, it no longer is divided into specific traits and functions whose only connection was the force of some dark necessity. (ii:130)

Similar schemes of final identity are expounded in Hegel's *Phenomenology of the Spirit* and in his writings on the philosophy of history and law. But nowhere are his arguments as "anthropological" as in his *Aesthetic*. For one thing, he soon overcomes earlier hesitation and extends his typology of art forms to all culture (see ii:232). His theory of art is a theory of culture:

> These ways of viewing the world constitute religion, the substantial spirit of peoples and times. They permeate art as much as all areas of a given living present. As every human being is in all his activities, be they political, religious, artistic, or scientific, a child of his time and has the task to work out the essential content and necessary form of his time, so is art destined to find the artistic expression appropriate to the spirit of a people. (ii:232)

The symbolic, however, clearly is the Other. Classic art appears as a transitory stage, a pale "logical" projection in this tripartite typology. It is admirable but does not inspire "uneasiness." The symbolic is the problem. It is in practical opposition to the romantic, and the romantic clearly serves as a description of Hegel's own nineteenth-century consciousness and sensibilities. The sovereign individual, free from the constraints of "natural" forms and aesthetic conventions, is the ideal of contemporary, modern man. To overcome the symbolic, historically and by conceptual anal-

ysis, constitutes a "task" for modern man: his self-constitu-
tion.

The symbolic-visual mode of expression is said to dominate the early stages of culture; it is ambiguous and tenuous, always in danger of turning into mere imagery or un-
controlled fancy. This is Hegel's counterimage to a culture
which has achieved "inner unity" of form and content. By
the logic of contrast and opposition one expects him to explore audial-verbal modes as appropriate expressions of romantic art. Such is indeed the case: "If we want to summa-
rize in one word the relationship of content and form in the
Romantic . . . we may say that its basic tone is . . . *musical*
and . . . *lyrical*" (II:141). He develops this insight systematically and in great detail in the third part of *Aesthetic* (III,
chapters on romantic music and poetry). There he speaks
of Time as that which is "dominant in music" (III:163), a
thought which links his theory of art to an idea pervading
his entire philosophical system. It has been said that Hegel's
philosophy of the human spirit is a philosophy of Time.[20]
Indeed, among the most beguiling of his insights are those
that contrast Time with Space, as Sound with Sight, History
with Nature. In the *Encyclopedia* Hegel formulates: "The au-
dible and temporal, and the visible and spatial each have
their own basis. They are, at first, equally valid." But—and
in this context he opposes writing and speaking—"visible
language relates to sounding (*tönend*) language only as a
sign." The catch is in the *only:* "true expression of the mind
occurs in speech" (see 1969:374, par. 459). We can, and must
go beyond signs and symbols.

The Other as Icon: The Case of "Symbolic Anthropology"

Contemporary symbolic anthropology can probably not be
blamed for (nor credited with) a historizing theory of the
symbolic. On the whole, it seems to have accepted Whitehead's verdict that symbolism as a culturally specific style (as
in "oriental symbolism," or "medieval symbolic architecture") is "on the fringe of life" (1959 [1927]:1). It opted for

an alternative that was rejected by Hegel, namely that the symbolic ought to be taken as a mode of all perception insofar as it is cultural.

It appears, however, if we let ourselves be guided by Whitehead's classical text, that a transhistorical theory of symbolization shares many of the assumptions we ascribed to a relativist, taxonomic, and generally visualist outlook. The constitutive act of knowledge—"selfproduction" in Whitehead's terminology—consists of bringing together into one sign-relation what was apart (1959:9). The temporal coexistence of perceptions and expressions is not considered problematic. It is an external, physical fact (see 1959:16, 21); what counts is the "scheme of spatial relatedness of the perceived things to each other and to the perceiving subject" (1959:22). This echoes Ramist epistemology and, as one might expect, has strong affinities to a classificatory, taxonomic stance. Spatial relations and sense data are both "generic abstactions" and

The main facts about presentational immediacy are: (i) that the sense-data involved depend on the percipient organism and its spatial relations to the perceived organisms; (ii) that the contemporary world is exhibited as extended and as a plenum of organisms; (iii) that presentational immediacy is an important factor in the experience of only a few high-grade organisms, and that for the others it is embryonic or entirely negligible. Thus the disclosure of a contemporary world by presentational immediacy is bound up with the disclosure of the solidarity of actual things by reason of their participation in an *impartial system of spatial extension.* (1959:23; my emphasis)

These premises are ingeniously developed until they lead to the conclusion that "Ultimately all observation, scientific or popular, consists in the determination of the spatial relation of the bodily organs of the observer to the location of 'projected' sense data" (1959:56). Furthermore, there is only a small step from spatialism to what I will refer to as the iconism of symbolic approaches: "Our relationships to these bodies are precisely our reactions to them.

The projection of our sensations is nothing else than the *illustration* of the world in partial accordance with the systematic scheme, in space and time, to which these reactions conform" (1959:58; my emphasis). Finally, by way of assumptions concerning the spatial-geographic "unity" of societies and the role of language as the most important "national symbolism" (see 1959:64, 66 f.) Whitehead's argument ends with statements of a political nature which today sound much like the commonplaces one is likely to encounter in anthropological and sociological texts:

When we examine how a society bends its individual members to function in conformity with its needs, we discover that one important operative agency is our vast system of inherited symbolism. (1959:73).

The self-organisation of society depends on commonly diffused symbols evoking commonly diffused ideas, and at the same time indicating commonly understood actions. (1959:76)

Whitehead is not the sole philosophical ancestor of symbolic anthropology, perhaps not even its most important one. And there is much more to his thought and the essay from which I quoted than its being an example of visualism.[21] Still, it is fair to say that *Symbolism: Its Meaning and Effect* contains some of the basic presuppositions of the symbolic approach in current anthropology. It holds that symbols are the mode of knowledge of the cultures we study, in fact of culture *tout court,* and that symbolic analysis or interpretation provide anthropology with adequate methods of describing and understanding other cultures. Symbolic anthropology shares with structuralism its contempt for crude empiricism; it is less enthusiastic about its concerns for classification and taxonomic description. I say "less" because the taste for taxonomies is not entirely absent. For instance, V. Turner's proposal to chart a symbol system in terms of dominant and instrumental symbols (1967:30 f.) clearly presupposes classificatory and hierarchical ordering which, as a method of description, could easily be presented as a taxonomy of symbols. Incidentally, Turner provides us with a striking example of an ethnographic translation from temporal to spatial schemes. At one point he notes that each of the symbols he identified as "dominant" is described by the Ndembu as *mukulumpi*, elder, senior (1967:31; see also 30). Relations based on seniority (especially when they are concretized as filiation or generation) and relations based on subsumption and dominance are of different types entirely. Of course it is the juxtaposition of the Ndembu term and its ethnographic gloss—a trace of field work carried out under conditions of coevalness—which permits this critique.

Symbolic anthropologists advocate hermeneutic approaches and perfer "thick" ethnographic accounts over anemic diagrams and tables. Very likely, they come closer than other schools to treating Others not just *in* but also *on* their own terms. Yet symbolic anthropology continues to speak not only of symbols but of symbol-systems; it strives to lay bare the symbolic structures and props of a culture. On the whole, it orients its discourse on root metaphors derived from vision. Consequently it exhibits more affinities to spatial order than to temporal process.

Rather than trying to confront symbolic anthropology in terms of its numerous philosophical and social-scientific sources, I will discuss one example documenting the *iconic* bent and then examine some further consequences in a recent case of conversion to symbolic anthropology.

My first example is James Boon's *The Anthropological Romance of Bali* (1977), a thoughtful and (in a positive sense) self-conscious work in the symbolic orientation. Boon's project is carried out with elegance and persuasiveness. His central concern might in fact be quite close to the one pursued in these essays: The ethnography of Bali must be understood in the context of "temporal perspectives" (thus the title of part 1) which, successively and cumulatively, have contributed to constituting "Bali" as a topos, i.e., a striking and significant place of return and reference in Western anthropological discourse. From the time of its discovery as a "paradise" by the Dutch, to Mead and Bateson's delight at finding its people superbly photogenic (1977:10, 67), down to the touristic packaging of the island in our days, there runs a history of visualization whose explicitness and intensity affords us an extreme example of stereotypical knowledge of an exotic people. Bali's ecological compactness, its striking relief, and the profusion of visual-spatial symbolism developed by its culture contributed further to making the island eminently suited to ethnographic description replete with visual rhetoric. Boon is critically aware that his own ethnographic research inserts itself into that history. He knows that he must work either with or against the transformation of Bali into an emblem of exoticism.

The image of Bali derives from visual-spatial reduction which is at the same time too concrete and too abstract: too concrete, inasmuch as it depicts the Balinese clothed in a confusing plethora of symbols; too abstract when it wrongly projects a hieratic continuity onto their troubled history. Despite reports on virulent political strife, and disregarding evidence of historical process in the pronounced syncretism of its religious beliefs and social institutions, the Western image of timeless Bali was maintained with unwavering tenacity. It spawned a long series of ever more daring visual reductions, including attempts to read the system of branching irrigation canals literally as diagrams of kinship and social structure (see Boon 1977:40). In sum, anthropological discourse on Bali has been given to excesses of visualism which have the cumulative effect of temporal distancing: Bali is paradisiacal, hieratic, emblematic—everything but coeval with the Western observer.

When Boon sets out to undo these delusions, however, he chooses a strategy whose prospects for breaking with the tradition he criticizes are not very good. This is not immediately apparent from his method of playing concepts derived from literary criticism against the iconism of earlier ethnography; the verbal serves here as an instance against the visual. He applies the conceptual apparatus used to distinguish between the genres of romance and epic to Balinese history, ancient and recent, and succeeds in conveying an impression of a highly flexible and dynamic culture. Details of his account need not concern us here. Suffice it to say that Boon's sensitivity to the effects of visualizing and spatializing devices in anthropological discourse comes to the point where he almost raises the issue of coevalness.

But, and there is a but, it is not likely that Boon will raise that problem in a fundamental way as long as he remains within the theoretical and methodological frame of symbolic anthropology. True, he denounces facile visual-spatial reduction. Yet his own approach is topical in the sense of a place-logic that permits him to attach his account to a few striking themes (those of romance and epic and a series of features, styles, and recurrent motifs which are used to define these genres). He thus constructs an architecture of interpretations whose rhetoric appeal bears more than a superficial resemblance to the "art of memory."[22] The result is an account which rises above its crudely visualist antecedents. If successful, such description moves the ethnographer's audience to approval or rejection, as the case may be, but it avoids calling the Knower and the Known into the same temporal arena. Like other symbolic anthropologists, Boon keeps his distance from the Other; in the end his critique amounts to posing one image of Bali against other images. This is inevitable as long as anthropology remains fixed on symbolic mediations whose importance no one denies but which, after all, should be the field of encounter with the Other in dialectical terms of confrontation, challenge, and contradiction, not the protective shield which cultures hold up against each other. So far, it seems, fixation on the symbolic favored maintaining the stance of the viewer, observer, perhaps the decipherer of cultural "texts"; The Other remains an object, albeit on a higher level than that of empiricist or positivist reification. The following passage from Boon confirms this beyond any doubt:

A major interest in the art of ethnology is to convey
a sense of the whole society, to typify it in some
vivid, compelling manner. Like any essentially metaphorical procedure, ethnology thus resembles the
arts of visual illusion, if one realizes there is no such
thing as simple "realism" and no possible one-to-
one correspondence between that which is "illu-
sioned to" and the perceptual or conceptual apparatus by which illusion is perpetrated. (1977:18)

Having moved to a higher level of visual-spatial reduction, and hence of temporal distancing, symbolic anthropol-

ogy may in fact be quite immune to the problem of coevalness. As an ideology it may widen and deepen the gap
between the West and its Other. At least, this is how I read
the following statement from the introduction to a reader
on symbolic anthropology:

Fundamental to the study of symbolic anthropology
is the concern with how people formulate their
reality. We must, if we are to understand this and
relate it to an understanding of their (and our own)
action, examine *their culture*, not *our theories* (and if
we study our theories, we must study them *as* "their
culture"); study their systems of symbols, not our *ad
hoc* presumptions about what it might or should be.
(Dolgin et al. 1977:34)

One can applaud the authors' intent when, in the same
passage, they call for a study of culture as praxis rather than
form. All the same, to insist on keeping "their culture" and
"our theories" apart countermands the call for "praxis." A
praxis that does not include the one who studies it can only
be confronted as an image of itself, as a representation, and
with that, anthropology is back to the interpretation of
(symbolic) forms.

This is exemplified by Marshall Sahlins in the account
of his conversion to symbolic anthropology, *Culture and
Practical Reason* (1976). The book is devoted to demonstrating the difference between symbolic culture and practical
responses to life's necessities or the prospects for profit. It
is of special interest here because it not only opposes two
modes of knowledge and action (in this it is hardly unique)
but it aligns these modes, very much in the manner of Hegel, with the differences between what Sahlins calls the West
and the Rest.

In his arguments Sahlins makes ample use of the term
primitive. It turns out, however, that he is not much interested in evolutionary distancing and perhaps even less in
romantic idealizing. He goes farther than both these forms.
Where the former projects developmental or historical distance and the latter a utopian-critical distance from Western
society, Sahlins introduces an ontological difference: As

symbolic and practical reason are two irreducible modes of thought and action, so are being primitive and being civilized two irreducible modes of existence. Consciously or not, Sahlins and other symbolic anthropologists promote fundamental oppositions which have left traces in almost every ideological camp of our discipline. Certainly the nature-culture dualism of the structuralists seems to be a legitimate heir to nineteenth century disjunctions. It creates dichotomies, first by attributing central importance to classification and exchange in primitive society in contrast to labor and production in Western society; second, by opposing historical ("hot") to ahistorical ("cold") societies and claiming the latter as the proper domain of anthropology.

But let us take a closer look at Sahlins' reasoning. To begin with, he cannot be accused of naïveté about the origin and effect of such dichotomizing:

One evident matter—for bourgeois society as much as the so-called primitive—is that material aspects are not usefully separated from the social, as if the first were referable to the satisfaction of needs by the exploitation of nature, the second to problems of the relations between men. Having made such a fateful differentiation of cultural components . . . we are forced to live forever with the intellectual consequences. . . .
Much of anthropology can be considered as a sustained effort at synthesizing an original segmentation of its object, an analytic distinction of cultural domains it made without due reflection, if clearly on the model presented by our own society. (1976:205)

So far, so good. But the history of anthropology does not contain its own justification. The energy allegedly spent on resynthesizing does not guarantee the success of these efforts. Sahlins himself illustrates this by the way he carries out his project. Three-fourths of his book is devoted to showing that varieties of practical reason, in particular historical materialism, generate theories that are only applicable to Western society. Primitive societies, we are told, are guided by, and must be understood in terms of, "cultural (symbolic) reason." If this were taken to its radical conclusions one would have to assert that sense and meaning are to be found in primitive societies only, whereas Western civilization is but the result of economic mechanisms and pragmatic adjustments.[23]

Sahlins does not pose the problem in such a radical way.[24] The remainder of his book is devoted to uncovering "some semiotic dimensions of *our* economy" (1976:165; my emphasis). In other words, he proposes to show that even contemporary American society has "culture," i.e., is in some ways governed by symbolic reason whose logic is not reducible to practical concerns. With that he takes back what his central thesis states.

This attempt at synthesizing cultural and practical reason was doomed from the beginning because Sahlins tries to carry it out in terms of the disjunction it was supposed to overcome. Throughout, he clings to the notion of primitive society. In fact it is quite clear that he cannot do without it if he is to take the first step in his argument *for* culture *against* practical reason. To identify, as he does, in Western society the continued existence of symbolic representations characteristic of primitive society was a favorite strategy of nineteenth-century evolutionist comparative method: one is tempted to state that Sahlins resurrects the doctrine of survivals. Little if anything, is gained for our understanding of the symbolic if it is opposed to the practical.

M. Foucault observed, in the *Order of Things* (1973), that since Ricardo and certainly since Marx, economic theory went through a profound change. At one time, the relationship between value and labor had been seen as one of representation or signification. Value was conceived as a *sign* of human activity (axiom: "A thing is representable in units of work"). Ricardo and Marx redefined the relationship as one of origin and result: "Value has ceased to be a sign, it has become a product" (Foucault 1973:253). If this observation is correct it throws further light on current anthropological dichotomies. Culture, according to predominant opinion, relates to human activitity in symbolic or semiotic ways; it *represents* practical activities but is not studied as their product. Sahlins and other symbolic anthropologists who sub-

scribe to this view and who are out to assert the autonomous, irreducible character of symbolic culture, cut
themselves off from human praxis, which alone can account
for the emergence and existence of cultural orders. Illustrating Marx's First Thesis on Feuerbach, with which I pre-
faced this chapter, they advocate an anthropology for which
culture remains an "object of contemplation."

To criticize such "symbolism" is not to deny all usefulness to semiotic approaches. What should be rejected is the
ideological closure of semiotic and symbolic types of anthropological analysis. That closure is usually achieved by asserting the functional autonomy of symbolic relations and
systems, and by relegating all questions that regard their
production, their being anchored in a nonrepresentational
world of real space and time, to economics (as in Sahlins'
"practical reason") or to neurophysiology (as in Lévi-Strauss'
"human mind").

To insist on production besides, or against, representation is not to assert an ontological difference between the
two. There is no ontological necessity to regard culture as a
product rather than a sign. The distinction must be maintained for epistemological reasons. Proclaiming the symbolic autonomy of culture and practicing some sort of semiotic analysis on aspects of it really works only within one's
own culture (as demonstrated brilliantly by R. Barthes and
J. Baudrillard). When the analyst participates in the praxis
that produces the system he analyzes, he may bracket out
the question of production without doing too much harm
to his material. Semiotic analysis applied to other cultures
(especially when it is carried out without immerson into the
praxis of these cultures) can only be realized as a form of
arbitrary imposition—call it constructing the myth of a myth
(as Lévi-Strauss defines the task of the anthropologist) or
applying Occam's razor (as it is often put by his empiricist
counterparts). Arbitrary imposition *works*—witness the out-
put of various semiotic and symbolic schools in anthropology—but only on the condition that the one who employs it
exercises a kind of epistemological dictatorship reflecting the
real political relations between the society that studies and
societies that are studied.

With these remarks, our critique of symbolic anthropology converges with P. Bourdieu's objections to what he
calls *objectivism* in anthropology (aiming mainly at French
structuralism). Most of the issues are summarized in this
passage from his *Outline of a Theory of Practice:*

Objectivism constitutes the social world as a spectacle presented to an observer who takes up a "point
of view" on the action, who stands back so as to observe it and, transferring into the object the principles of his relation to the object, conceives of it as a
totality intended for cognition alone, in which all
interactions are reduced to symbolic exchanges.
This point of view is the one afforded by high positions in the social structure, from which the social
world appears as a representation (in the sense of
idealist philosophy but also as used in painting or
the theatre) and practices are no more than "execu-
tions," stage parts, performances of scores, or the
implementing of plans. (1977:96)

Chapter Five / Conclusions

*These petrified relations must be forced to dance by singing
to them their own melody.*

Karl Marx [1]

*All knowledge, taken at the moment of its constitution, is
polemical knowledge.*

Gaston Bachelard [2]

FORMULATED AS A QUESTION, the topic of these essays was: How has anthropology been defining or construing its object—the Other? Search for an answer has been guided by a thesis: Anthropology emerged and established itself as an allochronic discourse; it is a science of other men in another Time. It is a discourse whose referent has been removed from the present of the speaking/writing subject. This "petrified relation" is a scandal. Anthropology's Other is, ultimately, other people who are our contemporaries. No matter whether its intent is historical (*ideographic*) or generalizing, (*nomothetic*), anthropology cannot do without anchoring its knowledge, through research, in specific groups or societies; otherwise it would no longer be anthropology but metaphysical speculation disguised as an empirical science. As relationships between peoples and societies that study and those that are studied, relationships between anthropology and its object are inevitably political; production of knowledge occurs in a public forum of intergroup, inter-class, and international relations. Among the historical conditions under which our discipline emerged and which affected its growth and differentiation were the rise of capitalism and its colonialist-imperialist expansion into the very societies which became the target of our inquiries. For this to occur, the expansive, aggressive, and oppressive societies which we collectively and inaccurately call the West needed Space to occupy. More profoundly and problematically, they required Time to accomodate the schemes of a one-way history: progress, development, modernity (and their negative mirror images: stagnation, underdevelopment, tradition). In short, *geopolitics* has its ideological foundations in *chronopolitics*.

Retrospect and Summary

Neither political Space nor political Time are natural resources. They are ideologically construed instruments of power. Most critics of imperialism are prepared to admit this with regard to Space. It has long been recognized that imperialist claims to the right of occupying "empty," underused, undeveloped space for the common good of mankind should be taken for what they really are: a monstrous lie perpetuated for the benefit of one part of humanity, for a few societies of that part, and, in the end, for one part of these societies, its dominant classes. But by and large, we remain under the spell of an equally mendacious fiction: that interpersonal, intergroup, indeed, international Time is "public Time"—there to be occupied, measured, and allotted by the powers that be.

There is evidence—to my knowledge not touched upon by historians of anthropology—that such a political idea of public Time was developed in the years after World War II, with help from anthropology. Perhaps it was needed to fill the interstices between relativist culture gardens when, after cataclysmic struggle between the great powers and just before accession to political independence of most former colonies, it became impossible to maintain temporal pluralism in a radical way. Theoreticians and apologists of a new international order perceived the need to safeguard the position of the West. The necessity arose to provide an objective, transcultural temporal medium for theories of *change* that were to dominate Western social science in the decades that followed.[3]

F. S. C. Northrop was an important figure during that period. As a thinker who had achieved an astounding command and synthesis of logic, philosophy of science, political theory, and international law, he radiated the optimism of Western science on the threshold of new discoveries. It is impossible to do justice to his prolific writings by quoting a few passages. Nevertheless, to recall some of Northrop's ideas will help to clarify our argument about political uses of Time and the role anthropology was to play in this. The scene may be set, as it were, by quoting from his programmatic essay, "A New Approach to Politics":

The political problems of today's world, both domestic and international, center in the mentalities and customs of people and only secondarily and afterwards in their tools—whether those tools be economic, military, technological or eschatological in the sense of the Reverend Reinhold Niebuhr. *Since customs are anthropological and sociological, contemporary politics must be also.* (1960:15; my emphasis)

Northrop expected much from anthropology and took initiatives to prod anthropologists into formulating their contributions to a new theory of international relations. At a time when he served as the moderator of a symposium on "Cross-Cultural Understanding"[4] he professed to be guided by two premises. One was the anthropological doctrine of cultural relativism which he accepted as an appropriate philosophical and factual foundation of international pluralism. The other was his interpretation of the epistemological consequences of Einstein's space-time postulates. In a formula he also uses in other writings Northrop describes these consequences as "anyone's knowledge of the publicly meaningful simultaneity of spatially separated events" (1964:10). While the premises of cultural relativism posed the problem (the multiplicity of cultures as spatially separated events), the Einsteinian conception of relativity suggested to Northrop the solution. "Public" Time provided meaningful simultaneity, i.e., a kind of simultaneity that is natural because it is neural and independent of ideology or individual consciousness.[5] With that solution (which, I believe, is identical with Lévi-Strauss' recourse to neural structure) coevalness as the *problematic* simultaneity of different, conflicting, and contradictory forms of consciousness was removed from the agenda of international relations. Anthropology, of whose accomplishments Northrop had the highest regard, was to continue its role as the provider of cultural difference as distance. Distance, in turn, is what the forces of progress need so that it may be overcome *in time.*

That is the frame for an autocritique of anthropology which might have a chance to amount to more than a global confession of guilt or to ad hoc adjustments in theory and method designed to fit the neocolonial situation. Let me now recapitulate my attempts to draw at least the outlines of the task that lies before us.

In chapter 1 the terms of the argument were laid down. The rise of modern anthropology is inseparable from the emergence of new conceptions of Time in the wake of a thorough secularization of the Judeo-Christian idea of history. The transformation that occurred involved, first, a generalization of historical Time, its extension, as it were, from the circum-Mediterranean stage of events to the whole world. Once that was achieved, movement in space could become secularized, too. The notion of travel as science, that is, as the temporal/spatial "completion" of human history, emerged and produced, by the end of the eighteenth century, research projects and institutions which can be called anthropological in a strict sense. Precursors of modern anthropology in the eighteenth century have been called "time voyagers,"[6] a characterization which is acceptable as long as one keeps in mind that their fascination with Time was a prerequisite as much as a result of travels in space. It would be naïve to think that Enlightenment conceptions of Time were the simple result of empirical induction. As the "myth-history of reason," they were ideological constructs and projections: Secularized Time had become a means to occupy space, a title conferring on its holders the right to "save" the expanse of the world for history.

The secularization of Judeo-Christian Time was a mild

change, however, compared to its eventual naturalization which had been under way for several generations until it became finalized in the first third of the nineteenth century. Naturalization of Time involved a quantitative explosion of earlier chronologies so as to make available enough time to account for processes of geological history and biological evolution without recourse to supernatural intervention. Qualitatively, it completed the process of generalization by postulating coextensiveness of Time and planetary (or cosmic) Space. Natural history—a notion unthinkable until the coextensiveness of Time and Space had been accepted—was based on a thoroughly spatialized conception of Time and provided the paradigm for anthropology as the science of cultural evolution. Its manifest concerns were progress and "history," but its theories and methods, inspired by geology, comparative anatomy, and related scientific disciplines, were taxonomic rather than genetic-processual. Most importantly, by allowing Time to be resorbed by the tabular space of classification, nineteenth-century anthropology sanctioned an ideological process by which relations between the West and its Other, between anthropology and its object, were conceived not only as difference, but as distance in space *and* Time. Protoanthropologists of the Renaissance and Enlightenment *philosophes* often accepted the simultaneity or temporal coexistence of savagery and civilization because they were convinced of the cultural, merely conventional nature of the differences they perceived;[7] evolutionary anthropologists made difference "natural," the inevitable outcome of the operation of natural laws. What was left, after primitive societies had been assigned their slots in evolutionary schemes, was the abstract, merely physical simultaneity of natural law.

When, in the course of disciplinary growth and differentiation, evolutionism was attacked and all but discarded as the reigning paradigm of anthropology, the temporal conceptions it had helped to establish remained unchanged. They had long become part of the common epistemological ground and a common discursive idiom of competing schools and approaches. As conceptions of Physical, Typological and Intersubjective Time informed anthropological writing in turn, or in concert, each became a means toward the end of keeping anthropology's Other in another Time. There was one historical development, though, which prevented anthropology from finally dissolving into a "temporal illusion," from becoming a hallucinatory discourse about an Other of its own making. That was the undisputed rule requiring field research carried out through direct, personal encounter with the Other. Ever since, ethnography as an activity, not just as a method or a type of information, has been regarded as the legitimation of anthropological knowledge, no matter whether, in a given school, rationalist-deductive or empiricist-inductive conceptions of science prevailed. The integration of fieldwork into anthropological praxis had several consequences. Sociologically, field research became an institution which consolidated anthropology as a science and academic discipline; it was to serve as the principal mechanism of training and socializing new members. Epistemologically, however, the rule of fieldwork made anthropology an aporetic enterprise because it resulted in a contradictory praxis. This remained by and large unnoticed as long as ethnographic research was thought to be governed by positivist canons of "scientific observation." As soon as it is realized that fieldwork is a form of communicative interaction with an Other, one that must be carried out coevally, on the basis of shared intersubjective Time and intersocietal contemporaneity, a contradiction had to appear between research and writing because anthropological writing had become suffused with the strategies and devices of an allochronic discourse.[8] That ethnography involves communication through language is, of course, not a recent insight (Degérando insisted on that point; see 1969:68 ff). However, the importance of language was almost always conceived *methodologically*. Because linguistic method has been predominantly taxonomic, the "turn to language" actually reinforced allochronic tendencies in anthropological discourse.

There are ways to sidestep the contradiction. One can compartmentalize theoretical discourse and empirical research; or one defends the contradiction aggressively, insisting that fieldwork is a requisite of the professionalization of anthropology, a ritual of initiation, a social mechanism that only has incidental connections with the substance of anthropological thought. Both strategies provide a cover-up, they do nothing to resolve the contradiction. Worse, they obstruct critical insight into the possibility that those ritually repetitive confrontations with the Other which we call fieldwork may be but special instances of the general struggle between the West and its Other. A persistent myth shared by imperialists and many (Western) critics of imperialism alike has been that of a single, decisive conquista, occupation, or establishment of colonial power, a myth which has its complement in similar notions of sudden decolonization and accession to independence. Both have worked against giving proper theoretical importance to overwhelming evidence for *repeated* acts of oppression,[9] campaigns of pacification, and suppression of rebellions, no matter whether these were carried out by military means, by religious and educational indoctrination, by administrative measures, or, as is more common now, by intricate monetary and economic manipulations under the cover of foreign aid. The ideological function of schemes promoting progress, advancement, and development has been to hide the temporal contingency of imperialist expansion. We cannot exclude the possibility, to say the very least, that repetitive enactment of field research by thousands of aspiring and established practitioners of anthropology has been part of a sustained effort to maintain a certain type of relation between the West and its Other. To *maintain* and *renew* these relations has always required coeval recognition of the Other as the object of power and/or knowledge; to rationalize and ideologically justify these relations has always needed schemes of allochronic distancing. The praxis of field research, even in its most routinized and professionalized conception, never ceased to be an objective reflex of antagonistic political relations and, by the same token, a point of departure for a radical critique of anthropology.[10]

There is a need to formulate these conclusions simply and brutally. At the same time, one must avoid the mistake of concluding from the simplicity of effect to a simplicity of intellectual efforts that brought it about. In chapter 2

I analyzed two major strategies for what I called the denial of coevalness. Relativism, in its functionalist and culturalist varieties, undoubtedly has its roots in romantic reactions against Enlightenment rational absolutism. But romantic ideas regarding the historical uniqueness of cultural creations were only too vulnerable to chauvinistic perversion. What started perhaps as a movement of defiance, of an appropriation of "our Time" by peoples (and intellectuals) resisting French intellectual imperialism, soon became a way of encapsulating Time as "their Time" or, in the form of taxonomic approaches to culture, a plea for ignoring Time altogether. The purpose of that chapter was to illustrate accomplished forms of the denial of coevalness as these express dominant trends in modern anthropology. Continued efforts to counteract these dominant trends were, therefore, not given adequate attention and this remains, of course, a historical gap. I doubt that it will be closed soon. As long as the historiography of anthropology continues to be the story of those schools and thinkers who can be credited with the "success" of our discipline we cannot expect to find much in it that allows us to appreciate its failure.

Having demonstrated allochronism as a pervasive strategy of anthropological discourse, I tried in chapter 3 to address the problem in a more pointed fashion. Above all, my questions were directed to one of the more powerful defenses construed at about the same time that anthropology's aggressive allochronism became entrenched: Can we accept the claim that anthropology's allochronic conception of its object may be carried out with impunity because that object is, after all, "only" semiotic? If the Other is but a semiotic Other, goes the argument, then he remains internal to the discourse; he is signified in sign relations and must not be confused with the victim of "real" relations. We found that a semiotic approach is useful, up to a point, when it comes to analyzing the intricacies of temporalization. Yet when we proceeded from general considerations to reflexions on two specific discursive practices—the ethnographic present and the autobiographic past—we found serious limitations. In both cases, semiotic, i.e., self-contained linguistic explanations proved to be afflicted by logical "leaks" causing critical analysis to consider links between communicative practices (or literary conventions) and the political economy of scientific activities: Time, the real Time of human action and interaction, does seep into the systems of signs which we construct as representations of knowledge. We may even have to consider, following a suggestion by M. Serres, that setting up a semiotic relation, especially if it is part of a taxonomy of relations, is itself a temporal act. While pretending to move in the flat space of classification, the taxonomist in fact takes a position on a temporal slope—uphill, or upstream, from the object of his scientific desire.

The allegation that sign theories of culture inevitably rest on temporal distancing between the decoding subject and the encoded object can obviously not be demonstrated "semiotically;" such a project would necessarily get lost in an infinite regress of sign-relations upon sign-relations. There is a point at which sign-theories must be questioned epistemologically. What sort of theory of knowledge do they presuppose, or: what sort of theory of knowledge can be inferred from the history of sign-theories bearing on anthropology? Chapter 4 attempts to probe into such deeper connections by tracing the current prominence of semiotics and semiology to a long history of visualist and spatialist conceptions of knowledge. Specifically, I situated "symbolic anthropology" in a tradition dominated by the "art of memory" and Ramist pedagogy. The gist of that argument was that sign-theories of culture are theories of representation, not of production; of exchange or "traffic,"[11] not of creation; of meaning, not of praxis. Potentially, and perhaps inevitably, they have a tendency to reinforce the basic premises of an allochronic discourse in that they consistently align the Here and Now of the signifier (the form, the structure, the meaning) with the Knower, and the There and Then of the signified (the content, the function or event, the symbol or icon) with the Known. It was this assertiveness of visual-spatial presentation, its authoritative role in the transmission of knowledge, which I designated as the "rhetoric of vision." As long as anthropology presents its object primarily as seen, as long as ethnographic knowledge is conceived primarily as observation and/or representation (in terms of models, symbol systems, and so forth) it is likely to persist in denying coevalness to its Other.

Issues for Debate

I expect that the sweeping character of this account of temporal distancing might be disturbing to many readers. My intent has not been to express a summary repudiation of anthropology. Rather, I wanted to outline a program for dismantling identifiable ideological devices and strategies which have been functioning to protect our discipline from radical epistemological critique. I do believe that allochronism consists of more than occasional lapses. It is expressive of a political cosmology, that is, a kind of myth. Like other myths, allochronism has the tendency to establish a total grip on our discourse. It must therefore be met by a "total" response, which is not to say that the critical work can be accomplished in one fell swoop.

Such a project must be carried out as a polemic. However, polemic is not just a matter of style or taste—bad taste by some canons of academic civility. Polemic belongs to the substance of arguments if and when it expresses intent on the part of the writer to address opponents or opposing views in an antagonistic fashion; it is a way of arguing that does not dress up what really amounts to dismissal of the other as "respect" for his position; nor does it reject the other view as *dépassé*. The ideal of coevalness must of course also guide the critique of the many forms in which coevalness is denied in anthropological discourse. This is perhaps a utopian goal. I realize that certain ways of summarily designating trends and approaches as so many *isms* border on allochronic dismissal. For instance, anthropologists have used the term *animism* (which they invented in order to separate primitive mentality from modern rationality) as a means to indicate that an opponent is no longer in the contemporary arena of debate.[12] That sort of arguing from upstream of historical progress is unproductive; it merely reproduces allochronic discourse. In contrast, polemic irreverence is, or ought to be, an acknowledgment of the coeval conditions of the production of knowledge.

Above all, polemic is future oriented. By conquering the past, it strives to imagine the future course of ideas. It is conceived as a *project* and it recognizes that many of the ideas it needs to overcome have been both self-serving, interest oriented *and* objective, project oriented. Evolutionism established anthropological discourse as allochronic, but was also an attempt to overcome a paralyzing disjunction between the science of nature and the science of man. Diffusionism ended in positivist pedantry; it also hoped to vindicate the historicity of mankind by taking seriously its "accidental" dispersal in geographic space. Relativist culturalism encapsulated Time in culture gardens; it derived much of its élan from arguments for the unity of mankind against racist determinisms,[13] a project that, in a somewhat different fashion, is carried on by taxonomic structuralism.

All these endeavors and struggles are present and co-present with this critique of anthropology. To incorporate them into an account of the history of allochronism makes them past, not *passé*. That which is past enters the dialectics of the present—if it is granted coevalness.

Another objection could be formulated as follows: Aren't you in fact compounding allochronism by examining anthropology's uses of Time while disregarding time-conceptions in other cultures? There is no simple way to counter that objection. I am not ready to accept the categorical verdict that Western anthropology is so corrupt that any further exercise of it, including its critique by insiders, will only aggravate the situation. I also believe that the substance of a theory of coevalness, and certainly coevalness as praxis, will have to be the result of actual confrontation with the Time of the Other. I am not prepared to offer an opinion on how much of this has been accomplished by extant ethnographies of Time. If there is any merit to my arguments one would expect that anthropology, in studying Time as much as in other areas, has been its own obstacle against coeval confrontation with its Other. This is putting it mildly, for denial of coevalness is a political act, not just a discursive fact. The absence of the Other from our Time has been his mode of presence in our discourse—as an object and victim. That is what needs to be overcome; more ethnography of Time will not change the situation.

Other questions are even more vexing. Is not the theory of coevalness which is implied (but by no means fully developed) in these arguments a program for ultimate temporal absorption of the Other, just the kind of theory needed to make sense of present history as a "world-system," totally dominated by monopoly- and state-capitalism?[14] When we allege that the Other has been a political victim; when we, therefore, assert, that the West has been victorious; when we then go on to "explain" that situation with theories of social change, modernization, and so forth, all of which identify the agents of history as the ones that hold economic, military, and technological power; in short, when we accept domination as a fact, are we not actually playing into the hands of those who dominate? Or, if we hold that the political-cognitive interests of Western anthropology have been manipulation and control of knowledge about the Other, and if it is true (as argued by critics of our discipline) that precisely the scientistic-positivistic orientation which fostered domineering approaches has *prevented* anthropology from ever really "getting through" to the Other, should we then conclude that, as a by and large unsuccessful attempt to be a "science of mankind," Western anthropology helped to save other cultures from total alienation?

Are there, finally, criteria by which to distinguish denial of coevalness as a condition of domination from refusal of coevalness as an act of liberation?

Answers to these questions, if there are any at the present time, would depend on what can be said, positively, about coevalness. If it meant the oneness of Time as identity, coevalness would indeed amount to a theory of appropriation (as, for instance, in the idea of *one* history of salvation or *one* myth-history of reason). As it is understood in these essays, coevalness aims at recognizing cotemporality as the condition for truly dialectical confrontation between persons as well as societies. It militates against false conceptions of dialectics—all those watered-down binary abstractions which are passed off as oppositions: left vs. right, past vs. present, primitive vs. modern. Tradition and modernity are not "opposed" (except semiotically), nor are they in "conflict." All this is (bad) metaphorical talk. What are opposed, in conflict, in fact, locked in antagonistic struggle, are not the same societies at different stages of development, but different societies facing each other at the same Time. As J. Duvignaud, and others, are reminding us, the "savage and the proletarian" are in equivalent positions vis-à-vis domination (see 1973:ch. 1). Marx in the nineteenth century may be excused for not giving enough theoretical recognition to that equivalence; certain contemporary "Marxist" anthropologists have no excuse.

The question of Marxist anthropology is not resolved in my mind.[15] In part this is so because we have (in the West) as yet little Marxist praxis on the level of the *production* of ethnographic knowledge. As long as such a practical basis is lacking or badly developed, most of what goes by the name of Marxist anthropology amounts to little more than theoretical exercises in the style of Marx and Engels. These exercises have their merits: the best among them have helped to confound earlier approaches and analyses. They are bound to remain disconnected forays, however, as long as their authors share with bourgeois positivist anthropology certain fundamental assumptions concerning the nature of ethnographic data and the use of "objective" methods.

An even more serious problem with Marxist anthropology appears when we view it in the perspective of this book: the construction of anthropology's object. In what sense can Marxist anthropology be said to offer a counterposition to the deep-rooted allochronic tendencies that inform our discourse? Do allochronic periodizations of human history wich play such an important role in Marxist analyses belong to the substance of Marxist thought or are they just a matter of style inherited from the nineteenth century? How is the Other construed in the anthropological discourse generated in societies which are not part of the West-and-the-Rest complex? Antagonism with the capitalist world notwithstanding, these societies have built analogous spheres of colonial expansion and, more recently, of foreign aid and development. Does the routinized world revolution construe a different Other than the capitalist world market?[16]

Coevalness: Points of Departure

Those who have given the matter some thought developed outlines of a theory of coevalness through critical confrontation with Hegel. Here I can offer little more than a few comments on what I consider significant steps in the development of Hegel's insights. In doing so I want to indicate points of departure, not solutions; appeals to the history of philosophy as such will not save the history of anthropology. There is no need for a "Hegelian" anthropology. What must be developed are the elements of a *processual and materialist* theory apt to counteract the hegemony of taxonomic and representational approaches which we identified as the principal sources of anthropology's allochronic orientation.[17] Affirmations of coevalness will not "make good" for the denial of coevalness. Critique proceeds as the negation of a negation; it calls for deconstructive labor whose aim cannot be simply to establish a Marxist "alternative" to Western bougeois anthropology, one that would have to beg for recognition as just another paradigm or scientific culture garden.

This being said, what are the points of departure for a theory of coevalness? A first step, I believe, must be to recuperate the idea of totality. Almost all the approaches we touched on in these essays affirm such a notion—up to a point. This explains why the (totalizing) concept of culture could have been shared by so many different schools. Practically everybody agrees that we can make sense of another society only to the extent that we grasp it as a whole, an organism, a configuration, a system. Such holism, however, usually misses its professed aims on at least two accounts.

First, by insisting that culture is a system (ethos, model, blueprint, and so forth) which "informs" or "regulates" action, holistic social science fails to provide a theory of praxis; it commits anthropology forever to imputing (if not outright imposing) motives, beliefs, meanings, and functions to the societies it studies from a perspective outside and above. Moral compliance, aesthetic conformity, or systemic integration are, as bad substitutes for dialectic conceptions of process, projected onto other societies. As demonstrated by Kroeber, T. Parsons, and more recently by M. Sahlins, culture will then be ontologized, i.e., given an existence apart. These so-called holistic approaches to culture result in a dualistic theory of society which, in turn, invites spurious solutions of the kind represented by M. Harris' cultural materialism.

Second, failure to conceive a theory of praxis blocks the possibility, even for those who are prepared to reject a positivistic epistemological stance, to perceive anthropology as an activity which is part of what it studies. Scientistic objectivism and hermeneutic textualism often converge.[18] The We of anthropology then remains an exclusive We, one that leaves its Other outside on all levels of theorizing except on the plane of ideological obfuscation, where everyone pays lip service to the "unity of mankind."

Among the most scandalizing of Hegel's pronouncements have been those that affirm the all-inclusiveness of historical process—its totality—and, as a consequence, the copresence of the different "moments" through which the totality realizes itself. In the *Phenomenology of the Spirit* he stated: "Reason (*Vernunft*) now has a general interest in the world because it is assured to have presence in the world, or, that the present is reasonable (*vernünftig*)" (1973 [1807]:144).

To be sure, that sort of equation of the reasonable and the present can serve to justify evolutionist *Realpolitik*, which would argue that a state of affairs must be accepted because it is a present reality. Marx criticized Hegel for just that. At the same time he insisted, with Hegel, on the present as the frame for historical analysis. Here the present is conceived, not as a point in time nor as a modality of language (i.e. a tense) but as the copresence of basic acts of production and reproduction—eating, drinking, providing shelter, clothes, "and several other things." In the *German Ideology* Marx ridicules German historians and their penchant for "prehistory" as a field of speculation, an area outside of *present* history. Research into the principles of social organization must not be relegated to a mythical time of origins, nor can it be reduced to the construction of stages. Forms of social differentiation must be seen as "moments" which, "from the beginning of history, and ever since human beings lived, have existed *simultaneously* and still determine history" (1953:355 f; my emphasis; see also 354 f.). This is the "materialist connection among human beings which is conditioned by their needs and the mode of production and is as old as mankind itself" (*ibid.* 356). To be sure, there are problems with the concept of needs; and Marx did return to phases, periods, and stages (even in the text from which we just quoted) but the point is that a Hegelian view of the totality of historical forces, including their cotemporality at any given time, prepared Marx to conceive his theory of economy as a political one. The same awareness underlies his critique of Proudhon:

The relations of production of every society form a totality. Mr. Proudhon looks at economic relations as so many social phases generating one another such that one can be derived from the other. . . . The only bad thing about this method is that Mr. Proudhon, as soon as he wants to analyze one of these phases separately, must take recourse to other social relations. . . . Mr. Proudhon goes on to generate the other phases with the help of pure reason, he pretends to be facing newborn babies and forgets that they are *of the same age* as the first one. (1953:498; my emphasis)

This is the passage—from *The Poverty of Philosophy*—which was to be a cornerstone for L. Althusser's arguments for a structuralist interpretation of Marx. In *Reading Capital* he concluded "that it is essential to reverse the order of reflection and think first the specific structure of totality in order to understand both the form in which its limbs and constitutive relations co-exist and the peculiar structure of history (1970 [1966]:98). The valid point in Althusser's reading is to have demonstrated that Marx cannot be dismissed as just another historicist. Marx's contribution to critical social thought has been his radical presentism which, in spite of all the revolutionary talk to which Marx and especially Engels resorted, contained the theoretical possibility for a negation of allochronic distancing. What else is coevalness but recognizing that all human societies and all major aspects of a human society are "of the same age" (a distinctly romantic idea, incidentally, if we remember Herder and Ratzel (see chapter 1). This does not mean that, within the totality of human history, developments did not occur which can be viewed in chronological succession. T. Adorno, in a reflection on Hegel, summarized the difference between allochronic historism and a dialectical conception of coevalness in one of his inimitable aphorisms: "No universal history leads from the savage to humanity, but there *is* one that leads from the slingshot to the megabomb" (1966:312).

Hegel and some of his critical successors[19] opened up a global perspective onto questions which we raised from the particular vantage point of anthropology. If allochronism is expressive of a vast, entrenched political cosmology, if it has deep historical roots, and if it rests on some of the fundamental epistemological convictions of Western culture, what can be done about it? If it is true that ultimate justification is provided by a certain theory of knowledge, it would follow that critical work must be directed to epistemology, notably to the unfinished project of a materialist conception of knowledge "as sensuous-human activity [conceived as] praxis, subjectively." Concrete, practical contradiction between coeval research and allochronic interpretation constitutes the *crux* of anthropology, the crossroads, as it were, from which critique must take off and to which it must return. We need to overcome the contemplative stance (in Marx's sense) and dismantle the edifices of spatiotemporal distancing that characterize the contemplative view. Its fundamental assumption seems to be that the basic act of knowledge consists of somehow structuring (ordering, classifying) ethnographic *data* (sense data, fundamentally, but there are levels of information beyond that). It matters little whether or not one posits an objective reality beneath the phenomenal world that is accessible to experience. What counts is that some kind of primitive, original separation between a thing and its appearance, an original and its reproduction, provide the starting point. This fateful separation is the ultimate reason for what Durkheim (following Kant, up to a point) perceived as the "necessity" of culturally structuring the material of primitive perception. It is the necessity to impose order *and* the necessity of whatever order a society imposes. From Durkheim's theory of the sacred and the profane, to Kroeber's notion of the superorganic and Malinowski's culture as "second nature" down to Lévi-Strauss' ultimate "opposition" of nature and culture—anthropology has been asserting that mankind is bound together in communities of necessity.

So much is clear and readily admitted by most anthropologists who care to be explicit about their theories of knowledge. But one issue is usually left in the dark of undisputable assumptions and that is the Lockean phenomenalism shared by empiricists and rationalists alike. No matter whether one professes belief in the inductive nature of ethnography and ethnology or whether one thinks of anthropology as a deductive, constructive science (or whether one posits a sequence of an inductive ethnographic phase and a constructive theoretical phase), the primitive assumption, the root metaphor of knowledge remains that of a difference, and a distance, between thing and image, reality and representation. Inevitably, this establishes and reinforces models of cognition stressing difference and distance between a beholder and an object.

From detaching concepts (*abstraction*) to overlaying interpretive schemes (*imposition*), from linking together (*correlation*) to matching (*isomorphism*)—a plethora of visually-spatially derived notions dominate a discourse founded on contemplative theories of knowledge. As we have seen, hegemony of the visual-spatial had its price which was, first, to detemporalize the process of knowledge and, second, to promote ideological temporalization of relations between the Knower and the Known.

Spatialization is carried on and completed on the next level, that of arranging data and tokens in systems of one kind or another. In this respect there is little that divides otherwise opposed schools of anthropology, be they committed to a superorganic concept of culture, to a Saussurean model, or to Max Weber's *Eigengesetzlichkeit*. In fact, even vulgar biological and economic determinism should be added to the list. Nor does it really matter—and this is certain to scandalize some—that several of these schools profess to follow an historical, even processual approach to culture (as opposed to those that stress systemic and synchronic analysis). All of them have strained, at one time or another, to attain scientific status by protecting themselves against the "irruption of Time," that is, against the demands of coevalness which would have to be met if anthropology really took its relation to its Other to constitute a *praxis*. Anthropology's allochronic discourse is, therefore, the product of an *idealist* position (in Marxian terms) and that includes practically all forms of "materialism," from nineteenth-century bourgeois evolutionism to current cultural materialism. A first and fundamental assumption of a materialist theory of knowledge, and this may sound paradoxical, is to make consciousness, individual and collective, the starting point. Not disembodied consciousness, however, but "consciousness with a body," inextricably bound up with language. A fundamental role for language must be postulated, not because consciousness is conceived as a state internal to an individual organism which would then need to be "expressed" or "represented" through language (taking that term in the widest sense, including gestures, postures, attitudes, and so forth). Rather, the only way to think of consciousness without separating it from the organism or banning it to some kind of *forum internum* is to insist on its sensuous nature; and one way to conceive of that sensuous nature (above the level of motor activities) is to tie consciousness as an activity to the production of meaningful sound. Inasmuch as the production of meaningful sound involves the labor of transforming, shaping matter, it may still be possible to distinguish form and content, but the relationship between the two will then be *constitutive* of consciousness. Only in a secondary, derived sense (one in which the conscious organism is presupposed rather than accounted for) can that relationship be called representational (significative, symbolic), or informative in the sense of being a tool or carrier of information. It may come as a surprise but on this account I find myself in agreement with N. Chomsky when he states:

it is wrong to think of the human use of language as characteristically informative, in fact or in intention. Human language can be used to inform or mislead, to clarify one's own thoughts or to display one's cleverness, or simply for play. If I speak with no concern for modifying your behavior or thoughts, I am not using language any less than if I say exactly the same things *with* such intention. If we hope to understand human language and the psychological capacities on which it rests, we must first ask what it is, not how or for what purpose it is used. (1972:70)

Man does not "need" language; man, in the dialectical, transitive understanding of *to be*, *is* language (much like he does not need food, shelter, and so on, but *is* his food and house).

Consciousness, realized by the [producing] meaningful sound, is self-conscious. The Self, however, is constituted fully as a speaking and hearing Self. Awareness, if we may thus designate the first stirrings of knowledge beyond the registering of tactile impressions, is fundamentally based on hearing meaningful sounds produced by self *and* others. If there needs to be a contest for man's noblest sense (and there are reasons to doubt that) it should be hearing, not sight that wins. Not solitary perception but social communication is the starting point for a materialist anthropology, provided that we keep in mind that man does not "need" language as a means of communication, or by extension, society as a means of survival. Man *is* communication and society.

What saves these assumptions from evaporating in the clouds of speculative metaphysics is, I repeat, a dialectical understanding of the verb *to be* in these propositions. Language is not predicated on man (nor is the "human mind" or "culture"). Language produces man as man produces language. *Production* is the pivotal concept of a materialist anthropology.

Marx was aware of the material nature of language as well as of the material link between language and consciousness. In the light of what has been argued so far, the following two passages need no comment:

The element of thought itself—the element of thought's living expression—*language*—is of a sensuous nature. The *social* reality of nature, and *human* natural science, or *the natural science about man*, are identical terms. (Marx 1953:245 f.) Translation from *The Economic and Philosophic Manuscripts of 1844* 1964:143).

Only now, after having considered four moments, four aspects of the fundamental historical relationships, do we find that man also possesses "consciousness"; but, even so, not inherent, not "pure" consciousness. From the start the "spirit" is afflicted with the curse of being "burdened" with matter, which here makes its appearance in the form of agitated layers of air, sounds—in short of language. Language is as old as consciousness; language is practical consciousness, as it exists for other men, and for that reason is really beginning to exist for me personally as well (see Marx 1953:356 f. Translation quoted from *Marx and Engels* 1959:251)

A production theory of knowledge and language (in spite of Engels and Lenin) cannot be built on "abstraction" or "reflection" (*Widerspiegelung*) or any other conception that postulates fundamental acts of cognition to consist of the detachment of some kind of image or token from perceived objects. Concepts are products of sensuous interaction; they themselves are of a sensuous nature inasmuch as their formation and use is inextricably bound up with language. One cannot insist enough on that point because it is the sensuous nature of language, its being an activity of concrete organisms and the embodiment of consciousness in a material medium—sound—which makes language an eminently *temporal* phenomenon. Clearly, language is not *material* if that were to mean possessing properties of, or in, space: volume, shape, color (or even opposition, distribution, division, etc.). Its materiality is based on articulation, on frequencies, pitch, tempo, all of which are realized in the dimension of time. These essentially temporal properties can be translated, or transcribed, as spatial relations. That is an undisputable fact—this sentence proves it. What remains highly disputable is that visualization-spatialization of consciousness, and especially historically and culturally contingent spatializations such as a certain rhetorical "art of memory," can be made *the* measure of development of human consciousness.

The denial of coevalness which we diagnosed on secondary and tertiary levels of anthropological discourse can be traced to a fundamental epistemological issue. Ultimately it rests on the negation of the temporal materiality of communication through language. For the temporality of speaking (other than the temporality of physical movements, chemical processes, astronomic events, and organic growth and decay) implies cotemporality of producer and product, speaker and listener, Self and Other. Whether a detemporalized, idealist theory of knowledge is the result of certain cultural, ideological, and political positions, or whether it works the other way round is perhaps a moot question. That there is a connection between them which is in need of critical examination, is not.

At one time I maintained that the project of dismantling anthropology's intellectual imperialism must begin with alternatives to positivist conceptions of ethnography (Fabian 1971). I advocated a turn to language and a conception of ethnographic objectivity as communicative, intersubjective objectivity. Perhaps I failed to make it clear that I wanted language and communication to be understood as a kind of praxis in which the Knower cannot claim ascendancy over the Known (nor, for that matter, one Knower over another). As I see it now, the anthropologist and his interlocutors only "know" when they meet each other in one and the same cotemporality (see Fabian 1979a). If ascendancy— rising to a hierarchical position—is precluded, their relationships must be on the same plane: they will be frontal. Anthropology as the study of cultural difference can be productive only if difference is drawn into the arena of dialectical contradiction. To go on proclaiming, and believing, that anthropology is nothing but a more or less successful effort to abstract general knowledge from concrete experience and that, as such, it serves universal goals and human interests, should be difficult if the arguments advanced in these essays are valid. In order to claim that primitive societies (or whatever replaces them now as the object of anthropology) are the reality and our conceptualizations the theory, one must keep anthropology standing on its head. If we can show that our theories of their societies are *our praxis*—the way in which we produce and reproduce knowledge of the Other for our societies—we may (paraphrasing Marx and Hegel) put anthropology back on its feet. Renewed interest in the history of our discipline and disciplined inquiry into the history of confrontation between anthropology and its Other are therefore not escapes from empiry; they are practical and realistic. They are ways to meet the Other on the same ground, in the same Time.

Notes

1. Time and the Emerging Other

1. 'Ausser der Zeit gibt es noch ein anderes Mittel, grosse Veränderungen hervorzubringen, und das ist die—Gewalt. Wenn die eine zu langsam geht, so tut die andere öfters die Sache vorher' (Lichtenberg 1975:142). All translations into English are my own unless an English version is cited.
2. Tylor 1958:529.
3. The most influential modern statement of this idea was Mircea Eliade's *Mythe de l'éternel retour* (1949). How much the linear-cyclical opposition continues to dominate inquiry into conceptions of time is shown in a more recent collection of essays edited by P. Ricoeur (1975). Similar in outlook and somewhat broader in scope was the volume *Man and Time* (1957).
4. The point that philosophy and the social sciences missed the Copernican revolution or, at any rate, failed to produce *their* Copernican revolution was made by G. Gusdorf: 'Ainsi la Renaissance est vraiment, pour les sciences humaines, une occasion manquée' (1968:1781, see also 1778).
5. For Gusdorf's discussion of Bossuet see 1973:379 ff. See also an essay by Koselleck, on "History, Stories, and Formal Structures of Time" in which he points to the Augustinian origins of Bossuet's "order of times" (1973:211–222) and a study by Klempt (1960).
6. These are connotations, not strict definitions of *universal*. They indicate two major tendencies or intentions behind anthropological search for universals of culture. One follows a rationalist tradition and often takes recourse to linguistics. The other has an empiricist orientation and seeks statistical proof for universal occurrence of certain traits, institutions, or customs. The most obvious example for the former is the work of Lévi-Strauss (especially his writing on the elementary structures of kinship and on totemism). For a statement of the problem from the point of view of anthropological linguistics see the chapters on "synchronic universals" and "diachronic generalization" in Greenberg 1968:175. A major representative of the "generalizing" search for universals has been G. P. Murdock (1949).
7. The continued influence of both traditions will be discussed in chapter 4. On the rhetorical devices used by Bossuet see O. Ranum in his introduction to a recent English edition of the *Discours* (1976:xxi–xxviii).
8. Concise and informative overviews over the opening of "human space" and the processing of that information in a vast literature during the eighteenth century may be found in the first two chapters of Michèle Duchet's work on anthro-

pology and history during the Enlightenment (1971:25–136). See also a dissertation, "The Geography of the Philosophes" by Broc (1972).

9. W. Lepenies does not seem to take into account this possibility in his important essay on temporalization in the eighteenth century (1976). As he tells the story, the breakthrough into the dimension of time responded to "empirical pressure" (*Erfahrungsdruck*); the mass of available data could no longer be contained in spatial, achronic schemes. I do not find this very convincing, especially not in the case of anthropology, where it is manifest that temporal devices have been ideologically mediated, never direct responses to experienced reality.

10. The term *episteme* was introduced by M. Foucault. Much of what I will have to say about "spatialized" Time has been inspired by a reading of his *The Order of Things* (1973; originally published as *Les Mots et les choses* 1966).

11. First published in 1874 by the British Association for the Advancement of Science. The project goes back to the work of a committee of three physicians (!) initiated in 1839 (see Voget 1975:105).

12. On the *Société*, see Stocking 1968: ch. 2, Moravia 1973:88 ff, Copans and Jamin n.d. [1978]. On Degérando (also written de Gérando) see F. C. T. Moore's translator's introduction to the English edition (1969). On the *Institutio*, see Moravia 1967:958. Lepenies also mentions this work and links it to later treatises by Blumenbach, Lamarck, and Cuvier (1976:55). As recent work by J. Stagl shows, however, Linnaeus was by no means an "ancestor." He wrote in an established tradition whose roots must be sought in humanist educational treatises and Ramist "method" (Stagl 1980). On Ramism see chapter 4.

13. L. White's *The Evolution of Culture* (1959) has been hailed as "the modern equivalent of Morgan's *Ancient Society*" by M. Harris who, in the same sentence, shows how little it matters to him that Morgan's historical context was quite different from White's. We are told that the "only difference" between the two works is "the updating of some of the ethnography and the greater consistence of the cultural-materialist thread" (1968:643). This is typical of Harris' historiography. His tale of anthropology is confessional, aggressive, and often entertaining, but not critical. Sahlins and Service's *Evolution and Culture* (1960) and Julian Steward's *Theory of Culture Change* (1955) have been among the most influential statements of neoevolutionism in anthropology.

14. Numerous publications attest to a renewed interest in Vico; see for instance the collections of essays assembled in two issues of the journal *Social Research* (Giorgio Tagliacozzo, ed., 1976).

15. Perhaps there is a tendency, fostered by Darwin, to give too much credit to Lyell. The "crisis of chronology" goes back to the sixteenth century and courage to think in millions of years was demonstrated by Kant and Buffon, among others, in the eighteenth century (see Lepenies 1976:9–15, 42 ff). Nevertheless, it remains important that evolutionist thought owed its temporal liberation to geology, a science which perhaps more than any other, astronomy excepted, construes Time from spatial relation and distribution. On predecessors of Lyell, see Eiseley 1961.

16. Peel uses *naturalizing* in a similar sense. Although he does not develop this further, his statement is worth quoting here: "In an obvious sense social evolution is easily the most time-oriented style of sociology, and many writers, Collingwood and Toulmin among them, have seen the dominance of evolutionary modes of thought as a sign of the conquest of science by history. Up to a point

this is doubtless so; but it must not blind us to a profoundly anti-historical bias in social evolution. For in one respect evolution was not so much a victory of the historical style of explanation as a denaturing, or rather naturalization, of the proper study of society and history" (1971:158).

17. Kroeber attacks those who invoke biological or mechanical causality in order to explain *history* (his term for cultural anthropology). But when he says (in Profession 16) *"History deals with conditions sine qua non, not with causes"* (1915:287), he seems to concur with Morgan.

18. A fair historical and historiographic appreciation of what is customarily lumped together as "German diffusionism" is another matter. Remarks on that school in recent textbooks usually betray a dismal ignorance of its intellectual sources and background. Close links between German *Kulturkreis*-thought and early American anthropology are all but forgotten, as is Edward Sapir's work, *Time Perspective in Aboriginal American Culture: A Study in Method*, published only five years after Graebner's *Methode* (in 1916).

19. For Parsons see the book edited by J. Toby (Parsons 1977). Peel discusses the revival of evolutionism in contemporary sociology and anthropology (1971:ch. 10); Toulmin coauthored a major work on conceptions of Time (see Toulmin and Goodfield 1961); Donald T. Campbell stated his position in an essay titled "Natural Selection as an Epistemological Model" (1970). Much of the Habermas-Luhman controversy and the literature it generated remains all but inaccessible because it is expressed in a forbidding jargon. For a statement of the importance of evolutionary arguments see an essay by Klaus Eder (1973). Halfmann (1979) identifies the opponents as Darwinists vs. critical theories of development.

20. However, when the necessity to consider Time arises, anthropologists in the culturalist tradition remember the eighteenth century. D. Bidney states in *Theoretical Anthropology:* "The problem still remains, however, as to the relation of historical, evolutionary culture to human nature. If culture is a direct, necessary expression of human nature, how is one to explain the evolution of culture patterns in time? In my opinion the problem remains insoluble as long as one does not admit that human nature, like culture, evolves or unfolds in time. This may be understood on the assumption that while the innate biological potentialities of man remain more or less constant the actual, effective psychophysical powers and capabilities are subject to development in time. What I am suggesting is comparable to the eighteenth-century notion of the perfectibility of human nature, which seems to have dropped out of the picture in contemporary ethnological thought" (1953:76).

21. Radiocarbon dating was fully established by W. F. Libby (1949); its wider acceptance in anthropology was aided by symposia and publications sponsored by the Wenner-Gren Foundation. By 1964 (the date of publication of works by Oakley and Butzer) it had attained "normal scientific" status (in T. S. Kuhn's terms) on the level of textbooks. While it was revolutionary in the sense of providing hitherto unattainable chronometric certainty, it changed little as regards certain long-established convictions about the relatively "timeless" nature of early human evolution. Compare the following statement by Oakley with the passage from Graebner (1911) quoted above: "At the present time, in almost all parts of the world, cultures of many kinds and varying levels of complexity occur within short distances of one another, but before the Neolithic Revolution this was not so. The

cultures of the early hunters and foodgatherers evolved slowly and their traditions spread widely long before there was any marked change. Where a paleolithic culture can be defined and identified on the basis of sufficiently large assemblages of artifacts, it is legitimate to regard its "industries" as approximately contemporaneous throughout their area of distribution. Until recently this view was based wholly on theory, but radiocarbon dating of early archeological horizons in Africa at least supports the conclusion that in pre-Neolithic times cultural evolution was proceeding contemporaneously over very large areas. To that extent paleolithic industries may be used as means of approximate synchronic dating of Pleistocene deposits" (1964:9). Of course, both Graebner and Oakley base their statements on the little disputed assumption that material, technical products of culture ("industries")—those that result in a record of *spatial* distribution—are key indicators of the evolution of human culture *tout court*.

22. Originally published in 1966 and reprinted in Geertz 1973: ch. 14. An analysis of time conceptions in Zulu myth and ritual, based on Schutz, was made by I. Szombati-Fabian (1969). Among the writings of A. Schutz see especially 1967. One of his more accessible essays, 'Making Music Together' (originally published in 1951), was reprinted in the reader *Symbolic Anthropology* (J. L. Dolgin et al., eds., 1977:106–119). Whereas Husserl and Heidegger were primarily concerned with Time as it needs to be thought in the context of human perception and "internal consciousness," Schutz analyzed its role in communication. He states in the conclusion of the essay just cited: "It appears that all possible communication presupposes a mutual tuning-in relationship between the communicator and the addressee of the communication. This relationship is established by the reciprocal sharing of the Other's flux of experiences in inner time, by living through a vivid present together, by experiencing this togetherness as 'We' " (Schutz 1977:118). It is in this context of intersubjectivity and of the problem of shared Time that some of the insights of phenomenological philosophy continue to influence anthropology, sociology, and also linguistics. Examples for this are R. Rommetveit's incisive critique of generativist hegemony in linguistics (1974) and my own reappraisal of sociolinguistics (Fabian 1979a). This paper should be consulted by readers who are interested in the practical-ethnographic problematics of intersubjective Time.

23. In a thoughtful book on the intellectual history of anthropological research among Australian "aborigines," K. Burridge develops this point at greater length (1973:13 ff). However, where I see breaks and discontinuity, he regards the Christian conception of otherness as the main continuous source of anthropological curiosity. This leads him to ascribe a fundamental role to missionary practice as a model for anthropology (1973:18, 83 f). I don't think that his view is borne out by the history of our discipline. Throughout, Burridge stresses moral commitment as the common element of religious and scientific encounter with the Other which, in my view, prevents him from properly appreciating the intellectual, cognitive side of it.

24. K. G. Jayne notes that Prince Henry the Navigator used the myth of Prester John to justify an enterprise designed to "outflank" Islam through the circumnavigation of Africa (1970 [1910]:13). For an historical and literary analysis of the Prester John myth as a "spatial" dream and a utopia before Moore see ch. 5 in F. M. Rogers (1961; with references to the voluminous literature on the subject).

The story came to a conclusion of sorts with a Portugese mission to Ethiopia in 1520, the account of which was written by Father Francisco Alvares, an extraordinary document for the transition from myth to ethnography (see Beckingham and Huntingford 1961).

25. Marshall Sahlins uses this formula with disarming frankness in his recent attempt to set up a basic opposition between "practical reason" (the West's) and "culture" (the Rest's); see Sahlins 1976 and my comments in chapter.4.

26. David Bohm states in a textbook on relativity theory: "The notion that there is one unique universal order and measure of time is only a habit of thought built up in the limited domain of Newtonian mechanics" (1965:175). Ernst Bloch, citing developments in physics and mathematics, proposed to extend the notion of relativity to human time. We must recognize its "elasticity" and multiplicity. This, he argues, will be the only way to subsume Africa and Asia under a common human history without stretching them over the Western linear conception of progress (see 1963:176–203).

27. Apparently it is not dead in philosophy either, at least to judge from K. Wagn's *What Time Does* (1976). For an especially lucid "outline of the argument from time to space" see Lucas 1973:99 ff.

28. Malinowski's candid revelation about his obsession with sex, drugs, race and political chauvinism caught the prurient interest when the diary was first published. Its importance as an epistemological document was overlooked by most (but not by C. Geertz, see 1979:225 f). Malinowski carefully recorded his struggle with "the uncreative demon of escape from reality" by reading novels rather than pursuing his research work (1967:86). At least twenty times he reports on situations where the present with its demands became too much to bear. Once he notes: "Profound intellectual laziness; I enjoyed things retrospectively, as experiences recorded in memory, rather than immediately, because of my miserable state" (1967:35). All this, I believe, is not only evidence of Malinowski's psychological problems with fieldwork, it documents his struggle with an epistemological problem—coevalness.

2. Our Time, Their Time, No Time: Coevalness Denied

1. 'Überhaupt ist der Primat des Raumes über die Zeit ein untrügliches Kennzeichen reaktonärer Sprache' (E. Bloch 1962:322).

2. Lévi-Strauss 1963:39.

3. In my own development, critical questioning of ethnoscientific procedures as to their ability to deal with the "irruptive force of time" has been crucial. My views are expressed in an essay "Taxonomy and Ideology" (1975), one reason why I do not want to address this issue again. M. Durbin's paper "Models of Simultaneity and Sequentiality in Human Cognition" (1975) in the same volume might be read as an attempt to raise the problem of Time within the confines of a taxonomic approach.

4. For a critical appraisal of functionalist inability to deal with change and a plea for the Popperian approach see Jarvie (1964). In his partisan defense of functionalism ("Without any doubt, the single most significant body of theory in the

social sciences in the present century") R. A. Nisbet ignores critiques such as Jarvie's and speaks of functionalism under the heading of Neo-Evolutionism (see
1969:223 ff).

5. See Malinowski 1945:34. At the same time he relegates that element to the
study of change which, with the straightforwardness that was characteristic of him,
he identifies as anthropology's response to problems of maintaining political power
over colonized populations (see 1945:4 f).

6. Georges Gurvitch, one of the few sociologists comparable in stature to T.
Parsons, summarized his views in a treatise on social time. His "dialectical" orientation produced insights of great depth and comprehensiveness. But he, too, starts
from an unquestioned assumption: Some societies are "promethean," i.e., history-
and time-centered, while others, notably those that are studied by "ethnography,"
are not (see 1964 [1962]:6). In the end his typological approach to the problem
leads him to assert a relativist "temporal pluralism." Similar in approach and intent
is the excellent, if fragmentary, essay "On Social Time" by V. Gioscia (1971). Gioscia, however, is aware of the political nature of social conceptions of Time as well
as of the visualist bias resulting in theoretical suppression of Time (see chapter 4).

7. A valuable summary of different genres of anthropological studies of Time
(including a bibliography containing references to most of the important articles
and monographs) may be found in the essay "Primitive Time-Reckoning as a Symbolic System" by D. N. Maltz (1968). R. J. Maxwell's contribution to the Yaker
volume is less useful (1971). To the list of Frazerian compilations of cultural conceptions of Time one could add the three volumes of F. K. Ginzel's "Manual of
Mathematical and Technical Chronology" (1906, 1911, 1914)—a misleading title
because the work examines only early historical, ethnographic, and folkloric evidence. A paper by W. Bogoras (1925) is remarkable mainly for an early attempt
to show similarities between relativity theory and primitive Time concepts. Among
more recent work one could cite Bourdieu (1963), a volume edited by Lacroix
(1972), an important paper by Turton and Ruggles (1978), and an essay by Kramer (1978). The list is by no means complete.

8. For a succinct summary of philosophical arguments relating to time and
communication see Lucas 1973:44 ff.

9. For instance by D. Bidney in his critique of Herskovits (1953:423 ff) and
more recently in a devastating essay by Nowell-Smith (1971). Relevant writings by
Herskovits were republished, with a positive introduction, by D. T. Campbell
(Herskovits 1972). Book-length appraisals were given by Rudolph (1968) and Tennekes (1971) and above all by Lemaire (1976). Serious counterarguments continue
to be formulated with respect to the question of linguistic relativity; see the volume
of essays edited by Pinxten (1976). See also Hanson's proposal for "contextualism"
as a mediation between relativism and objectivism (1979).

10. And, one might add, the outlook of American politics: "We cannot hope
to discharge satisfactorily to ourselves or to other peoples the leadership that history has forced upon us at this time unless we act upon reasoned and clearly stated
standards of evaluation. Finally, all talk of an eventual peaceful and orderly world
is but pious cant or sentimental fantasy unless there are, in fact, some simple but
powerful beliefs to which all men hold, some codes or canons that have or can
obtain universal acceptance." This is not an American president preaching his doc-

trine of human rights in 1982, but Clyde Kluckhohn in a cold war essay "Education, Values, and Anthropological Relativity" (1962 [1952]:286 f).

11. It is intriguing to note that a coherent critical account of the "war effort" in American anthropology is conspicuously absent from M. Harris' history of anthropology, although he gives a cursory review of some studies of that period (1968:413–418). The same holds for Honigman, who mentions "national character" in connection with Vico, Montesquieu, Hume, and Herder (1976:99 f), and for Voget who does, however, provide an informative section on Kluckhohn's project of "covert" value studies in five cultures of the Southwest (1975:414–421). It is even more surprising that, as far as I can see, none of the contributors to Hymes' *Reinventing Anthropology* (1974) felt the need to drag that particular skeleton out of the closet. Incidentally, no reference is made in these books to the Mead and Métreaux manual on which I will comment below. One important critical appraisal, focusing on studies of Japanese national character by W. La Barr, was recently made by P. T. Suzuki (1980).

12. But this is only a passing impression. Elsewhere M. Mead stated: "These contemporary national character studies of culture at a distance resemble attempts to reconstruct the cultural character of societies of the past . . . in which the study of documents and monuments has to be substituted for the direct study of individuals interacting in observable social situations. However they differ from historical reconstruction in that, whether they are done at a distance or through field-work in the given nation, they are based primarily on interviews with and observation of living human beings" (1962:396). Note that the allochronic intent of the statement is reinforced, not mitigated by reference to living human beings.

13. This intent is expressed in the title of a paper by Hall and William Foote Whyte (1966): "Intercultural Communication: A Guide to Men of Action." The section on time provides a catalog of how-to recommendations for American businessmen having to deal with Latin Americans, Greeks, Japanese, and Indians and concludes with this anthropological malapropos: "If you haven't been needled by an Arab, you just haven't been needled" (1966:570).

14. Margaret Mead formulated that presupposition as follows: "Cultural understanding of the sort discussed in this Manual can only be achieved within a frame of reference that recognizes the internal consistency of the premises of each human culture and also recognizes that much of this consistency is unconscious; that is, is not available to the average member of the culture" (Mead and Métreaux 1953:399 f).

15. Perhaps one should not even attempt a bibliographic note (a useful working bibliography on Lévi-Strauss and his critics—containing 1,384 titles!—is now available: Lapointe and Lapointe 1977). Nevertheless, here are some titles, all primarily concerned with a systematic interpretation of Lévi-Strauss' work, which I would recommend for consultation. In English: Leach (1970)—readable but to be taken with caution; Scholte (1974a), the most concise and differentiated introduction by an anthropologist; Rossi (1974); and most recently Jenkins (1979). In French: Simonis (1968) and Marc-Lipianski (1973), the latter being mainly a study guide. In German: Lepenies and Ritter (1970), a collective volume especially valuable as a study of Lévi-Strauss' intellectual sources and affinities. Generally, I have found F. Jameson's *The Prison House of Language* (1972) to be a most convincing critique

of structuralism (including related movements such as Russian formalism and the Prague school). He is especially insightful with regard to the problem of Time.

16. See Lévi-Strauss 1976:12. It should be clear that *taxonomic* is here being used to designate an episteme (see Foucault 1973 and Lepenies 1976) and not in a narrow technical sense of one type of classification (see Durbin 1975).

17. See also the excellent essay on Lévi-Strauss and Sartre by Rosen (1971).

18. One of Lévi-Strauss' most famous statements should be quoted here. Speaking of myth and music, he observes that both require "a temporal dimension in which to unfold. But this relation to time is of a rather special nature: it is as if music and mythology needed time only in order to deny it. Both, indeed, are instruments for the obliteration of time" (1970 [1964]:15 f). Incidentally, when Lévi-Strauss later tries to correct misunderstandings with regard to the distinction of synchrony and diachrony he reaffirms the antitemporal intent; see 1976:16 f.

19. G. Bachelard argues similarly and concludes: "Subrepticement, on a remlacé la locution *durer dans le temps* par la locution *demeurer dans l'espace* et c'est l'intuition grossière du plein qui donne l'impression vague de plénitude. Voilà le prix dont il faut payer la continuité établie entre la connaissance objective et la connaissance subjective" (1950:27).

20. In this respect, Lévi-Strauss' position is identical to L. H. Morgan's (see the quotation from Morgan, chapter 1). Appropriately, *The Elementary Structures of Kinship* is dedicated to Morgan.

21. Absence of a theory of production is not a mere side effect of a radically taxonomic approach. Structuralism is a theory of *non-production:* ostensibly, because it is a theory tailored to non- or preindustrial societies which are based on symbolic exchange; in reality, because it is a theory produced by a society whose "industrial" phase has long been terminated by what Baudrillard calls the "end of production." As the writings of Baudrillard show (see especially 1976) structuralism as the theory of the "simulation of the code" can be put to use for a shattering critique of late capitalist "culture" but only at the expense of primitive society from which it must continuously extract its insights. Lévi-Strauss expresses awareness of this in his famous bon mot on anthropology as *entropology* (1963:397).

22. See also a statement from the introduction to *The Raw and the Cooked:* "Throughout, my intention remains unchanged. Starting from ethnographic experience, I have always aimed at drawing up an inventory of mental patterns, to reduce apparently arbitrary data to some kind of order, and to attain a level at which a kind of necessity becomes apparent, underlying the illusion of liberty" (Lévi-Strauss 1970:10).

23. Elsewhere I argue that the silence and secrecy surrounding the ethnographic act are comparable to the removal of fundamental religious acts from the everyday sphere. I then ask: "Could it be that in anthropology, as in many religious movements, there is a censoring-out of its constitutive acts, expressing conscious or unconscious efforts to protect the discipline from realizing that, after all, it rests on a historically situated praxis, a mode of producing knowledge in which personal mediation is essential and must be 'accounted for' instead of being simply presumed in such fuzzy axioms as 'anthropology should be based on field work' " (Fabian 1979b:25).

24. The colonial involvement of British anthropology has been well docu-

mented, which is one reason why it will be little discussed in these essays. See Asad 1973, Leclerc 1971, Kuper 1973.

3. Time and Writing About the Other

1. Bohm 1965:175 f.
2. La Fontaine 1962:Fable X.
3. Evans-Pritchard found it "surprising that, with the exception of Morgan's study of the Iroquois [1851] not a single anthropologist conducted field studies till the end of the nineteenth century." He undoubtedly exaggerated, but his observation underscored the insight that the eventual incorporation of field research into the praxis of anthropology was not so much due to a need for empirical confirmation as it was expressive of the professionalization of a discipline: "Anthropology became more and more a whole-time professional study, and some field experience came to be regarded as an essential part of the training of its students" (see 1962:71 f, 73).
4. For a recent statement of this see an otherwise disappointing essay by F. A. Salamone (1979, with useful bibliographic references to the literature on fieldwork). Notice a remarkable shift in these debates from a scientific orientation inspired by an "Einsteinian" notion of epistemology in Northrop and Livingston (1964) toward the communicative legitimation of anthropological knowledge.
5. My own contribution to this debate was an essay, "Language, History and Anthropology" (1971), which occasioned an article by Jarvie (1975). Bob Scholte contributed several important essays (see 1971, 1974b) as did K. Dwyer (1977, 1979), J. P. Dumont (1978), B. Jules-Rosette (1978), and D. Tedlock (1979), among others.
6. This can be done in a critical and fruitful fashion, as, e.g., by Hayden White (1973). His analyses of historical discourse in terms of metaphorical strategies permit, at the very least, interesting comparisons between different historians. However, when all discourse on Time, history, and change is denounced, rather than analyzed, as metaphorical the results can be stultifying; see Nisbet (1969). Used judiciously or not, I find *metaphor* to be of limited use for the critical project of this book. No doubt many allochronic devices are metaphoric—but that is, I am tempted to say, no excuse.
7. This has been asserted, incidentally, about "Time and Physical Language." According to Schumacher, who qualifies special relativity as a "rule of communication" in a frame separating subject and object, "the idea of the progress of time is an outgrowth of the linguistic forms for physical communications" (see 1967:196, 203).
8. What Greimas has in mind seems to be illustrated by Evans-Pritchard when he states: "Every kind of social relationship, every belief, every technological process—in fact everything in the life of the natives—is expressed in words as well as in action, and when one has fully understood the meaning of all the words of their language and all their situations of reference one has finished one's study of the society" (1962a:79 f).
9. For a radical critique of claims that historical discourse might, or should be,

viewed as self-contained see Mairet (1974). A similar concern, combined with a critique of the "positivist illusion" akin to that expressed by anthropologists (see note 5 above), characterizes the work of B. Verhaegen (see 1974). The many facets of the problem of history qua discourse are discussed in a collective volume edited by Koselleck and Stempel (1973; see also Greimas' essay "Sur l'histoire événementielle et l'histoire fondamentale" in that collection).

10. Two sentences from Herodotus' *Histories,* chosen at random, illustrate this. Notice that they could also occur in modern ethnographies: "The only deities to whom Egyptians consider it proper to sacrifice pigs are Dionysus and the Moon" (1972:148); "It is the custom [of the Lybian tribes], at a man's first marriage, to give a party, at which the bride is enjoyed by each of the guests in turn. . . ." (1972:329). On early ethnological theorizing, see Müller 1972. Examples of recent criticism in anthropological textbooks are Vansina (1970, see p. 165 where he calls the ethnographic present a "zero-time fiction") and Anderson (1973:205 f).

11. This does not cancel earlier remarks on terminological allochronism; it makes them more precise. A further point of clarification: What is gained or changed if primitive is used in quotation marks, or preceded by *so-called* and similar disclaimers (see some random examples in Lévi-Strauss which are representative of a widespread usage: 1966:222, 243, 267; 1976:19 [in his Inaugural Lecture])? Perhaps these modifiers signal the label-character of the term, its conventional, classificatory function in a technical vocabulary. But disclaimers may be indexical rather than referential. In that case they point to the position of the primitive in anthropological discourse. Who calls the primitive *so-called?* Anthropologists. In that case the modifier may not dissociate its user from anthropological praxis; nor does it soften the blow of allochronism. Because the use of primitive is not just a matter of definition but expressive of a historically established praxis, the term may become a starting point for fruitful philosophical analysis (see Dupré 1975:16ff) and, indeed, for a general critique of Western society (see Diamond 1974), an intention that must also be granted to Lévi-Strauss. Yet there remains the question to what extent the political conditions of established anthropological praxis legitimate the use epistemologically, even if ethical intentions are beyond doubt. For the wider history of *primitivism* see the standard work edited by Lovejoy et al. (1935).

12. I believe that this is illustrated by a statement from one of anthropology's ancestors: "I have studied men, and I think I am a fairly good observer. But all the same I do not know how to see what is before my eyes; I can only see clearly in retrospect, it is only in my memories that my mind can work. I have neither feeling nor understanding for anything that is said or done or that happens before my eyes. All that strikes me is the external manifestation. But afterwards it all comes back to me, I remember the place and the time, nothing escapes me. Then from what a man has done or said I can read his thoughts, and I am rarely mistaken" (J. J. Rousseau 1977 [1781]:114).

13. *Hermeneutics* (much like *phenomenology*) retains a distinctly European-continental flavor. When it crosses the Atlantic it seems to arrive as a fashionable jargon rather than a style of thought with serious practical consequences. Nevertheless, there are now signs that it begins to have substantial influence on the social sciences in the English-speaking world. G. Radnitsky's *Continental Schools of Metascience* (1968, with later editions), K. O. Apel's *Analytic Philosophy of Language and*

the Geisteswissenschaften (1967), and Palmer's *Hermeneutics* (1969) provide clear and compact introductions in English. Two recent publications, an historical study by Z. Bauman (1978) and a reader edited by Rabinow and Sullivan (1979), attest to the reception of hermeneutics in the social sciences, including anthropology.

14. See also the reflections on fieldwork and time by J. P. Dumont (1978:47 f) but notice his taking recourse to visual-spatial representation when he reports on "Social Time and Social Space as Context" (*ibid.*, ch. 5). Dumont illustrates my point regarding "contradictions" between temporal sensibility in doing research and visualist distancing in writing anthropology (see ch. 4).

15. The process by which money and language, merchandise and information, become less and less distinguishable had been observed by thinkers at least since the seventeenth century. Kant's critic, J. G. Hamann noted (with a reference to Leibniz): "Money and language are two things whose study is as profound and abstract as their use is general. Both are more closely related than one would suspect. The theory of one explains the theory of the other; it appears, therefore, that they derive from common grounds" (1967 [1761]:97). Incidentally, this was written almost a century and a half before de Saussure found in the economic theory of value a model for his structural linguistics (see, e.g., 1975 [1916]:114 f, 157). Data storage and computer use in anthropology are discussed in a volume edited by Dell Hymes (1965).

16. On Trille's fraudulent ethnography of West-African pygmies see Piskaty (1957); for a useful survey of the muddled debates concerning Castaneda see Murray (1979).

17. For a theoretical discussion of this last point see our essay "Folk Art from an Anthropological Perspective" (Fabian and Szombati-Fabian 1980).

18. Dell Hymes considers this in his introduction to *Reinventing Anthropology* (1974:48 ff) and quotes J. Galtung on "scientific colonialism": "There are many ways in which this can happen. One is to claim the right of unlimited access to data from other countries. Another is to export data about the country to one's own home country for processing into 'manufactured goods,' such as books and articles. . . . This is essentially similar to what happens when raw materials are exported at a low price and reimported as manufactured goods at a very high cost" (Galtung 1967:296). See also the introduction to A. Wilden (1972, "The Scientific Discourse: Knowledge as a Commodity").

19. G. Gusdorf gives an account of the rise of modern linguistics in a context of struggle between old and new interpretations of the Western "tradition" (1973: part 3). See also Gadamer on the connection between theological and philological hermeneutics (1965:162 ff; based on an earlier study by Dilthey). Gadamer notes that the origins of the modern concept of "system" must be sought in attempts to reconcile the old and the new in theology and in a phase that prepared the separation of science from philosophy (1965:164n2). In other words, "system" always has served as a figure of thought related to Time. Its currency in taxonomic anthropology (and other approaches stressing the scientific character of our discipline) is indicative of allochronic tendencies. (We will have more to say about these connections in the following chapter).

20. The following reflections were inspired by my reading of an essay by Michel Serres, "Le Jeu du Loup" (1977:89–104). I am grateful to Josué V. Harari who brought the piece to my attention. He has since published an English version of

Serres' essay which includes the text of La Fontaine's fable "The Wolf and the Lamb" (see Harari 1979:260–276).

4. The Other and the Eye: Time and the Rhetoric of Vision

1. Thomas Hobbes, *Leviathan* (1962 [1651]:21).
2. Karl Marx, "First Thesis on Feuerbach" (1953:339).
3. Without attempting to document here what is by now a considerable literature on fieldwork and methods one may note a development from the catalogue-genre of the eighteenth and nineteenth centuries (see chapter 1, note 12) toward more and more "graphic" instructions. Thus Marcel Mauss declared in his *Manuel d'Ethnographie:* "Le premier point dans l'étude d'une société consiste à savoir de qui l'on parle. Pour cela, on établira la cartographie complète de la société observée" (1974:13). Notice the massing of visual-graphic and tabular material in the sections on field methods in the Naroll and Cohen (1970: part 2) and the Honigmann handbooks (1976: ch. 6); also in the more recent manual by Cresswell and Godelier (1976). Much less frequently does one come upon statements like "Understanding in field research is very much like the aural learning of a language" (Wax 1971:12). But Rosalie Wax does not develop her insight and her own account is dominated by the spatial image of inside/outside.
4. See Givner's essay "Scientific Preconceptions in Locke's Philosophy of Language" (1962).
5. On "The Sense of Vision and the Origins of Modern Science" see Lindberg and Steneck (1972); see also Lindberg's book *Theories of Vision from Al-Kindi to Kepler* (1976).
6. See Feyerabend 1975:157 (with a reference to Koyré's studies of Galileo); Kuhn 1970 [1962]:47 f seems to restrict the importance of "debates" to preparadigm periods. Wilden analyses "binarism" fashionable in anthropology and elsewhere under the heading "The Scientific Discourse as Propaganda" (1972: ch. 14).
7. Perhaps one should distinguish several ways in which topoi and topical logic inform anthropological discourse: (1) *Through time,* often with astonishing continuity down to the beginnings of recorded Western intellectual history, philosophers, *philosophes,* and anthropologists have returned to the same common places (often copying from each other)—savagery, barbarism, cannibalism (see the latest fashion in books on that topos) and certain tenacious elements of ethnographic lore (see Vajda 1964). (2) *At any given time,* anthropologists have been visiting and revisiting familiar intellectual places—matriarchy, couvade, mana, incest, totem and taboo, culture heroes, kula, potlatch, Crow kinship systems, and so on. (3) Finally, there have been attempts to chart topoi—Murdock's ethnographic sample, preceded by Tylor's classical study of marriage and descent, is an instrument for statistical calculations but also an *atlas* mapping topoi (see Tylor 1889, Murdock 1949: app. A). The Hall and Trager inventory may be read as a sort of periodic chart of culture elements; its mnemonic character is obvious (Hall 1959:174 f). Even Hymes' "SPEAKING"—the mnemonic summary of components in a speech event—may belong here (Hymes 1972:65 ff).
8. For further references to the *ars mnemonica,* to the history of scientific illustration and related currents in the eighteenth century, see Lepenies 1976:32 ff.

4. The Other and the Eye   179

9. This had ancient precedents in the Pythagorean and (neo-) Platonic traditions. Iamblichos (who died around 330 AD) reports in his book on Pythagoras that the master "called geometry 'history.'" He also notes that his followers avoided common and popular expressions in their publications; rather, "following the command of Pythagoras to be silent about divine mysteries, they chose figures of speech whose meaning remained incomprehensible to the non-initiated and they protected their discussions and writings through the use of agreed-upon *symbols*" (see Iamblichos 1963:97, 111; my emphasis).

10. Notice that in this chapter I concentrate on tracing a general history of visualism. For an account of Renaissance attempts to incorporate the newly found savage into such visual-spatial schemes as the "chain of being" see Hodgen 1964: ch. 10 (especially the tree- and ladder-diagrams of hierarchy, pp. 399, 401, both from works by Raymond Lull, one of Ramus' precursors).

11. See Goody (1977) on tables, lists, formulae, and other devices.

12. This evokes, of course, the "medium-is-the-message" slogan to which M. McLuhan's brilliant insights seem to have been reduced by now. Ong, by the way, acknowledges intellectual debts to McLuhan who in turn builds on Ong's studies in his *The Gutenberg Galaxy* (1962:144 ff., 159 f., 162 f.).

13. Because methodology remained tied to the business of disseminating and transmitting knowledge. Rhetoric as *pédagogie*, incidentally, was the "narrow door" (M. Halbwachs) through which Durkheim—and with him sociology—gained admission to the Sorbonne. He was first hired to teach education. His lectures on the history of higher education in France up to the Renaissance were later published as a book (Durkheim 1938).

14. Especially in his *The Presence of the Word* (Ong 1970 [1967]) to which I have paid little attention in these essays.

15. See Derrida 1976, especially part 2, ch. 1. At this point, I am not prepared to confront Derrida's undoubtedly important theses regarding writing and violence. Inasmuch as he seems to equate writing with taxonomy (see 1976:109 f.) our arguments may converge. As regards his charge of "epistemological phonologism" (against Lévi-Strauss) I would think that his critique is aimed in the same direction as my views on visualism.

16. On the ritual-initiatory character of fieldwork see chapter 2; on its relatively late appearance as a required practice, see chapter 3. Notice that in both these contexts the point was to stress the institution of field research as a routine, as something that was almost incidental to the rise of anthropology. This indicated the tenuous *practical* integration of empiry and theory. *Ideologically*, it became all the more important to insist on a tough, visualist ideal of scientific observation. However, this was ideologization with a vengeance insofar as our clinging to fieldwork also produced the aporetic situation which allowed us to identify denial of coevalness as the key to anthropology's allochronism (see chapter 1).

17. T. Todorov (1977) traces theories of symbols to the origins of our Western tradition. J. Boon explores connections between symbolism and French structuralism (1972). R. Firth's study is the most comprehensive attempt by an anthropologist to provide a systematic treatise on symbols (1973). Works by Victor Turner (e.g. 1967) and Mary Douglas (1966), as well as the writings of C. Geertz (e.g., 1973), among others, have been influential. Geertz, especially, acknowledges the influence of Susanne K. Langer (e.g., 1951 [1942]). There exists a reader on sym-

bolic anthropology (Dolgin et al. 1977), perhaps a symptom of its aspiring to normal scientific status. Several works document the many points of contact and contrast between structuralism and symbolic approaches, see Sperber (1975), and Basso and Selby (1976). The latter, incidentally, evokes a related trend, expressive of the influence of K. Burke, which concentrates on the notion of metaphor and on rhetoric models for cultural analysis (see the seminal article by Fernandez, 1974, and the collection of essays edited by Sapir and Crocker, 1977). A concise overview of "symbolic interactionism," a movement closely related to symbolic anthropology, was given by Meltzer et al. 1975. On *symbol* in social anthropology see Skorupski 1976.

18. I am using the three-volume study edition, Hegel, *Vorlesungen über die Aesthetik* (1970) referred to in the following as *Aesthetic* I, II, III.

19. Hegel refers to Friedrich von Schlegel and to Friedrich Creuzer. Kramer traces Creuzer's influence in creating the "myth of the Orient" (1977:20 ff.).

20. See the commentary by Kojève (1969:134 f.) especially the important remark on Hegel's historical Time being conceived as a movement that starts with the future and moves through the past into the present. Kojève notes "It may be that the Time in which the Present takes primacy is cosmic or physical Time, whereas biological Time would be characterized by the primacy of the Past" (1969:134n21).

21. In fairness to Whitehead and to contemporary symbolic anthropologists one must acknowledge a *critical* intent directed against crude empiricism and positivism. As has been noted by others (e.g., Apel 1970, Habermas 1972: chs. 5 and 6) there are many points of contact between pragmatic philosophy, hermeneutics, and critical theory inspired by a Marxist theory of praxis. Roy Wagner's original and insightful approach to symbolization (e.g., 1975) exemplifies critical and autocritical symbolic anthropology. See also V. Turner's essay reviewing current symbolic studies (1975).

22. Ironically, in view of the critique expressed here, I must express my gratitude to J. Boon for having brought to my attention, with much enthusiasm, the work of Frances Yates. I also know of his interest in the history and semiotics of ethnographic illustration and I look forward to the results of his research.

23. For a critique of a similar argument expounded in another account of conversion to symbolic anthropology see my review of R. Rappaport's *Ecology, Meaning, and Religion* (1979), Fabian 1982.

24. That is done in the writings of J. Baudrillard (whom Sahlins quotes), especially in his *L'Échange symbolique et la mort* (1976). To realize that Baudrillard, too, feeds on the primitive-civilized dichotomy is perhaps the best antidote against the spell cast by this brilliant new proponent of "philosophy with a hammer" (see S. K. Levine's review of Baudrillard's *Mirror of Production,* Levine 1976).

5. Conclusions

1. "Man muss diese versteinerten Verhältnisse dadurch zum Tanzen zwingen, dass man ihnen ihre eigene Melodie vorsingt!" (Marx 1953:311).

2. "Toute connaissance prise au moment de sa constitution est une connaissance polémique" (Bachelard 1950:14).

3. A document for the spirit of that time is an essay by Julian Huxley titled

"Unesco: Its Purpose and its Philosophy" (1949). He had been the executive secretary of the Preparatory Commission to Unesco in 1946. Although he insists that he is speaking only for himself he clearly was influential in shaping policies and, above all, in providing them with a temporal perspective. The objective basis for international cultural politics, he argues, must be an "evolutionary approach" based on "scientific method," i.e., a transcultural theory of change. He undoubtedly had anthropology in mind when he stated that "the necessary bridge between the realm of fact and the realm of value . . . can be strengthened by those social sciences which utilize the scientific method but endeavor to apply it to values" (1949:315).

4. Northrop presumably qualified for that role as the author of *The Meeting of East and West* (1946) and editor of *Ideological Differences and World Order* (1949). The latter included contributions by D. Bidney ("The Concept of Meta-Anthropology") and C. Kluckhohn ("The Philosophy of the Navaho Indians").

5. Northrop's view is expressed obliquely in this remark about Bergson: "It was because Bergson assumed that a publicly meaningful neurological epistemic correlate of introspected memory is impossible to find that he relapsed into his purely intuitive philosophy which accounted for impressionistic art and the introspected private flow of time which he confused with public time and called 'durée,' but which left no meaning for public space and time, the public events and objects in it or a public self, all of which he called 'falsifications of fact' or the 'misuse of the mind' " (1960:51). The quotation is from the essay "The Neurological Epistemic Correlates of Introspected Ideas."

6. This is the heading of a chapter on De Maillet, Buffon, and others in Loren Eiseley's *Darwin's Century* (1961).

7. Remember that Montaigne ended his essay "Des Cannibales" (based, incidentally, on conversations with one of them) with this ironical remark: "All this isn't so bad but, imagine, they don't wear breeches" ("Tout cela ne va pas trop mal: mais quoy! ils ne portent point de hault de chausses." See Montaigne 1925 [1595]:248). Two centuries later, Georg Forster noted: "We never consider how similar we are to the savages and we call, quite improperly, everyone by that name who lives on a different continent and does not dress according to Parisian Fashion" ("denn wir bedenken nie, wie ähnlich wir den Wilden sind und geben diesen Namen sehr uneigentlich allem, was in einem anderen Weltteile nicht parisisch gekleidet ist." See Forster 1968 [1791]:398 f).

8. On "Linguistic Method in Ethnography" see Hymes 1970; on "Ethnography of Communication" see Schmitz 1975. On epistemological problems with the "ethnography of speaking" see my paper "Rule and Process" (1979a).

9. Although this was recognized by F. Fanon and others there is a need to remind ourselves of the fact that colonial regimes "aim at the repeated defeat of resistance" (see Wamba-dia-Wamba in an essay on philosophy in Africa, 1979:225). On the general issue of sustained oppression see S. Amin 1976.

10. This was noted by many critics of anthropology, especially in France; see the critical account of African Studies by Leclerc (1971) and of ethnology in Latin America by Jaulin (1970). In a similar vein are the essays by Duvignaud (1973) and Copans (1974). More recently, a collection of articles (many of them discussing the thesis of Jaulin) was edited by Amselle (1979).

11. C. Geertz (with a reference to G. Ryle) posited that thought consists of "a traffic in significant symbols," a view which "makes of the study of culture a positive science like any other" (1973:362). I suspect that he would rather not be re-

minded of statements such as the one just quoted since he has been advocating a hermeneutic stance in recent writings. Whether one really can hold both, a representational theory of culture and a hermeneutic approach in the sense in which it is intended, for instance, by Gadamer (1965) is in my view an open question.

12. A. Kroeber and L. White used animism as an invective in their debates (see Bidney 1953:110). Lévi-Strauss says about Sartre's notion of the practico-inert that it "quite simply revives the language of animism" (1966:249), and in the same context he dismisses Sartre's *Critique de la raison dialectique* as a myth and therefore an "ethnographic document" (What does this make of Sartre—a "primitive"? See also Scholte's comments on this, 1974a:648).

13. I am sure that the glaring absence of the issue of race from these essays will be noted. It would be foolish to deny its importance in the rise of anthropology (see Stocking 1968). Upon reflection, my failure to discuss race may have something to do with the fact that it was not considered a problem in the training I received (and that may be indicative of the rift between academe and the wider American society). Apart from offering the lame excuse that one cannot speak about everything, I would argue that a clear conception of allochronism is the prerequisite and frame for a critique of racism. Refutations of racist thought from genetics and psychology are useful, but they will not as such do away with race as an ideological and, indeed, cosmological concept.

14. Without any doubt, the politics of Time which provided a motor for the development of anthropology is somehow connected with the phenomena analyzed by I. Wallerstein (1974). But I see a major difficulty in the notion of system itself. Can it ever accommodate coevalness, i.e., a dialectical concept of Time? N. Luhmann seems to think so but I find his arguments inconclusive to say the least. See his important essay "The Future Cannot Begin: Temporal Structures in Modern Society" (1976).

15. And it remains problematic in the minds of anthropologists whose oeuvre is commonly recognized as Marxist; see the preface to Godelier 1973; see the volume edited by M. Bloch (1975; especially R. Firth's contribution), and the first chapter in Abeles 1976.

16. As far as Soviet ethnology is concerned, the situation is unclear to say the least. We owe to Stephen and Ethel Dunn an important *Introduction to Soviet Ethnography* (1974) but their interpretations have been hotly disputed by Soviet émigré anthropologists such as David Zil'berman (see 1976, including replies by the Dunns).

17. There are signs that anthropologists have begun to develop elements of such a theory, see Bourdieu (1977) on a theory of practice, Friedrich (1980) on the material-chaotic aspects of language, Goody (1977) on the material conditions of communication, to name but three examples.

18. In this respect, Bourdieu's quasi-synonymous use of hermeneutic interpretation and structuralist decoding is justified (see 1977:1). It is another question whether this does justice to recent proposals for a critical hermeneutic.

19. E. Bloch formulated thoughts on *Gleichzeitigkeit* and *Ungleichzeitigkeit* which are too complex to be dealt with in this context. I want to note, though, that totality was central to him and that he anticipated the critique of visualism when he insisted that use of the concept of "totality must not only be critical, but above all non-contemplative" (1962 [1932]:125).

References Cited

Abeles, Marc. 1976. *Anthropologie et marxisme*. Brussels: Editions Complexe.

Adams, Charles R. 1979. "Aurality and Consciousness: Basotho Production of Significance." In Bruce T. Grindal and Dennis M. Warren, eds., *Essays in Humanistic Anthropology: A Festschrift in Honor of David Bidney*, pp. 303–325. Washington, D.C.: University Press of America.

Adorno, Theodor W. 1966. *Negative Dialektik*. Frankfurt: Suhrkamp.

Althusser, Louis and Étienne Balibar. 1970. *Reading Capital*. London: NLB.

Amin, Samir. 1976. *Unequal Development: An Essay on the Social Formations of Peripheral Capitalism*. Sussex: Harvester Press.

Amselle, Jean-Loup, ed. 1979. *Le Sauvage à la mode*. Paris: Editions le Sycomore.

Anderson, James N. 1973. "Ecological Anthropology and Anthropological Ecology." In John J. Honigman, ed., *Handbook of Social and Cultural Anthropology*, pp. 179–239. Chicago: Rand McNally.

Apel, Karl-Otto. 1967. *Analytic Philosophy of Language and the Geisteswissenschaften*. Dordrecht: Reidel.

—— 1970. "Szientismus oder transzendentale Hermeneutik?" In Rüdiger Bubner, Konrad Cramer, and Reiner Wiehl, eds., *Hermeneutik und Dialektik*, 2:105–144. Tübingen: J. C. B. Mohr (Paul Siebeck).

Arens, W. 1979. *The Man-Eating Myth. Anthropology and Anthropophagy*. New York: Oxford University Press.

Asad, Talal, ed. 1973. *Anthropology and the Colonial Encounter*. New York: Humanities Press.

Bachelard, Gaston. 1950. *La Dialectique de la durée*. Paris: PUF.

Barthes, Roland. 1970. *Writing Degree Zero and Elements of Semiology*. Boston: Beacon.

Basso, Keith H. and Henry A. Selby, eds. 1976. *Meaning in Anthropology*. Albuquerque: University of New Mexico Press.

Bastian, Adolf. 1881. *Die Vorgeschichte der Ethnologie. Deutschlands Denkfreunden gewidmet für eine Mussestunde*. Berlin: Dümmler.

Baudrillard, Jean. 1976. *L'Échange symbolique et la mort*. Paris: Gallimard.

Bauman, Zygmunt. 1978. *Hermeneutics and Social Science*. New York: Columbia University Press.

Becker, Carl L. 1963 [1932]. *The Heavenly City of the Eighteenth-Century Philosophers.* New Haven: Yale University Press.

Beckingham, C. F. and G. W. Huntingford, eds. 1961. *The Prester John of the Indies.* 2 vols. Cambridge: Cambridge University Press.

Benedict, Ruth. 1934. *Patterns of Culture.* New York: Houghton Mifflin.

—— 1967 [1946]. *The Chrysanthemum and the Sword: Patterns of Japanese Culture.* Cleveland: World.

Benveniste, Emile. 1971 [1956]. *Problems in General Linguistics.* Coral Gables: University of Miami Press.

Bidney, David. 1953. *Theoretical Anthropology.* New York: Columbia University Press.

Bloch, Ernst. 1962 [1932]. "Ungleichzeitigket und Pflicht zu ihrer Dialektik." In *Erbschaft dieser Zeit,* pp. 104–126. Frankfurt: Suhrkamp.

—— 1963. *Tübinger Einleitung in die Philosophie,* vol. 1. Frankfurt: Suhrkamp.

Bloch, Maurice. 1977. "The Past and the Present in the Present." *Man* (N.S.), 12:278–292.

Bloch, Maurice, ed. 1975. *Marxist Analyses and Social Anthropology.* London: Malaby Press.

Bogoras, Waldemar. 1925. "Ideas of Space and Time in the Conception of Primitive Religion." *American Anthropologist* 27:205–266.

Bohm, David. 1965. *The Special Theory of Relativity.* New York: W. A. Benjamin.

Boon, James. 1972. *From Symbolism to Structuralism.* New York: Harper Torchbooks.

—— 1977. *The Anthropological Romance of Bali, 1597–1972.* New York: Cambridge University Press.

Bossuet, Jacques Bénigne. 1845. *Discours sur l'histoire universelle.* Paris: Firmin Didot Frères.

—— 1976. *Discourse on Universal History.* O. Ranum, ed., trans. Chicago: University of Chicago Press.

Bourdieu, Pierre. 1963. "The Attitude of the Algerian Peasant Toward Time." In J. Pitt-Rivers, ed., *Mediterranean Countrymen: Essays in the Social Anthropology of the Mediterranean.,* pp. 55–72. Paris: Mouton.

—— 1977. *Outline of a Theory of Practice.* Cambridge: Cambridge University Press.

Broc, Numa. 1972. *La Géographie des philosophes: Géographes et voyageurs français au XVIIIᵉ siècle.* Lille: Service de reproduction des thèses.

Burridge, Kenelm. 1973. *Encountering Aborigines.* New York: Pergamon Press.

Burrow, J. W. 1966. *Evolution and Society. A Study in Victorian Social Theory.* Cambridge: Cambridge University Press.

Butzer, Karl W. 1964. *Environment and Archaeology: An Introduction to Pleistocene Geography.* Chicago: Aldine.

Cahiers Internationaux de Sociologie. 1979. Issues on "Temps et société" and "Temps et pensée."

Campbell, Donald T. 1970. "Natural Selection as an Epistemological Model." In Raoul Naroll and Ronald Cohen, eds., *A Handbook of Method in Cultural Anthropology,* pp. 51–85. Garden City, N.Y.: Natural History Press.

Chomsky, Noam. 1972. *Language and Mind.* Enlarged edition. New York: Harcourt Brace Jovanovich.

Copans, Jean. 1974. *Critiques et politiques de l'anthropologie.* Paris: Maspéro.

—— and Jean Jamin. 1978. *Aux origines de l'anthropologie française.* Paris: Editions le Sycomore.

Creswell, Robert and Maurice Godelier. 1976. *Outils d'enquête et d'analyse anthropologiques.* Paris: Maspéro.

Darwin, Charles. 1861. *On the Origin of Species by Means of Natural Selection.* 3d ed. London: J. Murray.

Degérando, Joseph-Marie. 1969 [1800]. *The Observation of Savage Peoples.* F. C. T. Moore, ed. and Berkeley: University of California Press.

Derrida, Jacques. 1976. *Of Grammatology.* Gayatri Chakravarty Spivak, trans. Baltimore, Md.: Johns Hopkins University Press.

Diamond, Stanley. 1974. *In Search of the Primitive: A Critique of Civilization.* New Brunswick, N.J.: Transaction.

Dolgin, Janet L., David S. Kemnitzer, and David M. Schneider, eds. 1977. *Symbolic Anthropology: A Reader in the Study of Symbols and Meaning.* New York: Columbia University Press.

Doob, L. W. 1971. *Patterning of Time.* New Haven: Yale University Press.

Douglas, Mary. 1966. *Purity and Danger.* London: Routledge and Kegan Paul.

Duchet, Michèle. 1971. *Anthropologie et histoire au siècle des lumières.* Paris: Maspéro.

Dumont, Jean-Paul. 1978. *The Headman and I: Ambiguity and Ambivalence in the Fieldworking Experience.* Austin: University of Texas Press.

Dunn, Stephen P. and Ethel Dunn, eds. 1974. *Introduction to Soviet Ethnography.* Berkeley: Highgate Social Science Research Station.

Dupré, Wilhelm. 1975. *Religion in Primitive Cultures. A Study in Ethnophilosophy.* The Hague: Mouton.

Durand, Gilbert. 1979. *Science de l'homme et tradition.* Paris: Berg International.

Durbin, Marshall. 1975. "Models of Simultaneity and Sequentiality in Human Cognition." In M. Dale Kinkade, Kenneth L. Hale, and Oswald Werner, eds., *Linguistics and Anthropology: In Honor of C. F. Voegelin,* pp. 113–135. Lisse: Peter de Ridder.

Durkheim, Émile. 1938. *L'Évolution pédagogique en France des origines à la Renaissance*. Paris: Félix Alcan.

Duvignaud, J. 1973. *Le Language perdu. Essai sur la différence anthropologique*. Paris: PUF.

Dwyer, Kevin. 1977. "On the Dialogic of Field Work." *Dialectical Anthropology* 2:143–151.

⸻ 1979. "The Dialogic of Ethnology." *Dialectical Anthropology* 4:205–224.

Eder, Klaus. 1973. "Komplexität, Evolution und Geschichte." In Franz Maciejewski, ed., *Theorie der Gesellschaft oder Sozialtechnologie. Theorie Diskussion*, supplement 1, pp. 9–42. Frankfurt: Suhrkamp.

Eiseley, Loren. 1961. *Darwin's Century: Evolution and the Men Who Discovered It*. New York: Doubleday Anchor.

Eliade, Mircea. 1949. *Mythe de l'éternel retour*. Paris: Gallimard.

Evans-Pritchard, E. E. 1962a. "Fieldwork and the Empirical Tradition." In *Social Anthropology and Other Essays*, pp. 64–85. New York: Free Press.

⸻ 1962b. "Anthropology and History." In *Social Anthropology and Other Essays*, pp. 172–191. New York: Free Press.

Fabian, Johannes. 1971. "Language, History, and Anthropology." *Philosophy of the Social Sciences* 1:19–47.

⸻ 1975. "Taxonomy and Ideology: On the Boundaries of Concept-Classification." In M. Dale Kinkade, Kenneth L. Hale, and Oswald Werner, eds., *Linguistics and Anthropology: In Honor of C. F. Voegelin*, pp. 183–197. Lisse: Peter de Ridder.

⸻ 1979a. "Rule and Process: Thoughts on Ethnography as Communication." *Philosophy of the Social Sciences* 9:1–26.

⸻ 1979b. "The Anthropology of Religious Movements: From Explanation to Interpretation." *Social Research* 46: 4–35.

⸻ 1982. "On Rappaport's *Ecology, Meaning, and Religion*," *Current Anthropology* 23:205–209.

Fabian, Johannes and Ilona Szombati-Fabian. 1980. "Folk Art from an Anthropological Perspective." In M. G. Quimby and Scott T. Swank, eds., *Perspectives on American Folk Art*, pp. 247–292. New York: Norton.

Fernandez, James W. 1974. "The Mission of Metaphor in Expressive Culture." *Current Anthropology* 15:119–145.

Feyerabend, Paul. 1975. *Against Method: Outline of an Anarchistic Theory of Knowledge*. London: NLB.

Firth, Raymond, 1973. *Symbols: Public and Private*. London Allen and Unwin.

Forster, Georg. 1968. [1791]. *Ansichten vom Niederrhein*. Collected Works. Vol. 2 Gerhard Steiner, ed. Berlin: Aufbau Verlag.

Foucault, Michel. 1973. *The Order of Things: An Archeology of the Human Science*. New York: Vintage Books.

Fraser, J. T., ed. 1966. *The Voices of Time: A Cooperative Survey of Man's*

Views of Time as Expressed by the Sciences and by the Humanities. New York: George Braziller.

Fraser, J. T., F. C. Haber, and G. H. Muller, eds. 1972. *The Study of Time.* Vol. 1. New York: Springer. (Vols. 2–4 published 1975–1979).

Freyer, Hans. 1959 [1931]. "Typen und Stufen der Kultur." In A. Vierkandt, ed., *Handwörterbuch der Soziologie,* pp. 294–308. Stuttgart: Ferdinand Enke.

Friedrich, Paul. 1980. "Linguistic Relativity and the Order-to-Chaos Continuum." In Jacques Maquet, ed., *On Linguistic Anthropology: Essays in Honor of Harry Hoijer 1979,* pp. 89–139. Malibu: Undina Publications.

Gadamer, Hans-Georg. 1965. *Wahrheit und Methode.* Second edition. Tübingen: J. C. B. Mohr (Paul Siebeck).

Galtung, Johann. 1967. "After Camelot." In Irving L. Horowitz, ed., *The Rise and Fall of Project Camelot: Studies in the Relationship Between Social Science and Practical Politics,* pp. 281–312. Cambridge: MIT. Press.

Geertz, Clifford. 1973. *The Interpretation of Cultures.* New York: Basic Books.

—— 1979. "From the Native's Point of View: On the Nature of Anthropological Understanding." In Paul Rabinow and William N. Sullivan, eds., *Interpretive Social Science: A Reader,* pp. 225–241. Berkeley: University of California Press.

Gellner, Ernest. 1964. *Thought and Change.* Chicago: University of Chicago Press.

Ginzel, F. K. 1906, 1911, 1914. *Handbuch der mathematischen und technischen Chronologie: Das Zeitrechnungswesen der Völker.* 3 vols. Leipzig: J. C. Hinrich.

Gioscia, Victor. 1971. "On Social Time." In Henri Yaker, Humphry Osmond, and Frances Cheek, eds., *The Future of Time,* pp. 73–141. Garden City, N.Y.: Doubleday.

Givner, David A. 1962. "Scientific Preconceptions in Locke's Philosophy of Language." *Journal for the History of Ideas* 23:340–354.

Gluckman, Max. 1963. *Order and Rebellion in Tribal Africa.* London: Cohen and West.

Godelier, Maurice. 1973. *Horizons, trajects marxistes en anthropologie.* Paris: Maspéro.

Goody, Jack. 1977. *The Domestication of the Savage Mind.* Cambridge: Cambridge University Press.

Graebner, Fritz. 1911. *Methode der Ethnologie.* Heidelberg: C. Winter.

Greenberg, J. H. 1968. Anthropological Linguistics: An Introduction. New York: Random House.

Greimas, Algirdas Julien. 1973. "Sur l'histoire événementielle et l'histoire fondamentale." In Reinhart Koselleck and Wolf-Dieter Stempel, eds., *Geschichte—Ereignis und Erzählung,* pp. 139–153. Munich: Wilhelm Fink.

—— 1976. *Sémiotique et sciences sociales.* Paris: Seuil.

Gurvitch, Georges. 1961. *La Multiplicité des temps sociaux*. Paris: Centre de Documentation Universitaire.

—— 1964. *The Spectrum of Social Time*. Dordrecht: Reidel.

Gusdorf, Georges. 1968. "Ethnologie et métaphysique." In Jean Poirier, ed., *Ethnologie générale*, pp. 1772–1815. Paris: Gallimard.

—— 1973. *L'Avènement des sciences humaines au siècle des lumières*. Paris: Payot.

Habermas, Jürgen. 1972. *Knowledge and Human Interests*. London: Heinemann.

Halfmann, Jost. 1979. "Wissenschaftliche Entwicklung und Evolutionstheorie." *Europäisches Archiv für Soziologie* 20: 245–298.

Hall, Edward T. 1959. *The Silent Language*. Greenwich, Conn.: Fawcett.

Hall, Edward T. and William Foote Whyte. 1966. "Intercultural Communication: A Guide to Men of Action." In Alfred G. Smith, ed., *Communication and Culture*, pp. 567–576. New York: Holt, Rinehart, and Winston.

Hamann, Johann Georg. 1967. *Schriften zur Sprache*, Wolfgang Rödel, ed. Frankfurt: Suhkamp.

Hanson, F. Allan. 1979. "Does God Have a Body? Truth, Reality and Cultural Relativism." *Man* (N.S.), 14:515–529.

Harari, Josué V., ed. 1979. *Textual Strategies. Perspectives in Post-Structuralist Criticism*. Ithaca, N.Y.: Cornell University Press.

Harris, Marvin. 1968. *The Rise of Anthropological Theory*. New York: Thomas Y. Crowell.

Hegel, G. F. W. 1969 [1830]. *Enzyklopädie der philosophischen Wissenschaften im Grundrisse*. Friedhelm Nicolin and Otto Pöggeler, eds. Berlin: Akademie Verlag.

—— 1970 [1835]. *Vorlesungen über die Aesthetik*. 3 vols. Frankfurt: Suhrkamp.

—— 1973 [1807]. *Phänomenologie des Geistes*. Gerhard Göhler, ed. Frankfurt: Ullstein.

Herodotus. 1972. *The Histories*. Aubrey de Sélincourt, trans. Baltimore: Penguin Books.

Herskovits, Melville J. 1972. *Cultural Relativism: Perspectives in Cultural Pluralism*. Frances Herskovits, ed. New York: Random House.

History and Theory. 1966. *History and the Concept of Time*. Beiheft 6. Middletown, Conn.: Wesleyan University Press.

Hobbes, Thomas. 1962 [1651]. *Leviathan or the Matter, Forme and Power of a Commonwealth Ecclesiastical and Civil*. Michael Oakeshott, ed. New York: Collier.

Hodgen, Margaret E. 1964. *Early Anthropology in the Sixteenth and Seventeenth Centuries*. Philadelphia: University of Pennsylvania Press.

Honigmann, John J. 1976. *The Development of Anthropological Ideas*. Homewood, Ill.: Dorsey.

Huizer, Gerrit and Bruce Mannheim, eds. 1979. *The Politics of Anthropology*. The Hague: Mouton.

Huxley, Julian. 1949. "Unesco: Its Purpose and its Philosophy." In F. S. C. Northrop, ed., *Ideological Differences and World Order*, pp. 305–322. New Haven: Yale University Press.

Hymes, Dell. 1970. "Linguistic Method in Ethnography: Its Development in the United States." In Paul L. Garvin, ed., *Method and Theory in Linguistics*, pp. 249–325. The Hague: Mouton.

—— 1972. "Models of the Interaction of Language and Social Life." In John J. Gumperz and Dell Hymes, eds., *Directions in Sociolinguistics*, pp. 35–71. New York: Holt, Rinehart and Winston.

Hymes, Dell, ed. 1965. *The Use of Computers in Anthropology*. The Hague: Mouton.

—— 1974. *Reinventing Anthropology*. New York: Random House, Vintage Books.

Iamblichos. 1963. *Pythagoras*. Michael von Albrecht, ed., trans. Zürich: Artemis.

Jameson, Fredric. 1972. *The Prison House of Language: A Critical Account of Structuralism and Russian Formalism*. Princeton: Princeton University Press.

Jarvie, Ian C. 1964. *The Revolution in Anthropology*. New York: Humanities Press.

—— 1975. "Epistle to the Anthropologists." *American Anthropologist* 77:253–266.

Jaulin, R. 1970. *La Paix blanche*. Paris: Seuil.

Jayne, K. G. 1970 [1910]. *Vasco da Gama and His Successors 1460–1580*. New York: Barnes and Noble.

Jenkins, Alan. 1979. *The Social Theory of Claude Lévi-Strauss*. London: Macmillan.

Jules-Rosette, Bennetta. 1978. "The Veil of Objectivity: Prophecy, Divination and Social Inquiry." *American Anthropologist* 80:549–570.

Klempt, Adalbert. 1960. *Die Säkularisierung der universal-historischen Auffassung. Zum Wandel des Geschichtsdenkens im 16. und 17. Jahrhundert*. Göttingen: Musterschmidt.

Kluckhohn, Clyde. 1962. *Culture and Behavior*. Richard Kluckhohn, ed. New York: Free Press.

Kojève, Alexandre. 1969. *Introduction to the Reading of Hegel*. New York: Basic Books.

Koselleck, Reinhart. 1973. "Geschichte, Geschichten und formale Zeitstrukturen." In Reinhart Koselleck and Wolf-Dieter Stempel, eds., *Geschichte—Ereignis und Erzählung*, pp. 211–222. Munich: Wilhelm Fink.

Koselleck, Reinhart and Wolf-Dieter Stempel, eds. 1973. *Geschichte—Ereignis und Erzählung*. Munich: Wilhelm Fink.

Kramer, Fritz. 1977. *Verkehrte Welten. Zur imaginären Ethnographie des 19. Jahrhunderts.* Frankfurt: Syndikat.

—— 1978. "Über Zeit, Genealogie und solidarische Beziehung." In Fritz Kramer and Christian Sigrist, eds., *Gesellschaften ohne Staat. Vol 2: Genealogie und Solidarität,* pp. 9–27. Frankfurt: Syndikat.

Kroeber, Alfred. 1915. "The Eighteen Professions." *American Anthropologist* 17:283–289.

Kubler, George. 1962. *The Shape of Time. Remarks on the History of Things.* New Haven: Yale University Press.

Kuhn, Thomas S. 1970. *The Structure of Scientific Revolutions.* Second enlarged edition. Chicago: University of Chicago Press.

Kuper, Adam. 1973. *Anthropologists and Anthropology. The British School, 1922–1972.* London: Allen Lane.

Lacroix, Pierre-Francis, ed. 1972. *L'Expression du temps dans quelques langues de l'ouest africain.* Paris: Selaf.

La Fontaine. 1962. *Fables choisies mises en vers.* Paris: Garnier Frères.

Langer, Susanne K. 1951. *Philosophy in a New Key. A Study in the Symbolism of Reason, Rite, and the Arts.* New York: Mentor Books.

Lapointe, François H. and Claire C. Lapointe. 1977. *Claude Lévi-Strauss and His Critics.* New York: Garland.

Leach, E. R. 1954. *Political Systems of Highland Burma: A Study of Kachin Social Structure.* London: Cohen and West.

—— 1970. *Claude Lévi-Strauss.* New York: Viking.

—— 1976. *Culture and Communication.* Cambridge: Cambridge University Press.

Leclerc, Gerard. 1971. *Anthropologie et colonialisme: Essai sur l'histoire de l'africanisme.* Paris: Fayard.

—— 1979. *L'Observation de l'homme: Une histoire des enquêtes sociales.* Paris: Seuil.

Lemaire, Ton. 1976. *Over de waarde van kulturen.* Baarn: Ambo.

Lepenies, Wolf. 1976. *Das Ende der Naturgeschichte.* Munich: C. Hanser.

Lepenies, Wolf and H. H. Ritter, eds. 1970. *Orte des Wilden Denkens. Zur Anthropologie von Claude Lévi-Strauss.* Frankfurt: Suhrkamp.

Lévi-Strauss, Claude. 1963. *Tristes Tropiques: An Anthropological Study of Primitive Societies in Brazil.* New York: Atheneum.

—— 1966. *The Savage Mind.* Chicago: University of Chicago Press.

—— 1967. *Structural Anthropology.* New York: Doubleday Anchor.

—— 1968. *L'Origine des manières de table. Mythologiques III.* Paris: Plon.

—— 1969 [1949]. *The Elementary Structures of Kinship.* Boston: Beacon Press.

—— 1970. *The Raw and the Cooked. Introduction to a Science of Mythology I.* New York: Harper Torchbooks.

—— 1976. *Structural Anthropology II.* New York: Basic Books.

Levine, S. K. 1976. "Review of J. Baudrillard, *The Mirror of Production.*" *Dialectical Anthropology* 1:395–397.

Libby, W. F. 1949. *Radiocarbon Dating.* Chicago: University of Chicago Press.

Lichtenberg, Georg Christoph. 1975. *Werke in einem Band.* Hans Friederici, ed. Berlin: Aufbau Verlag.

Lindberg, David C. 1976. *Theories of Vision from Al-Kindi to Kepler.* Chicago: University of Chicago Press.

Lindberg, David C. and Nicholas H. Steneck. 1972. "The Sense of Vision and the Origins of Modern Science" In Allen G. Debus, ed., *Science, Medicine and Society in the Renaissance: Essays to Honor Walter Pagel,* 1:29–45. New York: Science History Publications.

Locke, John. 1964 [1689]. *An Essay Concerning Human Understanding.* A. D. Woozley, ed. New York: Meridian.

Lovejoy, Arthur O., Gilbert Chinard, George Boas, and Ronald S. Crane, eds. 1935. *A Documentary History of Primitivism and Related Ideas.* Baltimore, Md.: Johns Hopkins University Press.

Lucas, J. R. 1973. *A Treatise on Time and Space.* London: Methuen.

Luhmann, Niklas. 1976. "The Future Cannot Begin: Temporal Structures in Modern Society." *Social Research* 43:130–152.

Lyell, Charles. 1830. *Principles of Geology.* London: J. Murray.

Maffesoli, Michel, ed. 1980. *La Galaxie de l'imaginaire.* Paris: Berg International.

Mairet, Gérard. 1974. *Le Discours et l'historique. Essai sur la représentation historienne du temps.* Paris: Mame.

Malinowski, Bronislaw. 1945. *The Dynamics of Culture Change: An Inquiry into Race Relations in Africa.* Phyllis M. Kaberry, ed. New Haven: Yale University Press.

—— 1967. *A Diary in the Strict Sense of the Term.* New York: Harcourt, Brace, and World.

Maltz, D. N. 1968. "Primitive Time-Reckoning as a Symbolic System." *Cornell Journal of Social Relations* 3:85–111.

Man and Time. 1957. *Papers from the Eranos Yearbooks 3. Bollingen Series 30.* New York: Pantheon Books.

Marc-Lipiansky, Mireille. 1973. *Le Structuralisme de Lévi-Strauss.* Paris: Payot.

Marx, Karl. 1953. *Die Frühschriften.* Siegfried Landshut, ed. Stuttgart: A. Kröner.

—— 1964. *The Economic and Philosophic Manuscripts of 1844.* Dirk Struik, ed. New York: International.

Marx, Karl and Friedrich Engels. 1959. *Marx and Engels: Basic Writings on Politics and Philosophy.* Lewis S. Feuer, ed. Garden City, N.Y.: Doubleday.

Mauss, Marcel. 1974. *Manuel d'ethnographie*. Paris: Payot.

Maxwell, Robert J. 1971. "Anthropological Perspectives on Time." In Henri Yaker, Humphry Osmond, and Frances Cheek, eds., *The Future of Time*, pp. 36–72. Garden City, N.Y.: Doubleday.

McLuhan, Marshall. 1962. *The Gutenberg Galaxy*. Toronto: University of Toronto Press.

Mead, Margaret. 1962. "National Character." In Sol Tax, ed., *Anthropology Today: Selections*, pp. 396–421, Chicago: University of Chicago Press.

Mead, Margaret and Rhoda Métraux, eds. 1953. *The Study of Culture at a Distance*. Chicago: University of Chicago Press.

Meltzer, Bernard N., John W. Petras, and Larry T. Reynolds. 1975. *Symbolic Interactionism*. London: Routledge & Kegan Paul.

Montaigne. 1925 [1595]. *Essays de Montaigne*. M. J. V. Leclerc, ed. Paris: Garnier Frères.

Moravia, Sergio. 1967. "Philosophie et géographie à la fin du XVIIIᵉ siècle." *Studies on Voltaire and the Eighteenth Century*. 57:937–1011.

—— 1973. *Beobachtende Vernunft. Philosophie und Anthropologie in der Aufklärung*. Munich: C. Hanser.

—— 1976. "Les Idéologues et l'âge des lumières." *Studies on Voltaire and the Eighteenth Century* 151–155:1465–1486.

Morgan, L. H. 1877. *Ancient Society*. New York: World.

Müller, Klaus E. 1972. *Geschichte der antiken Ethnographie und ethnologischen Theoriebildung*. Part 1: *Von den Anfängen bis auf die byzantischen Historiographen*. Wiesbaden: Franz Steiner.

Murdock, G. P. 1949. *Social Structure*. New York: MacMillan.

Murray, Stephen O. 1979. "The Scientific Reception of Castaneda." *Contemporary Sociology* 8:189–196.

Naroll, Raoul and Ronald Cohen, eds. 1970. *A Handbook of Method in Cultural Anthropology*. Garden City, N.Y.: Natural History Press.

Nilsson, Martin P. 1920. *Primitive Time-Reckoning: A Study in the Origin and First Development of the Art of Counting Time Among Primitive and Early Culture Peoples*. Oxford: Oxford University Press.

Nisbet, Robert A. 1969. *Social Change and History. Aspects of the Western Theory of Development*. Oxford: Oxford University Press.

Northrop, F. S. C. 1946. *The Meeting of East and West*. New York: Macmillan.

—— 1960. *Philosophical Anthropology and Practical Politics*. New York: Macmillan.

Northrop, F. S. C., ed. 1949. *Ideological Differences and World Order: Studies in the Philosophy and Science of the World's Cultures*. New Haven: Yale University Press.

Northrop, F. S. C. and Helen Livingston, eds. 1964. *Cross-Cultural Understanding: Epistemology in Anthropology*. New York: Harper and Row.

Nowell-Smith, P. H. 1971. "Cultural Relativism." *Philosophy of the Social Sciences* 1:1–17.

Oakley, Kenneth P. 1964. *Framework for Dating Fossil Man.* Chicago: Aldine.

Ong, Walter J. 1958. Ramus: Method and the Decay of Dialogue. Cambridge: Harvard University Press.

—— 1970 [1967]. *The Presence of the Word.* New York: Simon and Schuster.

Owusu, Maxwell. 1978. "Ethnography of Africa: The Usefulness of the Useless." *American Anthropologist* 80:310–334.

Palmer, Richard E. 1969. *Hermeneutics.* Evanston: Northwestern University Press.

Parsons, Talcott. 1963. *The Social System.* New York: Free Press.

—— 1977. *The Evolution of Societies.* Jackson Toby, ed. Englewood Cliffs, N.J.: Prentice-Hall.

Peel, J. D. Y. 1971. *Herbert Spencer: The Evolution of a Sociologist.* New York: Basic Books.

Pinxten, Rik, ed. 1976. *Universalism Versus Relativism in Language and Thought.* The Hague: Mouton.

Piskaty, Kurt. 1957. "Ist das Pygmäenwerk von Henri Trilles eine zuverlässige Quelle?" *Anthropos* 52:33–48.

Poirier, Jean, ed. 1968. *Ethnologie générale: Encyclopédie de la Pléiade.* Paris: Gallimard.

Popper, Karl. 1966. *The Open Society and Its Enemies.* 2 vols. Princeton: Princeton University Press.

Rabinow, Paul. 1978. *Reflections on Fieldwork in Morocco.* Berkeley: University of California Press.

Rabinow, Paul and William M. Sullivan, eds. 1979. *Interpretive Social Science: A Reader.* Berkeley: University of California Press.

Radnitzky, Gerard. 1968. *Contemporary Schools of Metascience.* Vol. 2: *Continental Schools of Metascience.* Göteborg: Akademiefövlaget.

Ranum, Orest. 1976. "Editor's Introduction." In J. B. Bossuet, *Discourse on Universal History,* pp. xiii–xliv. Chicago: University of Chicago Press.

Rappaport, Roy A. 1979. *Ecology, Meaning, and Religion.* Richmond, Calif.: North Atlantic Books.

Ratzel, Friedrich. 1904. "Geschichte, Völkerkunde und historische Perspektive." In Hans Helmholt, ed., *Kleine Schriften,* 2:488–525. Munich: R. Oldenbourg.

Reid, Herbert G. 1972. "The Politics of Time: Conflicting Philosophical Perspectives and Trends." *The Human Context* 4:456–483.

Ricoeur, Paul, ed. 1975. *Les Cultures et le temps.* Paris: Payot.

Rogers, Francis M. 1961. *The Travels of the Infante Dom Pedro of Portugal.* Cambridge: Harvard University Press.

Rommetveit, Ragnar. 1974. *On Message Structure. A Framework for the Study of Language and Communication.* London: Wiley.

Rosen, Lawrence. 1971. "Language, History, and the Logic of Inquiry in Lévi-Strauss and Sartre." *History and Theory* 10:269–294.

Rossi, Ino. 1974. *The Unconscious in Culture: The Structuralism of Claude Lévi-Strauss.* New York: Dutton.

Rousseau, Jean-Jacques. 1977 [1781]. *Confessions.* New York: Penguin Classics.

Ruby, Jay. 1980. "Exposing Yourself: Reflexivity, Anthropology and Film." *Semiotica* 30:153–179.

Rudolph, W. 1968. *Der kulturelle Relativismus.* Berlin: Duncker und Humblot.

Sahlins, Marshall. 1976. *Culture and Practical Reason.* Chicago: University of Chicago Press.

Sahlins, Marshall and Elmer Service. 1960. *Evolution and Culture.* Ann Arbor: University of Michigan Press.

Said, Edward W. 1979. *Orientalism.* New York: Random House, Vintage Books.

Salamone, Frank A. 1979. "Epistemological Implications of Fieldwork and Their Consequences." *American Anthropologist* 81:46–60.

Sapir, Edward. 1916. *Time Perspective in Aboriginal American Culture: A Study in Method.* Memoir 90, Geological Survey of Canada, Anthropological Series, no. 13. Ottawa.

Sapir, J. David and J. Christopher Crocker, eds. 1977. *The Social Use of Metaphor.* Philadelphia: University of Pennsylvania Press.

de Saussure, Ferdinand. 1975. *Cours de linguistique générale.* Tullio de Mauro, ed. Paris: Payot.

Schmitz, Heinrich Walter. 1975. *Ethnographie der Kommunikation. Kommunikationsbergriff und Ansätze zur Erforschung von Kommunikationsphänomenen in der Völkerkunde.* Hamburg: Helmut Buske.

Scholte, Bob. 1966. "Epistemic Paradigms: Some Problems in Cross-Cultural Research on Social Anthropological History and Theory." *American Anthropologist* 68:1192–1201.

—— 1971. "Discontents in Anthropology." *Social Research* 38:777–807.

—— 1974a. "The Structural Anthropology of Claude Lévi-Strauss." In J. J. Honigmann, ed., *Handbook of Social and Cultural Anthropology,* pp. 637–716. New York: Rand McNally.

—— 1974b. "Toward a Reflexive and Critical Anthropology.' In Dell Hymes, ed., *Reinventing Anthropology,* pp. 430–457. New York: Random House, Vintage Books.

Schumacher, D. L. 1967. "Time and Physical Language." In T. Gold and D. L. Schumacher, eds., *The Nature of Time,* pp. 196–213. Ithaca, N.Y.: Cornell University Press.

Schutz, Alfred. 1967. *The Phenomenology of the Social World.* Evanston, Ill.: Northwestern University Press.

—— 1977. "Making Music Together: A Study of Social Relationships." In Janet L. Dolgin, David S. Kemnitzer, and David M. Schneider, eds., *Symbolic Anthropology,* pp. 106–119. New York: Columbia University Press.

Serres, Michel. 1977. *Hermes IV: La distribution.* Paris: Minuit.

—— 1979. "The Algebra of Literature: The Wolf's Game." In Josué V. Harari, ed., *Textual Strategies,* pp. 260–276. Ithaca: N.Y. Cornell University Press.

Simonis, Yvan. 1968. *Claude Lévi-Strauss ou 'la passion de l'inceste': Introduction au structuralisme.* Paris: Aubier-Montaigne.

Skorupski, John. 1976. *Symbol and Theory.* Cambridge: Cambridge University Press.

Sperber, Dan. 1975. *Rethinking Symbolism.* Cambridge: Cambridge University Press.

Stagl, Justin. 1979. "Vom Dialog zum Fragebogen. Miszellen zur Geschichte der Umfrage." *Kölner Zeitschrift für Psychologie und Sozialpsychologie* 31:611–638.

—— 1980. "Der wohl unterwiesene Passagier. Reisekunst und Gesellschaftsbeschreibung vom 16. bis zum 18. Jahrhundert." In B. I. Krasnobaev, Gert Nobel, and Herbert Zimmermann, eds., *Reisen und Reisebeschreibungen im 18. und 19. Jahrhundert als Quellen der Kulturbeziehungsforschung,* pp. 353–384. Berlin: U. Camen.

Steward, Julian H. 1955. *Theory of Culture Change.* Urbana: University of Illinois Press.

Stocking, George. 1968. *Race, Culture, and Evolution.* New York: Free Press.

Suzuki, Peter T. 1980. "A Retrospective Analysis of Wartime 'National Character' Study." *Dialectical Anthropology* 5:33–46.

Szombati-Fabian, Ilona. 1969. "The Concept of Time in Zulu Myth and Ritual: An Application of A. Schutz's Phenomenology." M.A. thesis, Department of Anthropology, University of Chicago.

Tagliacozzo, Giorgio, ed. 1976. *Vico and Contemporary Thought, 1 and 2. Social Research* (Autumn and Winter), vol. 43.

Tedlock, Dennis. 1979. "The Analogical Tradition and the Emergence of a Dialogical Anthropology." *Journal of Anthropological Research* 35:387–400.

Tennekes, J. 1971. *Anthropology, Relativism and Method: An Inquiry into the Methodological Principles of a Science of Culture.* Assen: Van Gorkum.

Time and Its Mysteries. Series 1–3. 1936, 1940, 1949. New York: New York University Press.

Todorov, Tzvetan. 1977. *Théories du symbole.* Paris: Seuil.

Toulmin, S. E. and June Goodfield. 1961. *The Fabric of the Heavens. The Development of Astronomy and Dynamics.* New York: Harper.

Turnbull, Colin M. 1962. *The Forest People: A Study of the Pygmies of the Congo.* New York: Natural History Library-Anchor.

Turner, Victor. 1967. *The Forest of Symbols.* Ithaca, N.Y.: Cornell University Press.

—— 1975. "Symbolic Studies." In B. J. Siegel et al., eds., *Biennial Review of Anthropology,* Palo Alto: Annual Reviews.

Turton, David and Clive Ruggles. 1978. "Agreeing to Disagree: The Measurement of Duration in a Southwestern Ethiopian Community." *Current Anthropology* 19:585–600.

Tylor, E. B. 1889. "On a Method of Investigating the Development of Institutions: Applied to Laws of Marriage and Descent." *Journal of the Royal Anthropological Institute* 18:245–269.

—— 1958 [1871]. *Religion in Primitive Culture (Primitive Culture,* vol. 2). New York: Harper Torchbooks.

Vagdi, László. 1964. "Traditionelle Konzeption und Realität in der Ethnologie." In *Festschrift für Ad. E. Jensen,* pp. 759–790. Munich: Klaus Renner.

Vansina, Jan. 1970. "Cultures Through Time." In Raoul Naroll and Ronald Cohen, eds., *A Handbook of Method in Cultural Anthropology,* pp. 165–179. Garden City, N.Y.: Natural History Press.

Verhaegen, Benoît. 1974. *Introduction à l'histoire immédiate.* Gembloux: J. Duculot.

Voget, Fred W. 1975. *A History of Ethnology.* New York: Holt, Rinehart, and Winston.

Volney, C. F. 1830. *Les Ruines, ou méditation sur les révolutions des empires, suivies de la loi naturelle.* Brussels: Librairie Philosophique.

Wagn, Klaus. 1976. *What Time Does.* Munich: Caann Verlag.

Wagner, Roy. 1975. *The Invention of Culture.* Englewood Cliffs, N.J.: Prentice-Hall.

Wallerstein, Immanuel. 1974. *The Modern World-System: Capitalist Agriculture and the Origins of the European World-Economy in the Sixteenth Century.* New York: Academic Press.

Wamba-dia-Wamba. 1979. "La Philosophie en Afrique, ou les défis de l'Africain philosophe." *Revue Canadienne des Études Africaines* 13:225–244.

Wax, Rosalie H. 1971. *Doing Fieldwork: Warnings and Advice.* Chicago: University of Chicago Press.

Weber, Max. 1964. *Wirtschaft und Gesellschaft. Studienausgabe.* Cologne: Kiepenheuer und Witsch.

Weinrich, Harald. 1973. *Le Temps.* Paris: Seuil.

Weizsäcker, Carl Friedrich von. 1977. *Der Garten des Menschlichen. Beiträge zur geschichtlichen Anthropologie.* Munich: C. Hanser.

White, Hayden. 1973. *Metahistory: The Historical Imagination in Nineteenth-Century Europe*. Baltimore, Md.: Johns Hopkins University Press.

White, Leslie. 1959. *The Evolution of Culture*. New York: McGraw-Hill.

Whitehead, Alfred North. 1959 [1927]. *Symbolism: Its Meaning and Effect*. New York: Putnam.

Whitrow, G. 1963. *The Natural Philosophy of Time*. New York: Harper and Row.

Wilden, Anthony. 1972. *System and Structure: Essays in Communication and Exchange*. London: Tavistock.

Yaker, Henri. Humphry Osmond, and Frances Cheek, eds. 1971. *The Future of Time*. Garden City, N.Y.: Doubleday.

Yates, Frances A. 1966. *The Art of Memory*. Chicago: University of Chicago Press.

Zelkind, Irving and Joseph Sprug, eds. 1974. *Time Research: 1172 Studies*. Metuchen, N.J.: Scarecrow Press.

Zil'berman, David. 1976. "Ethnography in Soviet Russia." *Dialectical Anthropology* 1:135–153.

Index

200   Index